Legal
Anthropology

Legal
Anthropology

James M. Donovan

A Division of
ROWMAN & LITTLEFIELD PUBLISHERS, INC.
Lanham · New York · Toronto · Plymouth, UK

AltaMira Press
A division of Rowman & Littlefield Publishers, Inc.
A wholly owned subsidary of The Rowman & Littlefield Publishing Group,
Inc.
4501 Forbes Boulevard, Suite 200
Lanham, MD 20706
www.altamirapress.com

Estover Road
Plymouth PL6 7PY
United Kingdom

British Library Cataloguing in Publication Information Available

Library of Congress Cataloging-in-Publication Data

Donovan, James M.
  Legal anthropology : an introduction / James M. Donovan.
     p. cm.
  Includes bibliographical references and index.
  ISBN-13: 978-0-7591-0982-7 (cloth : alk. paper)
  ISBN-10: 0-7591-0982-6 (cloth : alk. paper)
  ISBN-13: 978-0-7591-0983-4 (pbk. : alk. paper)
  ISBN-10: 0-7591-0983-4 (pbk. : alk. paper)
  1. Law and anthropology. I. Title.
  K487.A57D663 2007
  340'.115—dc22   2007035151

Printed in the United States of America

Contents

Preface

Goals of the Book

Legal anthropology looks at "law" from a cross-cultural, comparative perspective. The goal of the enterprise is to identify general principles that characterize this slice of sociocultural life so as to understand this aspect of what can be termed the normative regulation of society: those social forces generally working to create and maintain the ties of cohesion that hold society together against the tidal pull of individual interests. At best, these principles will be nontrivial claims that are uniquely true of law (as that term is usefully understood). Specific questions would include relating law to other normative control systems, identifying how society and its representatives use law to heal divisions and resolve disputes, and following the individual as he or she negotiates among available choices in order to obtain justice in whatever form he or she conceives it, analyzing in the process the normative values that influence those choices.

This text aspires to guide the student through some of the fundamental history, concepts, and theories that have emerged from the works of the field's most prominent and influential authorities. Missing from its pages is a catalog of legal exotica from remote cultures around the globe. This omission is utterly pragmatic. Space does not permit the thrilling recounting of the varied and creative ways that the world's peoples have found to resolve their disputes and do the other work expected of law. The second justification is more philosophical: the ethnographic detail that can so enchant the reader already shapes the data that support the theoretical propositions I describe. Ethnography is represented herein more by the results it has generated than by the process by which it helped to arrive at them. In its stead, the text uses recurring examples from Western legal systems. At one level this should require no apology: our own legal system is as needful of anthropological scrutiny as any other. But the broader purpose of these local illustrations is that they help the reader to better understand his or her own background assumptions about just what law is like. Controlling those assumptions is a prerequisite to thoughtful analysis of more unfamiliar systems. Highlighting some of the surprising idiosyncrasies of the reader's legal system is a first step toward achieving the necessary control to reflect on the experiences of others.

Legal Anthropology: An Introduction was conceived as a brief, affordable overview of the specialty, to be used in the classroom in conjunction with the instructor's choice of more detailed case study materials. The hope is that this text will allow the student to put the case studies into theoretical perspective, without "tracking up the snow" of their rich local detail that draws so many to anthropology in the first place. My own classes, for example, incorporate the materials on the Canela of Amazonian Brazil. The available materials—a wonderfully digestible overview of the society (William H. Crocker and Jean G. Crocker, *The Canela: Kinship, Ritual, and Sex in an Amazonian Tribe* [2004]) as well as an accompanying video (*Mending Ways: The Canela Indians of Brazil* [2003])—provide the right balance between what is said and unsaid about the relevant issues, leaving the students able to "do" the legal anthropology on their own.

The book's intention to be included within the classroom in no way precludes its reading in less structured environments. Although there is no substitute for the challenging confrontation with the primary material, *Legal Anthropology*'s arguments are self-contained and presume access to no supplemental elaboration. I confess a hope that the nonspecialist reader will at its end feel both comfortable and interested in that deeper immersion. As one of its leading figures, Paul Bohannan, has observed, legal anthropology is "a small field in which the general quality of the work is extraordinarily high," one that can promise lasting rewards to everyone who ventures into its pages.

In part because the intended audience of *Legal Anthropology* extends beyond the classroom, its contents are also somewhat atypical for what might be expected in a "textbook."

By no means is this book a bloodless review of the established "truths" of legal anthropology. Far from a recitation of facts and history, the chapters are designed to tell a story on several levels and to offer a few suggestions of their own.

Much of law concerns just this telling of stories. Whether the need is to convince an opponent that he is wrong or persuade a judge that she should favor your argument or even instill the standards of living in relative peace, the mode of discourse often turns to framing the argument within a compelling narrative. This book, not least because it is about law, also tells stories.

Two themes run through the following pages. The first seeks to introduce "law" in terms that will allow the reader to distinguish it from its normative cousins. As in any good story, the character of the focus can be conveyed through recounting the things that it has done, and so too shall law be sketched in terms of its actions. The goal shall be to learn to refine the categories of thinking about law so that anthropologists can reach better conclusions about it.

A second story line involves recounting the historical development that has culminated in a curious situation. Ask anyone on the street what law "does" or is "about," and one is likely to elicit a laundry list of tasks the speaker assumes are the special concern of lawmakers, if not law. Ask the same question of traditional legal anthropologists, however, and the response is likely to be much shorter. In fact, the answer might get no further than identifying dispute resolution as what law is about. At least that seems to be their position given the literature generated by the specialty. How that limited interest in the scope of law's action has come to be the standard of practice in legal anthropology shall be the second of this book's narrative themes.

There are more stories than these within the field of legal anthropology, so why tell these? A useful application of the insights of the first story will be to understand which social problems are best addressed through legal solutions and which are best left to other means of social regulation. Not only may a wrong choice exacerbate the original problem, but the resulting abuse could undermine the effectiveness of law even within its own domain. The second—showing how the reduction of legal anthropology to dispute resolution was historically motivated, not theoretically required—frees the student to expand inquiry beyond the traditional topics without apology. In its tersest formulation, legal anthropology is about law, not simply dispute resolution.

The narrative structure of the text has impacted its pages in yet another way. I have not littered the pages with innumerable citations or quotations from countless scholars beyond the bare minimum. Annotations are ordinarily collected into general footnotes to guide interested readers toward further source materials. Where available, I have deliberately selected references and quotations from the same small core of legal anthropologists in hopes that this will heighten the reader's familiarity with the speaker through repeated appearances in the text. Iterative exposure to a few key personalities, goes the hope, will increase the student's ability to contextualize the quotation. If one of the themes of the book's construction is to tell a story of the discipline, like any tale it will benefit from recurring appearances by a short list of known characters.

Narrative necessarily reflects the perspective of the narrator. While intending to be as objective as possible, this book does not pretend that it communicates only orthodox conclusions of the field. Another writer could easily have selected different emphases and underscored other conclusions than those found in the following pages. Accordingly, it is only fair to the reader to forthrightly identify my own intellectual biases. Two underlying premises strike me as being particularly influential on the arguments that follow, one utterly pragmatic, the other more abstract.

First, the view of law that one takes perhaps varies according to one's ordinary relationship to it. Some like myself, who work with law at a practical level on a daily basis guiding law students through the techniques of legal scholarship and listening to the stories of pro se litigants hoping to find some understanding and control of their circumstances, may not look at law in the same way as someone who deals with law from a distance, as the object of intellectual scrutiny that must be left when other obligations demand priority. We probably have very different stories to tell about what law means to real people and how it is usefully approached.

Second, throughout this text is an embedded assumption about human nature, which it is the special task of anthropology to elucidate. In addition to advocating for the holistic study of human nature, I also assume that the most productive method in that project will be systematic, at times even rising to the level of the scientific. Systematicity implies that there is a "truth of the matter" to be understood and that new research can be evaluated as to whether it carries us further toward that goal. What questions have been answered, what problem identified and perhaps even resolved? This posture heavily informs my reading of the history of the theory of legal anthropology and differs from that held by scholars adhering to a different paradigm—one that I perhaps unfairly gloss as "postmodern," thereby lumping together a disparate assortment of theoretical stances—that would lead them to tell a very different story from that which follows.

Because of this pluralism of ideas about what anthropology should look like, the student is challenged not to accept every analysis as though it were a settled wisdom but to think where I might have erred in my reasoning. Has a particular assertion been adequately defended? Do the implications of that assertion follow as logical entailments or only as suggestive possibilities? Where alternative lines of argument are equally reasonable, have I justified my choice to the student's satisfaction? Or have I stacked the deck in favor of my own favored theses? Does the overall picture of legal anthropology that the text constructs "hang together," or does it, in the end, come off as a disjointed recitation of prior monographs and unrelated bracketed arguments?

Anthropology—and perhaps especially legal anthropology—is something one "does" and not something one passively imbibes. It would be no accident should the reader gain more from challenging my text than from uncritically absorbing it. Like all teachers, I adamantly encourage the former over the latter and wish *Legal Anthropology* to be more provocative than canonical. As I present my own view on the subject, the student should be stimulated to produce his or her countervision.

Structure of the Book

Part I grounds the discussion in fundamental concepts of the specialty. To study law presupposes an ability to identify law, and this immensely complicated question is initially addressed in chapter 1. Further methodological considerations are reviewed in chapter 2. Together, these chapters might be considered the "philosophical" discussions of the text, as they address matters that can be argued only one way or the other and are immune to the usual challenges from the scientific method. A definition of law cannot be true or false but only more or less useful or informative. The significant works pre-dating the appearance of a formal discipline of legal anthropology are briefly considered in part II, chapters 3 and 4, which cover the natural law theorists and the sociologists of law, respectively.

The first half of part III (chapters 5 to 10) reviews the major ethnographic foundations of legal anthropology, covering the classic period from the 1926 appearance of Malinowski's short yet influential *Crime and Custom in Savage Society* through Pospisil's ethnographic treatment of the Kapauku in 1958. Although focus will be on their most important monographs, an attempt will be made to consider the influence of each fieldworker over the course of his professional career. Each chapter contemplates an especially important theoretical issue addressed by the featured thinker. Two exemplars of postclassic ethnographic work are offered in chapters 11 and 12 as illustrations of some of the significant scholarship being performed by today's legal anthropologists.

The challenge of part IV, spanning chapters 13 to 15, is to attempt to place the disparate ethnographic data into comparative perspective. The discussion on dispute resolution will show both the strength and the weakness of the current direction of legal anthropology and features the only truly comparative work in the discipline. That this need not have been the case will be shown by addressing other topics given greater emphasis in non-American legal anthropology traditions, such as legal pluralism.

Applying the comparative method to arrive at general principles that are both meaningful and valid cross-culturally would be no mean accomplishment. However, most anthropologists today are rarely satisfied to accrue such knowledge for its own sake, hoping instead to be able to use these insights to improve the life conditions of the original ethnographic informants, if not all persons and cultures. Some possible venues for this exercise are suggested in part V. The discussions in chapters 16 to 19 underscore the insights legal anthropology can bring to the task of articulating the contents of a cross-culturally valid category of human rights as well as how its lessons can inform a fairer approach to intellectual property problems. This project to interrelate the local and global legal norms receives special study through the question of whether criminal courts should recognize the "culture defense," a claim that a defendant who observes the dictates of his or her own cultural norms should sometimes be treated leniently when the associated acts violate the local law of another society. Finally, legal anthropologists have a role to play in reducing concerns over international terrorism, not least by bringing clarity to the concept and pointing out how local laws interact in broader international forums.

Finally, part VI, chapters 20 and 21, offers my own perspective on the future direction of legal anthropology. From an emphasis on the study of disputing, I argue that the specialty would be better served by analyzing perceptions of fairness. Fairness studies subsume the primary questions of dispute resolution but also bring to the anthropologist's attention problems normally associated with "law" that have been recently overlooked.

Acknowledgments

I could never have mustered the confidence to attempt such a wide survey of the field if not for the support of the Thursday night Globes colleagues, especially Bram Tucker, John Turci-Escobar, and Leigh Willis. Between rounds of drinks and chips, they offered an opportunity to verbalize previously inchoate thoughts and challenged me to think in even broader terms.

My colleagues at the University of Georgia School of Law Library gracefully tolerated my distracted mind as I puzzled through the issues of whatever section I was working on. The students in my legal anthropology classes have been exceptionally motivated and challenging, for which I thank them. John Miller and Edgar Miller carefully read most chapters, sparing me much embarrassment and the reader great confusion. Any remaining errors are due either to my own blindness or to my stubborn refusal to take their good advice.

Finally, I dedicate this book to the late Jorge Vasconez, as one last public declaration. I shall never know your like again.

Why Study Legal Anthropology?

LEGAL ANTHROPOLOGY emerged as a distinct intellectual specialty in the 1920s with the publication of Bronislaw Malinowski's *Crime and Custom in Savage Society*. Scholars of various pedigrees had, of course, earlier attempted to isolate universal principles of law. They were limited, however, by the lack of solid ethnographic data on which to build their theoretical systems. The sea change represented by Malinowski for anthropology generally and not only legal anthropology was his long fieldwork among the Trobriand Islanders, conducted in the native language, for primarily scientific purposes. The systematic and meticulous record of his research was qualitatively superior to the travelogues and missionary reports that to that point had provided most of the information available to theorists working from their overstuffed armchairs and raised to new levels the earlier efforts of anthropological fieldwork, such as that of the Torres Strait Expedition of 1898.

One might wonder why yet another specialty of anthropology was needed either then or now. Two broad answers offer themselves. In the first, the attention to law is merely one piece in the broader picture of sociocultural life that ethnography strives to depict. Here, accounts of law are necessary for completeness but otherwise not particularly exciting or intrinsically interesting.

Alternatively, an anthropology of law collects not just more but also different data on a people. This kind of incompleteness differs in that insights into the legal consciousness of a society do not just fill gaps in the story but potentially change the plot. Law is not a detail, to be addressed time and space permitting; it is a prerequisite to anything claiming to be a description of a society.

In the first, the law life of a society may be interesting but remains essentially peripheral; in the second, it is essential, demanding the depth of study routinely exerted for religion, economics, and kinship. One goal of the present work shall be to defend the second position over the first. That task will be easier if we have some reasonably specific idea about what the something "different" and "essential" to be gained by the anthropological study of law might be.

Identifying the promised benefits of legal anthropology must be considered in light of the goal of anthropology generally. Recent years have seen a swirl of debate over just what the purpose of anthropology should be. No single theory clearly commands the field, and most would wish to include something offered by practically every suggestion. My own perspective is that, whatever the approach taken to anthropology, the field is unified by a premise that there is, in fact, an "anthropos" to be studied. Whatever our differences, we are all part of the same group of "humans" because we share an underlying something. Specialties and paradigms immediately diverge with any effort to clarify just what that "something" may be. But anthropology, by its name if not its nature, presumes the reality of that bond. From that view, the project of anthropology becomes the elucidation of the human condition. The key term in that charge is "human." What does it mean to be "human"? The articulation of those criteria is one of the principal undertakings of anthropology.

By way of comparison, consider what psychology characteristically studies: the mental functioning of the organism *Homo sapiens*. Psychology is not particularly concerned only with those functions that are reserved to "humans" but instead with all functioning possessed by people whether arising out of their "humanness" or as remnants of less lofty precursors. Only in specialized subfields of psychology, such as comparative psychology, might the question arise about what functions are the exclusive ability of the human being. In this sense its subject matter is overbroad as compared to anthropology.

Sociology, in contrast, is underinclusive. Because sociology is a sister discipline to anthropology, sharing several key founders and a large body of early literature, it is unsurprising that sociology tackles several of the same intellectual problems as anthropology. But as its name suggests, sociology is very focused on understanding social structures. Anthropology appreciates these structures but realizes that much of what makes humans "human" lies in cultural ideation. So while sociology (and, for that matter, all of the "social sciences") offers valuable contributions to the problem of anthropology, the full answer of what it means to be human must come from elsewhere. That challenge falls uniquely to anthropology.

In that context, legal studies have a special place because of the unique role that law plays in the formation of society and culture. While some have marshaled strong arguments that other institutions or forces have pride of place as the fount of culture, law has at least an equal claim to that status.

Early social philosophers, such as John Locke and Thomas Hobbes, explicitly argued that the transition from the original state of nature to that of early civilization occurred when individuals agreed to surrender some of their natural rights in order to institute law and form a government. While Locke and Hobbes differed dramatically in their speculations about the motivations for this concession and the shape and powers that a legitimate government would assume, they agreed on the instrument that lifted the savage *Homo sapiens* out of the realm of the wild, untamed animal into that of the social-dwelling human: law.

Thomas Hobbes published his classic work of political philosophy, *Leviathan*, in 1651, positing an initial natural condition where all men were equal in mind and body. However, "during the time men live without a common Power to keep them all in awe, they are in that condition which is called War; and such a war, as is of every man, against every man." So consumed were the original peoples with warring that there was "no place for Industry . . . and consequently no Culture of the Earth. . . . And the life of man [was] solitary, poor, nasty, brutish, and short." People being what they are, they cannot abide peacefully "without the terror of some Power." The solution, according to Hobbes, was to confer on one man "all their power and strength." Only by surrendering natural right to self-governance in order to find peace under an absolute monarch—what Hobbes calls the "great Leviathan" and "Mortal God"—can the transition from savagery to civilization be accomplished.

Part of Hobbes's mission was to justify the English monarchy as being the proper form of government. Whether by design or happy accident, John Locke rejected Hobbes's thesis (it is a point of debate whether Locke intended his work to be a reply to Hobbes or to another writer) and offered his own origin myth in his *Second Treatise of Government* (1689). Like Hobbes, Locke envisions the inhabitants of the state of nature to be equal. Each person has liberty but not license, each being bound to observe the laws of nature. In this natural state every individual is empowered to enforce that law: "If any one in the state of nature may punish another for any evil he has done, every one may do so." This arrangement has its disadvantages, however, because in any dispute "it is unreasonable for men to be judges in their own cases, [because] self-love will make men partial to themselves and their friends: and on the other side, . . . ill-nature, passion, and revenge will carry them too far in punishing others; and hence nothing but confusion and disorder will follow." Unlike Hobbes, then, the state of nature is not an unending war, but there is nothing in Locke's model that prevents that outcome. To remove the potential for war rather than end war per se, "therefore God hath certainly appointed government to restrain the partiality and violence of men."

The form of this government, according to Locke's reasoning, will be that of the "civil society," arrived at "in the consent of the people." Under this system, each man will be able to have the disagreement adjudicated by a third party. This condition precludes monarchy from the forms of civil government, says Locke, because the monarch—Hobbes's Mortal God—has no higher authority to which a disputant with him can appeal. That is to say, because civil society is that between two equals, there can be an appeal to settle disputes; but no such appeal is available from a conflict with an absolute monarch. Monarchy, then, is but an extension of the state of nature and is not a civil society at all. The highest form of political arrangement for Hobbes is as good as nothing to Locke.

The social contract theories of Hobbes and Locke diverge on a number of other points, not least being the elevated status Locke accords the natural right to private property. While we should not take the details of their political myths too seriously, we cannot deny that the image they portray has a peculiar resonance. What one does with this image is, of course, a very different question and marks the difference between a philosopher and a scientist.

But enough has been recounted here to illustrate the point that in the foundational thinkers of political philosophy, the transition from the state of nature to civilization was an agreement on how to structure social institutions in order to prevent and settle disputes, which is to say, the creation of law. Law and society bring each other into existence simultaneously. The relationship of law to society therefore appears to be especially intimate in a way that exceeds that of any of the other major contenders for the title of master key to unraveling society's meanings. While this initial premise may be difficult to defend, it does explain the linguistic datum that while it is not semantically nonsensical to speak of a "religionless society" (to recognize the inherent difficulty in that locution requires considerable study), the idea of "lawless society" is oxymoronic. Our common understanding of "law" forces the concession that if a group truly lacks law, it has ceased to be a society in any meaningful sense.

In this sense, at least, the project of anthropology not only benefits from the study of legal anthropology but is arguably handicapped without it. Without a grasp of how law helps to bind the elements of society together, the student approaches his or her study well after the drama has begun. Law is not all there is to society and culture, but without law there would be no society or culture to study.

BOX I.1

The Intellectual Relatives of Legal Anthropology

The obvious focus of the chapters that follow is legal anthropology. It can be useful to clarify what that label refers to by contrasting it with several closely related terms. Because each refers in some way to the study of law in its cultural context, for many ordinary purposes it may be possible to use them interchangeably without too much misunderstanding. But each has its specific nuance of which the student should be aware.

Political anthropology addresses the way a society establishes, orders, and maintains the power and authority necessary to keep it together. Because of its interest in power and authority, political anthropology frequently looks at state-level societies where these qualities are most easily discerned and most formally structured. In that context the political dimension subsumes the legal in the sense that the form of law normally correlated with states is that which flows from its political organs and designated authorities. This correlation has in the past been so taken for granted that the lack of the latter led writers to assume the absence of the former.

This tight association, however, loosens considerably when other forms of societies are taken into account. Here law's relationship to politics is less certain, and the subject matter diverges significantly. Other sources and forms of law can be noticed beyond that created by the state. While political and legal anthropologies will have many common interests, they remain distinct projects.

Sociology of law is a descriptive science that studies legal institutions as a fact of the world that is one part of a wider pattern of culture. By emphasizing law as a product of its milieu, it distinguishes itself from methods that adopt a more philosophical perspective. In its investigations, law is as likely as not to be a dependent variable, with research questioning how changes in one sociocultural variable changes observations about law. Formative sociologists of law are reviewed in chapter 4.

Sociological jurisprudence, on the other hand, while looking at much the same information as sociology of law, has almost the opposite goal. Here, law is the independent variable in the analysis. Sociological jurisprudence asks less what law is than what it needs to be to achieve some desirable end. As described by Roscoe Pound,

(Continued)

BOX I.1
The Intellectual Relatives of Legal Anthropology (Continued)

"The problem is not merely how law-making and law-administering functions are exercised [which are the foci of the sociology of law], but also how they may be exercised so as best to achieve their purpose, and what conception of these functions by those who perform them will conduce best thereto. . . . The true juristic theory, the true juristic method, is the one that brings forth good works."

The school of sociological jurisprudence arose in reaction to theories of legal formalism, which held that law unfolded because of its intrinsic logic. While placing law squarely in the world, sociological jurisprudents were not neutral observers of legal reality but were actively concerned to influence its development. In its literal sense, sociological jurisprudence remains more a social philosophy of law than a method of social science of the law. The enduring significance of Pound's sociological jurisprudence may be as the precursor of legal realism, a related orientation that would exert extraordinary influence within legal anthropology (see chapter 7).

Against the background of these related fields, it becomes easier to see the special features of **legal anthropology**. Although the lines dividing these enterprises can blur, legal anthropology is to be distinguished from its closest conceptual neighbor, the sociology of law, primarily by method. Anthropology, while being eclectic in the approaches it employs to collect its data, remains unique in its reliance on extended participant observation and qualitative ethnography based on long residence with the studied people. Even when investigating the same topic, a sociological project is (broadly speaking) more likely to rely on official records, survey data, or short-term interactions.

The two are to be distinguished at the theoretical level as well. While sociology is, by its very name, more narrow in its interest in society and social structures, anthropology, while also deeply invested in those same issues, is more apt to cast its net wider to include elements of culture such as the ideas, beliefs, symbols, and other internal dimensions of group living.

Law and society is the supercategory that encompasses all the foregoing (except sociological jurisprudence). In the words of one of its founders, Lawrence Friedman, "'Law and society movement' is a rather awkward term. But there is no other obvious collective label to describe the efforts of sociologists of law, anthropologists of law, political scientists who study judicial behavior, historians who explore the role of nineteenth century lawyers, psychologists who ask why juries behave as they do, and so on." For members of this movement, says Laura Nader, "law is not autonomous but embedded in society and explained by forces outside the law."

Anthropology and law: All the preceding labels in one sense or another treat law as an object of study, to be informed by the methods and perspectives of the social sciences. "Anthropology and law" adopts a different approach in that it treats each of the two fields as equal subjects in their own right. Problems addressed here concern how the practice of anthropology intersects with the practice of law. The legal requirements to excavate a site would be one example. The debate of the Kennewick Man raised questions about who should control excavated human remains. A growing body of literature looks at how anthropological insights are incorporated into the judicial process, including the use of anthropologists as expert witnesses—as was done in the famous Supreme Court case involving the clash with the Amish over mandatory education of children (*Yoder*)—or the crafting of the culture defense to serve as a mitigating circumstance in criminal cases (see chapter 18). The central tenet of this specialty is that neither field—anthropology nor law—is an intellectual subordinate to the other, each offering valuable insights and advantages to the other. This relationship has been termed a **balanced reciprocity**.

Suggestions for Further Reading

James M. Donovan and H. Edwin Anderson, *Anthropology and Law* (2003) (discussing the balanced reciprocity between law and anthropology), and Philip C. Kissam, *The Discipline of Law Schools: The Making of Modern Lawyers* (2003) (describing why the law and society movement has failed to gain a meaningful presence in the curricula of American law schools). Lawrence M. Friedman, "Coming of Age: Law and Society Enters an Exclusive Club," *Annual Review of Law and Social Science* 1 (2005): 1–16, offers a recent perspective on that project, while a synopsis of political anthropology can be found at Ronald Cohen, "Political Anthropology," *Handbook of Social and Cultural Anthropology* (1973), 861–81.

References

Lawrence M. Friedman, "The Law and Society Movement," *Stanford Law Review* 38 (1985–1986): 763–80, at 763; Thomas Hobbes, *Leviathan* (1909) (spellings modernized), chaps. 13, 17; John Locke, *The Second Treatise of Government* (1964), §§7, 13; Laura Nader, *The Life of the Law: Anthropological Projects* (2002), at 104; Roscoe Pound, "The Scope and Purpose of Sociological Jurisprudence," *Harvard Law Review* 24 (1911): 591–619, at 598.

I

General Theoretical Background

IN THE WESTERN intellectual tradition, the sciences emerged from philosophy through increased methodological empiricism. Every scientific exercise recapitulates this ancestry in that its first steps must be philosophical, not empirical. In those initial statements, the researcher settles on the terms, units, and definitions that establish the solid foundation on which any method must build.

Chapter 1 identifies a few of those philosophical landmarks that precede the study of legal anthropology. Most important, perhaps, are the definitions used to distinguish the subject and to identify its objects of study. Definitions fall into the realm of philosophy because they are not matters of proof or disproof; definitions simply are. Neither true nor false, right nor wrong, definitions can, however, be evaluated by standards of practical utility and theoretical fruitfulness that will vary with the demands of the specific context. Plato's not entirely serious definition of man as a "featherless biped," for example, might be useful when sorting humans from chickens but less so when separating humans from apes. Thorough consideration of the focus of legal anthropology studies will, in its course, reveal other philosophical foundations, such as assumptions about human nature. Clarification of these preliminary matters allows the researcher to ask the meaningful questions that are the first step in the advance of knowledge and to design methods that are appropriate to address those puzzles.

Those methodological issues are reviewed in chapter 2. Appropriate method is intimately tied to the questions to be answered, and there are at least three levels of anthropological inquiry, each requiring its own kind of data. This chapter presents only a broad perspective. Several methodological problems are deferred until later chapters, such as what is the most efficient vocabulary to describe legal relationships (see chapter 13).

CHAPTER 1

Philosophical Starting Points

IN A RECENT REVIEW, Mark Goodale observed that "within U.S. legal anthropology . . . there has been a marked reluctance to consider foundational issues." One of the most fundamental conceptual problems that the anthropology of law evades concerns the definition and identification of the focal phenomenon to be scrutinized, analyzed, and explained through systematic research. If the anthropologist "has no idea as to what constitutes law, he will be unable to see law" (Hoebel 1945–1946). While skipping this step in any individual work may not be injurious to the integrity of that particular effort (the worker may have a valid intuition about the contours of the phenomenon), the cumulative effect in a collaborative and comparative enterprise such as anthropology can be disastrous.

What, then, is "law"?

This chapter maps some of the initial intellectual terrain any answer to that question must travel. The goal is not to resolve the issues but to equip the student with some initial conceptual tools with which to confront the later ethnographic data. While some options are reviewed about the form such a definition can assume, the more important point is to indicate why the need for any definition at all is unavoidable.

On Definitions

As a rule, anthropologists hate definitions—and for good reason. A seemingly innocuous definition can be laden with hidden ethnocentric assumptions. Bad definitions can mislead research for generations. Even those poor outcomes presuppose that a consensus can be reached about what any particular definition ought to be, an almost impossible occurrence. What holds true generally applies especially for "law." Max Radin's conclusion describes the situation well: "Those of us who have learned humility have given over the attempt to define law."

Unfortunately, the difficulty of the task and the low expectation of resounding success in no way diminish the necessity of the undertaking. In order to gather for study a sample of the target phenomenon, some standard must be applied. Otherwise, there would be no principled basis on which to separate the "law" from the "nonlaw" stuff.

Law is one piece of social reality that it has been useful to treat as a separate idea. Law is—at this point, at least—not a real thing. It is not something appearing in the natural world to be picked up, examined, and classified. As Leopold Pospisil pointed out, "'Law' is a term applied to a concept, not a phenomenon. . . . [It] is a concept whose justification lies in its heuristic value, in its efficiency as an analytical tool in the hands of an ethnologist." Because the idea of law does not need to conform to anything in the real world, there indeed has been a tremendous range of proposed ways to define it. That freedom accordingly has made it that much more difficult to define law in a consistent and useful way, in a way that informs more than it confuses.

Some legal anthropologists do insist that defining the category is either unnecessary or undesirable. Their position appears to follow U.S. Supreme Court Justice Potter Stewart's famed conclusion about pornography to the effect that "we know it when we see it, but we don't have to articulate what it is that we are recognizing. Trust us." Of course, in practice these workers are quite able to define the concept for their own purposes; their only lapse is a failure to tell the reader what that definition is. Unless the reader can be assured that the sample has been drawn on some rationally consistent basis, she is right to be skeptical of any conclusions that may be drawn and should be especially cautious about any attempt to compare findings from different workers. Is "law" what is written in codes, for example, or what happens in courtrooms? Both of these approaches have been popular, yet the data sets for analysis that each creates are starkly different.

Contemporary legal anthropologists might reply that they avoid such philosophical conundrums by focusing attention on "disputes," not law. Disputes have the virtue of being observable—that is, a dispute is (to use Pospisil's terms) more phenomenon than concept and therefore a more suitable unit for cross-cultural analysis. This solution buries the foundational issue rather than resolves it. The working assumption it incorporates is that disputes bear some privileged relationship to the concept of law. While it would be difficult to imagine that disputing bears *no* relationship to law, the precise parameters of that relationship still must be outlined. Is it subsumed within the larger category, the category itself, or an overlapping but independent concept? If the first, what are the nondispute aspects of law, and how are they to be studied? So long as the field is identified as the anthropology of law, the whole of law must be accounted for and not only the most accessible subset.

Given that every legal anthropologist inescapably employs a definition of law, a burden exists to demonstrate that the science can profitably proceed without an explicit statement about what the term means. It may not be beneficial as a discipline to harangue over definitions, but neither is it productive to keep them hidden.

On matters of definition, rarely is there a "right" or "wrong" approach. This is especially true when the concept to be defined does not exist in the real world but is instead a category that has been carved out and separated from the rest of the sociocultural spectrum because of some intrinsic intellectual interest. Thinking with the concept produces useful results, and thus the concept itself becomes established.

More than a few sterile research programs have arisen, however, by taking this necessary step too far. As categories of thought become familiar, we tend to **reify** the concept, to treat as real what is only an abstract idea, resulting in at least two kinds of errors. First, reification of a nonreal concept can lead to the attribution of properties and qualities that are possible only with concrete entities. A common example is to describe abstracts as possessing psychological properties, as when a group is described as thinking or feeling. Imagine we are studying the Yanomamo of the Amazon Basin, made famous through the works of Napoleon Chagnon. Statements to the effect that "the Yanomamo X" or even "the law of the Yanomamo Xs" may hide potential lapses of reification.

A second error of reification is to confuse a conclusion based on definition with one grounded in reality. A current debate over same-sex marriage illustrates this mistake. It is one thing to claim that, as traditionally defined, marriage excludes gay couples but quite another to argue that marriage itself, as a simple entailment of current social reality, precludes that outcome. The first observation is an accurate description; the second is faulty reasoning based on the reification of the sociocultural concept and definition of marriage and subsequent treatment as a natural category.

The temptation to reify should be avoided, not least because it leads to flawed reasoning. If the concept has been forged in the first place because it is "good to think," then as little as possible should be done that interferes with that application. Concepts must not only be usefully constructed but also meaningfully applied.

Substantive versus Functional Definitions

We are at no loss of possible candidates for ways to define "law" (see box 1.1). Notice that these are not simple restatements of the same idea. Some are mutually exclusive: for Rousseau, law derives from the "general will," while for Austin it is the command of the sovereign. According to Cicero, law is a manifestation of justice; for Weber and Ihering, the central criterion to find law is sanction to enforce conformity (independent, presumably, of whether this policed conformity results in justice). How shall we decide which is best (keeping in mind that by "best" we mean only for intellectual inquiry; we do *not* mean "best" in the sense of more accurately reflecting "reality")?

BOX 1.1

Definitions of "Law" Proposed by Prominent Thinkers

Cicero:
"Law is the distinction between things just and unjust, made in agreement with that primal and most ancient of all things, Nature." (*De Legibus*, Book II, §5 [51 B.C.E.])

Thomas Aquinas:
"[Law is] nothing else than an ordinance of reason for the common good, made by him who has care of the community, and promulgated." (*Summa Theologica* Q.91, art. 4 [1265])

John Locke:
"For law, in its proper notion is not so much the limitation as the direction of a free and intelligent agent to his proper interest, and prescribes no farther than is for the general good of those under that law." (*Second Treatise of Government* §57 [1689])

Jean Jacques Rousseau:
"Laws . . . are acts of the general will." (*The Social Contract* [1762])

William Blackstone:
"A rule of civil conduct prescribed by the supreme power in a state, commanding what is right, and prohibiting what is wrong." (*Commentaries on the Laws of England*, Book 1 [1765])

John Austin:
"A law . . . may be said to be a rule laid down for the guidance of an intelligent being by an intelligent being having power over him. . . . Laws or rules, properly so called, are a species of commands." (*Lectures on Jurisprudence* [1869])

Rudolf von Ihering:
"The State is society as the bearer of the regulated and disciplined coercive force. The sum total of principles according to which it thus functions by a discipline of coercion is *Law*. . . . The current definition of law is as follows: law is the sum of the compulsory rules in force in a State, and in my opinion it has therewith hit the truth." (*Law as a Means to an End*, chap. 8, §§ 8, 10 [1877])

Oliver Wendell Holmes Jr.:
"The prophecies of what the courts will do . . . are what I mean by the law." (*The Path of the Law* [1897])

Max Weber:
"Law . . . exists if it is externally guaranteed by the probability of coercion (physical or psychological) to bring about conformity or avenge violation, and is applied by a staff of people holding themselves specially ready for that purpose." (*Law in Economy and Society* [1925])

Roscoe Pound:
"I think of law as in one sense a highly specialized form of social control in a developed politically organized society—a social control through the systematic and orderly application of the force of such a society. In this sense it is a regime—the regime which we call the legal order." (*My Philosophy of Law* [1941])

Within its extensive definition, the authoritative *Oxford English Dictionary* (*OED*) offers the following meanings of "law":

- A rule of conduct imposed by authority
- The body of rules, whether proceeding from formal enactment or from custom, which a particular state or community recognizes as binding on its members or subjects

These two definitions illustrate the broad families to which a definition of "law" can belong. The first defines law according to external criteria, in this case its pedigree as a rule pronounced by an authority. Such **substantive** definitions—into which category we can place the examples from Austin, Blackstone, Rousseau, and Weber—contrast with **functional** definitions, those that define the term on the basis of its effects, like those from

Cicero and Aquinas. The second *OED* definition fits into this second kind, finding law in whatever produces the result of being binding on the citizenry. Any rule can by this criterion properly be termed a "law," regardless of its source, form, or other external quality, so long as it has the required effect.

Substantive and functional approaches each have strengths and weaknesses. Substantive definitions are comparatively easy to use. To identify category members, one need only ascertain that the exemplar possesses the requisite traits. So, for Austinians, any rule that is the decree of the legislature belongs in the category of law. This strategy can be overbroad, however. In the United States, the legislature passes bills for many purposes, including some that few would wish to call a law. In the past, it has voted on motions declaring commemorative events, such as October as National Breast Cancer Awareness Month, and it continues to pass nonbinding resolutions expressing the "sense of Congress" on an issue that some other branch of government must actually decide.

The substantive approach can also be simultaneously underinclusive, omitting rules that we might expect to include in our analysis of law, like the unenacted rules of custom. Failure to surrender your seat on the bus to a pregnant woman or elderly man may not land you in jail, but it can earn you the scorn and derision of your companions. The loss of reputation for failing to observe standards of custom and etiquette has proven cross-culturally to be an effective form of sanction enforcing social norms. Any criterion for law that excludes such unenacted rules without accounting for their role in the normative order of society risks rendering problematic familiar terms such as "customary law"—where the adjective seeks to append criteria that have been expressly precluded in the meaning of the noun.

Functional definitions reverse these evaluations. They are much more difficult to apply. When working with a functional definition, we cannot determine whether any particular instance is a law merely by learning its content. Instead, we must inquire into its effects. What influence does this purported law have on its environment? How, for example, could we know that a rule is truly "binding"? Must adherence be perfect, or if only 80 percent of cases conform to the rule, can we still conclude that it is "binding"? What about 60 percent? Where is the line, and how is it drawn? Is it enough that people *believe* the rule is binding without actually obeying it, or is it the opposite, namely, that evidence of "bindingness" must be found in behavior regardless of oral reports? If it can be accomplished, this work will be rewarding because the collected instances of examples will conform much better to the intuitive scope of the intended category, being less likely to be either too broad or too narrow.

To define law substantively or functionally exerts considerable influence on the types of phenomena the scholar recognizes as law and consequently the kinds of generalizations that data will produce.

Ordinary versus Technical Definitions

Ordinary meanings of a term create expectations about what counts as a member of category. These common associations in turn inform research. Despite this foundation, the technical concept should not be slavishly bound to ordinary speech; otherwise, it will lack the necessary precision to do the systematic intellectual work we require. When that does happen, research priorities become reversed, serving mainly to reinforce the commonsense preconceptions about what the term describes rather than to generate new insights on the social phenomena. On the other hand, the philosopher Ludwig Wittgenstein, who held all meaning to be rooted in ordinary use, implied that technical language could not diverge too drastically from common understanding without becoming incomprehensible or counterintuitive. A middle ground must be sought when attempting to attach technical meanings to common words like "law."

An example from the history of jurisprudence illustrates these points. Law has been defined substantively by some as what legislators create. This definition indeed captures much of the common meaning of the term in modern American society, flowing naturally from observations of how that society works. The incorporation of that commonsense definition into scientific theorizing produced some unintended and undesirable consequences. When applied by anthropological study, the definition yielded the result that law must be a property of advanced societies only, while "primitive" societies (a term that will for the most part be avoided in this text) adhered mindlessly to custom. This distinction in turn implied that the mental faculties of moderns and "primitives" themselves differed fundamentally in order to render such a stark contrast. The lay equation of law with legislative lawmaking, then, smuggled into anthropological inquiry preconceptions that favored colonial mind-sets and ethnic/racial prejudices.

While anthropological study should not be limited to the ordinary meaning of its research terms, neither can its definitions remain ignorant of those lay understandings. When that happens, what looks like an easily comprehended word becomes a highly technical term of art, or **jargon**, that serves more to obfuscate understanding than to foster it. Ideally, the technical and the common definitions of a term should be mutually informed and never mutually exclusive. Moreover, the scholar should be able to articulate clearly the precise points at which his or her use of the word "law" diverges from the layperson's ordinary understanding.

Law as a Norm for Social Regulation

Norms

The search for a definition of law proceeds from a philosophical posture that it should favor the values of usefulness and productivity over mere theoretical elegance. Moreover, the most useful and relevant examples will be collected by a functional definition rather than a substantive one. The best definition, finally, will tend to refine rather than reject or contradict the commonsense meaning of the word.

If these premises are reasonable, we could choose a worse place to begin than with a look at the ordinary understanding of what it means for something to fall within the category of law.

Analyzing the definitions in box 1.1, we can construct something approximating a generic understanding of the meaning of "law":

- Although the details vary between societies, in general law is closely associated with the social life of a community. That intimacy contributes to the identification of the phenomena as belonging to the category of law. Even if a rule is labeled as law, when it applies to something excessively peripheral to the concerns of present-day social life (such as laws against tying a giraffe to a telephone pole), it no longer enjoys the high respect usually granted to laws.
- By means that vary with the context, law is expected to regulate the interactions between members of the group. Law accomplishes this goal by variously teaching the proper mode of behavior—its *aspirational* dimension, directing how one ought to behave—or, in its *prescriptive* aspect, declaring how one must behave by punishing those who veer too far outside the established standards of acceptability. Sanctions to achieve this goal can be either positive or negative, requiring some actions (such as paying taxes) and forbidding others (like murder and robbery).
- Whatever the form assumed by law in its local environment, it is presumed to be a binding obligation on the society's members rather than an optional standard or a discretionary preference. The law sets standards that everyone is expected to comply with or at least not deliberately flaunt. In ordinary discourse, "It's the law" is taken to provide sufficient reason to adopt a given course of action.
- Finally, laws are ordinarily expected to be enforced by some external authority rather than be an exercise solely of personal discipline.

Even if most readers agree that this summary captures the most common ideas of the concept, as framed it offers little guidance for social scientific inquiry. At a minimum, research requires a statement with terms that are better organized and more easily operationalized.

Beginning with the observation that law is a feature of social and not personal life, we can venture that a general intent of law is to canalize behaviors in predetermined directions. Whether by requiring external compliance or fostering internal acceptance, laws are intended to generate behavioral regularities in social actions. As we shall see later, their actual success in this enterprise has been mixed. To count as a successful law, it would not have to completely determine individual acts, but most events should fall within the range envisioned by the legislators.

This property—to generate a predetermined field of behavioral expectations—places law within the category of **social norms**. "Norm" is another contested term, but for present purposes we may accept the following definition offered by Jack Gibbs:

> A norm in the generic sense (i.e., encompassing all the various types of norms) involves: (1) a collective evaluation of behavior in terms of what it *ought* to be; (2) a collective expectation as to what behavior *will be*; and/or (3) particular *reactions* to behavior, including attempts to apply sanctions or otherwise induce a particular kind of conduct.

Immediately we can see that law falls into this category of social norm given the similarities of their generic definitions. Both deal in aspirations, prescriptions, and evaluations of collective or social (not personal or private) behaviors.

The need for norms that limit the range of possible actions by group members should be apparent. Despite the fact that group life satisfies requirements that could not otherwise be met, each individual continues to have his or her own objectives, desires, aspirations, and other personal motivations. The central tendency of those private goals is to drive the group—be it the family, clan, or even city or state—apart. These can be termed the **centrifugal social forces**.

We can expand on this metaphor from physics. In order to overcome forces that would disperse the group, there must be countervailing forces to hold it together. These are the **centripetal forces of social regulation**. Social regulation involves inculcating within group members the norms of acceptable behavior, goals, aspirations, and even emotions while allowing venting of inevitable frustrations, angers, and conflicts in ways that do not threaten the long-term stability of the group. In Gibbs's terms, norms guide the behaviors of the member, shape the expectations of the comembers, and motivate actions and reactions to minimize the impact of significant deviation from expectations through the use of coercive sanctions.

Successful regulation requires balancing the needs of the group against those of its individual members. The balance to be found is for enough of the needs of the members to be satisfied while still allowing for a stable corporate organization so that those needs, too, can be fulfilled.

This general description merely recapitulates points long recognized in anthropology. As Bronislaw Malinowski observed,

> Every cultural activity again is carried out through co-operation. This means that man has to obey rules of conduct: life in common, which is essential to co-operation, means sacrifices and joint effort, the harnessing of individual contributions and work to a common end, and the distribution of the results according to traditional claims. Life in close co-operation—that is, propinquity—offers temptations as regards sex and property. Co-operation implies leadership, authority, and hierarchy, and these, primitive or civilized, introduce the strain of competitive vanity and rivalries in ambition. The rules of conduct which define duty and privilege, harness concupiscences and jealousies, and lay down the charter of family, municipality, tribe, and of every cooperative group, must therefore not only be known in every society, but they must be sanctioned—that is, provided with means of effective enforcement.

Stated in these broad terms, we expect that society contains several methods of achieving social regulation through inculcating norms. As Paul Bohannan argued, some of these have been elaborated and elevated to the status of institutions. Legal anthropology specializes in only one, law, but it should remain an open question to what extent it can understand the one in isolation from the others. Our immediate need, therefore, is for a typology of these norms. Only then will we be in a position to conclude where the boundaries of legal anthropology lie.

Some workers have attempted to itemize these norms of social regulation. William Sumner identified two, "folkways" and "mores," while Pitirim Sorokin counted four: law-norms, technical norms, norms of etiquette and fashion, and a residual category containing everything else. Sir Paul Vinogradoff listed "fashions, manners and customs, conventional standards, precepts of morality, and laws," all of which are obligatory but laws being the "most obligatory" of them all. Richard Morris critiqued these earlier efforts and identified seventeen criteria to categorize norms, while Jack Gibbs used his three definitional attributes given above to generate a grid containing twenty types of norms. Few of these attempts are more than intellectual curiosities, not least because they do not translate well into the institutions of social norms with which we expect to deal. In other words, they tend to violate our standard of basing our study in the ordinary meanings of terms, producing instead technical jargon.

Despite these attempts, the unfortunate fact is that no accepted, principled typology of social norms is currently available. We have notions what some of those norms will need to be, however, if they are to accomplish the task of effective social regulation. Rules will be required to govern **intragroup** behaviors (those within the group) as well as **intergroup** behaviors (those between groups). Included in this set will be rules about rules (**metarules**) to determine when a situation should be treated as within or between groups, an assessment that cannot always be determined by the identities of the actors. As often as not, it is the *role* or *status* a person inhabits for purposes of that interaction and how these compare with the opponent that will determine how the altercation is to be resolved.

The intragroup/intergroup sets will probably not be mirror imaged. Intragroup norms will be numerous and detailed, as compared to intergroup norms, which will be fewer in absolute number, apply in limited situations, and be less closely monitored but more apt to be strictly and literally enforced against outsiders. The rationale behind these summary claims is that intragroup norms tend to have as the goal a peaceful settlement that preserves the group; intergroup norms will more easily tolerate retribution and punitive retaliation that directs disruptive aggressions outside the group onto comparative "strangers." Intragroup relations are more important than those between groups, and thus the former will be more closely scrutinized, monitored, and regulated. Among insiders, the rules foster peace; with outsiders, justice. Keep in mind, though, that these are only initial expectations. The ethnographic data in part III will help evaluate their validity and utility.

Summary and Conclusions

In order to think clearly about the problems of the cross-cultural study of law, it is first necessary to have a principled definition of the focal phenomenon if for no other purpose than as a selection criterion for social facts to be studied. Dimensions along which any preferred definition will fall include whether its identifying criteria are substantive or functional and whether it frames an ordinary or technical approach to the subject matter. Any plausible candidate will situate law within a theoretical framework describing the norms of social regulation. This a priori decision by the anthropologist should be made explicit because different definitions will carve out for study different segments of sociocultural reality, a fact that can make difficult any attempt at recognizing cross-cultural generalizations.

BOX 1.2
Norms and Institutions

The theoretical position of the present discussion depends greatly on maintaining a principled distinction between *norms* and *institutions*. Claims made about the one tend be nonsensical if misunderstood to apply equally to the other. For the most part, the fundamental assertions herein are about legal norms and only indirectly about legal institutions. What is the difference?

In the most general sense, *norms* are unobserved and unobservable. They do not exist in the real world but, like other mental operations, can only be inferred from the patterns of observable phenomena (much as the presence of an unseen planet can be detected by the movements of other celestial bodies).

According to George C. Homans, a norm is "an idea in the minds of members of a group, an idea that can be put in the form of a statement specifying what the members or other men should do, ought to do, are expected to do, under given circumstances." It does not necessarily follow that such prescriptive norms determine behavior to the extent that they become expressed as statistical norms, although that can often occur. The important point here is that norms are ideas about the way things at least ought to work.

Institutions arise when normative ideas become instantiated in social structures intended to advance the goals of those norms. Such a structure, explains William Sumner, "holds the concept and furnishes instrumentalities for bringing it into the world of facts and action." Nothing requires that institutions be "pure" in the sense of advancing the goals of only one kind of norm. Consequently, specific institutions can be quite heterogeneous either by design or by accident.

The relationship between legal norms and legal institutions, therefore, is neither simple nor direct and is always fact intensive rather than abstractly theoretical. It should be no surprise to observe, for example, that religious institutions advance legal norms (and vice versa), as when law is used in the service of religion. We have no a priori reason on this basis to conclude that societies lacking legal institutions also lack legal norms. On the other hand, the relationship between legal norms and legal institutions is taken to be more than linguistic. Legal institutions, where they appear, are recognized as such not because they are the sole "holders" of legal norms but because they contain the majority of those norms.

Suggestions for Further Reading

The discussion of the problems of definition draws heavily on James M. Donovan, "Defining Religion: Death and Anxiety in an Afro-Brazilian Cult" (1994); for an illustration of the contextual sensitivity of definition, see Donovan, "Defining Religion," in *Selected Readings in the Anthropology of Religion: Theoretical and Methodological Essays* (2003), 61–98.

References

Jack P. Gibbs, "Norms: The Problem of Definition and Classification," *American Journal of Sociology* 70 (1965): 586–94, at 589; Max Gluckman, *The Judicial Process among the Barotse of Northern Rhodesia* (1955); Mark Goodale, "Traversing Boundaries: New Anthropologies of Law," *American Anthropologist* 107 (2005): 505–8, at 506; E. Adamson Hoebel, "Law and Anthropology," *Virginia Law Review* 32 (1945–1946): 835–54, at 840; George C. Homans, *The Human Group* (1950), at 123; Anthony T. Kronman, *Max Weber* (1983); Bronislaw Malinowski, "The Group and the Individual in Functional Analysis," *American Journal of Sociology* 44 (1939): 938–64, at 949; Leopold Pospisil, *The Anthropology of Law* (1971), at 16; Max Radin, "A Restatement of Hohfeld," *Harvard Law Review* 51 (1938): 1141–64, at 1145; William G. Sumner, *Folkways* (1913), at 53; Paul Vinogradoff, *Common-Sense in Law* (1914), at 19, 21; Ludwig Wittgenstein, *Philosophical Investigations* (1963).

CHAPTER 2

Studying Law in the Field

THE PREVIOUS CHAPTER explored initial philosophical issues, assumptions, and definitions that provide the background for questions that the legal anthropologist hopes to study. These are points of stipulation, not proof. Usefulness in research offers the only standard against which they should be evaluated. Having moved those often hidden assumptions into explicit awareness, the anthropologist is now prepared to consider formulating hypotheses and gathering data as part of a research method. This chapter identifies some issues when approaching the *doing* of legal anthropology.

This is not the venue for a thoroughgoing treatment of the execution of a fieldwork project. Instead, attention is limited to matters of particular relevance to legal anthropology. In addition to the usual challenges confronting any fieldwork endeavor, the anthropology of law confronts a few special problems and has seen its share of unique debates over how one best goes about studying the legal system of a group.

Hierarchy of Research: The Three Levels

Data do not speak for themselves, nor, as the joke says, is "data" the plural of "anecdote." One cannot merely accumulate information and expect something useful or meaningful to emerge spontaneously. Questions must be asked of data that have been thoughtfully collected for that specific purpose. Although exploratory studies of first impression can also be insightful, better results follow when the data have been gathered to test a stated hypothesis or address a particular question. While it may not always be feasible or desirable to design research that satisfies a condition of Popperian falsifiability and the elimination of competing hypotheses, the end result should still intend to enlighten rather than obscure, clarify rather than obfuscate. The range of possible explanations for phenomena should be smaller at the end of research than it was at the beginning.

What kinds of data would be appropriate depend on the issues to be considered. While all disciplines like their questions "answered," anthropologists require that they be contextualized. If viewed as a holistic science, anthropology requires a range of data to resolve its problems, one broader than typically expected by other disciplines asking the same question.

Whatever the question, a complete solution can be helpfully broken down into three different levels of conceptualization, each requiring its own kind of data. These can be collectively referred to as the **three primary tasks of legal anthropology**:

- To *analyze* the local legal system (**descriptive legal ethnography**)
- To *compare/contrast* the local system with other local systems so as to extract nontrivial general principles (**comparative legal anthropology**)
- To *facilitate* integration of the legal system into broader global networks through the promotion of mutual understanding (**applied legal anthropology**)

Descriptive Legal Ethnography

Ethnographic description comprises the raw data of all anthropological inquiry, including legal anthropology. Everything that anthropology hopes to achieve as an intellectual endeavor depends completely on the quality of the description of the local ways of living from around the globe. Within this task, the fieldworker strives to capture and to communicate in a written work the elements of the target group's norms, institutions, and structures that bind these elements into an identifiable entity of a "culture" or "society." The studied group can be society as a whole or only a portion. Rarely today does an anthropologist aspire to study an entire culture.

Ethnography is the most atheoretical work undertaken in the discipline. This should not be construed in any pejorative sense. The relative lack of theory incorporated into the description endows the monograph with a life beyond the intentions of its author, allowing it to be fruitfully consulted by later anthropologists investigating completely different topics.

The lack of theory within ethnography is, however, relative. Description is never "pure" in the sense of being unfiltered and unmediated by the anthropologist's own interpretive schema. Every account necessarily includes some distorting perspective, if for no other reason than that the fieldworker must choose which behaviors to notice in the field and from these which to include in the written report. The attentive fieldworker will explain as much of this selection process as possible, a duty that has led to an increasingly reflexive presence of the ethnographer in the ethnography. No longer is the fieldworker an invisible presence among an alien people. Common explanations for gaps in the literature have included that males did not have unrestricted access to the women of the group, that his or her choice of sponsors in the group favored access to some parts of the group while precluding others, or that the time spent in the field did not allow observation of the full round of social life. Some rituals, for example, may occur only once in a generation.

Although the primary objective of ethnography is to describe in as full detail as possible the observed and collective account of sociocultural life, atop this inevitably biased sampling of social phenomena the fieldworker usually offers his or her own theoretical model to explain the patterns of behaviors. Ideally, the raw data will be kept separate from the writer's own interpretations so that later workers can rework the information to test new, different, and even competing explanations from those held by the original ethnographer.

The warning to keep these two aspects of the ethnography distinct was most pointedly given by Paul Bohannan (see chapter 9). He contrasted the group's **folk system** to be recorded with the anthropologist's interpretive **analytical system**. This tension between the raw (yet unintentionally pre-processed) data and the overt attempts to explain the observed patterns (which can further influence the kinds of data that get noticed or ignored, creating a circle of influences within an ethnography) has been variously expressed by sets of opposing terms. The essential element in Bohannan's suggestion may be better known as the emic/etic dichotomy, wherein the **emic** view is that of the informants reflecting the people's own understanding of what is going on, while the **etic** is the scheme imposed in an attempt to bring some kind of order and theoretical elegance to the messy data.

To the competing levels of analysis that plague all ethnographic inquiry, legal anthropology contributes its own special difficulties with its unique dichotomous perspectives. One binary opposition concerns the locus of the law to be studied. The anthropologist can choose to attend either to the group's legal **formalities** or to its legal **realities**. In the former, the fieldworker looks at the abstract rules claimed to apply to an episode and that represent the ideal response to a given situation. The underlying philosophical assumption beneath legal formalism treats law as a closed system of rules, much like mathematics. If the law says that the pedestrian stops when the crosswalk light is red, the formal picture of pedestrians on the street has them stopping at red lights, always. The ethnographer may write something like, "The X are a stopping-for-red-lights people." If people are observed to behave in ways contradicting the stated rule, the event may be labeled anomalous or the actors deviant nonconformists. The rule itself would rarely be called into question by evidence of these deviant occurrences.

Methodologically, given the initial premises of legal formalism, the challenge is to find the rule that covers a given set of facts. The fieldworker might question informants about the proper rules governing a specific situation. Legal formalism can influence the kinds of conclusions an anthropologist may offer about the people studied. Our imaginary ethnographer might continue, "The X are a stopping-for-red-lights people because they report a rule forbidding crossing against the light." The implicit assumption is that a direct relationship exists between behavior-governing norms (which are psychological phenomena) and stated rules or legislation. Any such relationship, however, is a hypothesis to be tested and not an a priori premise assumed to be valid.

We know from our own experiences that the relationship between what people *say* they (ought to) do and the internalized norm that influences their decisions will be much more complicated than the legal formalists imagine. The slippage between formal law and internalized norm can be significant.

Equally problematic can be any attempt to equate formal rules not just with oral reports but also with observed behaviors. While we have many laws against speeding, it cannot be said that we do not speed while driving. Even if most drivers have internalized the norm that speeding is "bad," the acceptance of this legal norm has not prevented almost every driver from routinely behaving to the contrary, perhaps even most of the time. Knowing laws, we cannot infer the existence of norms; knowing norms, we cannot predict individual behaviors. The problem for the legal anthropologist is to trace how one becomes translated into the other. Serious problems exist, then, with a methodology based in principles of legal formalism.

These problems led legal anthropologists, especially after the 1940s following on the work of Llewellyn and Hoebel (see chapter 7), to look at **trouble cases**, or accounts of how the law actually works in specific disputes. This approach is an application of the philosophy of legal realism articulated by such jurisprudents as Oliver Wendell Holmes and has exerted extraordinary influence over the field of legal anthropology.

By observing the manner in which real disputes are resolved, the fieldworker is better able to understand how people conduct their lives so as to function productively within the group, especially when those lives diverge from the idealized norms. The flow of inquiry has now reversed: instead of trying, like formalism, to move from stated laws and norms to evaluate behaviors, realists move from observed behaviors to their conclusions about laws and norms. From here one can ask questions like, Where the divergence is significant, why is the norm not altered? Do rules and judgments have different roles to play (suggesting that both formalism and realism have a contribution to make to the understanding of the working of law as a whole), or are rules merely the written embodiment of past judgments (as is often claimed about Anglo-American common law)? This new vein of problems would eventually lead to legal anthropology's process orientation (see chapter 10).

Before leaving this section, we should return briefly to the problem of fieldworker bias. It is not an insult or criticism of the hardworking anthropologist to acknowledge that no person can be perfectly objective when conducting research. Our backgrounds, including education, upbringing, and relationships, influence not only our approach to the world but also what we find interesting enough about a topic to spend years studying it.

According to Karl Llewellyn and E. Adamson Hoebel, "General theory"—which should include our commonsense assumptions—"guides inquiry. It conditions not only interpretation but recording. It conditions the very seeing of the data. It also lends to data their significance." In the specialty of legal anthropology, a particularly powerful yet often unacknowledged background influence is the anthropologist's own experiences with the legal system of his or her home culture. In the field, an event may be noticed or overlooked, depending on the way it challenges or reinforces the worker's initial assumptions about the way law should work or what law is expected to look like.

Unfortunately, many citizens are surprisingly ill informed about their own legal systems, raising significant obstacles to efforts to control for that perceptual bias. As an illustration, Americans often assume that their legal system is designed to find out the "truth" of a situation. Beyond a certain point, however, this is not an accurate assessment of its priorities. The American legal system is **adversarial**, meaning that while both parties have an affirmative duty not to lie or mislead, neither party has a duty to expose the truth if it is disadvantageous. The winner is not the innocent or the truthful but the side with the most persuasive argument. Actual innocence will not necessarily get a person out of jail if the courts conclude that the faulty conviction was the result of an errorless trial. In many states, persons exonerated postconviction by DNA evidence can be released from prison only through a governor's pardon since the legal process itself allows for no rehearing. This system can be instructively contrasted with other legal systems that are more **inquisitorial**, or designed to suss out the truth of the matter. Each type of legal system has its attendant features. Inquisitorial systems, for example, tend to recognize fewer inviolable civil rights than do adversarial ones (see chapter 9).

Because one's own culture always and necessarily provides the implicit standard of comparison when confronted with a new one, a flawed understanding of one's own legal system could undermine perceptions during fieldwork. This possibility raises the issue of what formal training is desirable in order to pursue this kind of research. Should legal anthropologists have to go to law school before heading into the field?

Comparative Legal Anthropology

With several ethnographies in hand, the anthropologist is now equipped to proceed to the next level of analysis: legal anthropology proper. Here the goal is to map the different local legal systems as points in conceptual space, hoping to tease out some patterns of cross-cultural validity that are both general enough to apply to a broad number of distinctive cultural contexts and specific enough to be intellectually interesting.

Despite being the touted hallmark of anthropology as a discipline, truly comparative work is surprisingly rare. The more common practice is for a book on an announced topic to present chapters that each addresses the issue from the perspective of a single ethnographic field site. Without anything more, this practice falls short of true comparison, which at its best requires the ethnographic study of several independent local sites coordinated to gather similar data on particular issues using standardized methods. The results are then pooled to examine a few relatively focused questions or to tease out common patterns, some perhaps earning the label "universal." Although the results are typically narrow, the power of the method is irresistible.

One obvious obstacle to comparative research is that it is extraordinarily difficult to do. The time, personnel, and money required to execute such projects make them rare creatures on the intellectual landscape. The studies in anthropology that meet these criteria are both enduring classics and few in number. In legal anthropology, far fewer rise to this level.

An alternative method involves drawing a random sample from the Human Relations Area File (HRAF; once a laborious process, the task has been greatly eased by its recent availability as an electronic database). The HRAF is an enormous collection of information culled from a variety of sources and coded for variables of research interest. While it makes available to all anthropologists data from far-flung localities across the globe, thus maximizing the sample size to be compared, the data are only as good as their original sources, which were often collected for unrelated purposes, such as missionary reports. This lack of control over the data collection process complicates any final conclusions.

The paucity of genuine comparative studies in legal anthropology is probably not due solely to the methodological difficulties. Anthropological comparison has always been a more contentious undertaking than ethnographic description. Some fieldworkers do not believe that comparison is either wise or possible, convinced that each culture should be analyzed as a sui generis phenomenon with little theoretical relevance to any other. They deny that the variations encountered in the field are principled in any way or are the output of any more general forces or influences. Others express the judgment that the theoretical preconditions that would support such comparisons, such as the demonstrated equivalence of units, can never be satisfied, precluding the exercise.

The act of comparison implies that, despite apparent differences, both the examples are instances of a single kind of thing. We earlier characterized the goal of anthropology as the search to understand what it means to be "human." Implied in this quest is the existence of some as yet undefined quality common to all creatures believed to fall into that category and that serves as the fount of the special constellation of abilities anthropologists have labeled as "culture." Without this underlying uniformity, no basis exists to isolate a "human" subset from the rest of the animal world and therefore to compare them.

Some anthropologists—sometimes collectively placed within the school of **postmodernism**—have found the concept of a universal human nature to be sufficiently problematic that they would deny either its reality or at least its usefulness. For them, such appeals to a human nature veer uncomfortably close to a type of biological essentialism that ignores the formative power of the symbolic culture that is equally a focus of anthropology.

While the debate continues, with points scored on both sides, the immediate lesson is that doing comparative anthropology becomes very difficult, if not impossible, from a philosophical posture that rejects human nature (or some equivalent concept). Postmodernism held particularly strong sway within the discipline from the mid-1980s until very recently, although Fran Mascia-Lees, writing from her perspective as former editor of the *American Anthropologist*, suggests that its currency has abated. Today anthropology exists in what Bruce Knauft has called a "post-paradigmatic" phase, with anthropologists moving "like *bricoleurs* to combine pieces of different perspectives—positivist and post-positivist, historical and genealogical, symbolic and political economic, theoretical and applied—in relation to particular projects and topics."

Against that earlier background, however, we can see an additional explanation why the legal anthropology corpus contains few completed comparative works.

Applied Legal Anthropology

Ethnography generates the data that feed into anthropological cross-cultural comparison, with the objective of deriving useful conclusions about the human condition. Applied anthropology hopes to use those conclusions to effect positive changes in the lives of all peoples, most especially among the peoples on whom the original ethnographies were based. In the broadest sense, it strives to facilitate integration of the local legal system into broader global networks through the promotion of mutual understanding based on the comparatively derived general principles.

It has not always been an acceptable practice for anthropologists to become directly involved in the lives of those they study. The methodological ideal of ethnography is that of **participant observation**, which requires a sensitive balance between involvement in the community so that its members become inured to the fieldworker's presence and open to his or her constant questions and objective observation of the behaviors to be studied. To become overinvolved risks influencing detrimentally the behaviors of the people studied; underinvolvement can lead to lack of access to those behaviors. Achieving the appropriate distance, neither too close nor too far, is one reason fieldwork can take years to master.

The reticence surrounding applied anthropology has its roots in the fear that as the ethnographer becomes more participant than observer, he or she will commit the worst of the methodological sins by "going native." This plunge negatively impacts the quality of the data ultimately collected. Would a deeply involved anthropologist, for example, be tempted to omit data that were potentially damaging to the position of the studied group, even if that data were intellectually valuable? Even if the fieldworker would not succumb to such temptations, putting him- or herself in a position for the question to be raised at all undermines the end product of the research. Best, it was thought, to avoid such issues, maintain the proper distance, and refuse to become involved in the group in any way that would be inappropriate for an objective "scientist."

Whatever the limitations on personal interventions, anthropologists are thankfully no longer reluctant to marshal the insights of their studies for the benefit of the studied, especially when exercised in appropriate forums and within reasonable limits. Later chapters shall examine a few of these special venues.

You're In the Field. Now What?

Once in the field, the ethnographer begins to collect data about this stuff called "law." Where to look?

This is the moment in which one's definition (see chapter 1) becomes especially crucial. In general, though, three types of information are likely to be of interest, broadly glossed as rules, behaviors, and institutions.

Rules are best exemplified by formal codes. These may be the enacted laws governing the citizens of a given jurisdiction. In the United States, for example, the worker would need to become familiar with such formal rules at the national, state, and municipal levels.

Formal laws can, however, be distilled by other methods than consulting published texts. The fieldworker may attempt to elicit rules from informants. One method would be to present them with the scenario of a dispute and ask what rules might be invoked to help resolve the case. Another approach involves summarizing statements from officials resolving actual arguments, hoping to distill from them some regularities.

In addition to linguistic data, the anthropologist would also study **behaviors,** the real-world interactions of people. It may not always be obvious which behaviors are relevant, leading some to begin their studies with accounts of disputes, expanding outward in directions that help clarify the issues raised as well as any underlying history between the complainants. In addition to dispute-resolving actions, attention should also be paid to dispute-prevention behaviors. These might include mechanisms by which group members, especially children, are inculcated with the norms of interacting with others, both inside and outside the group.

From these behaviors, the fieldworker might extract the presumed rules that guide the behaviors, whether or not the informants are consciously aware of those guidelines. This allows an additional method besides oral elicitations to derive the controlling rules of society, which may or may not be "official." Observation of individual behaviors can reveal a lack of fit between the system as it actually works and expectations by ordinary citizens about how it should be working.

Study of behavior should not be limited to the individual but extended to the formalized *relationships* between persons. What, for example, are the recognized rights, duties, and responsibilities? How are these created, modified, or extinguished? Which correlate with a person's status (e.g., as a male head of household) and which with a specific role the person currently holds (e.g., priest, voluntary association member)?

Finally, the thorough fieldworker would attend to any formal **institutions** that the society has created to promote the effectiveness of legal norms. These would include bodies charged to create new laws, enforce existing ones, adjudicate between disputants, or prosecute criminals.

These types of data interact with each other, encouraging the conscientious anthropologist to pursue all of them simultaneously.

Summary and Conclusions

Each of the succeeding parts III to V of this book focuses on one of the methodologically tiered tasks of legal anthropology. Part III recounts the major accomplishments of the classic legal ethnographies. The leading issues that have been studied comparatively are the topic for part IV, while part V outlines a few topics to which legal anthropological studies have been or could be productively applied outside the discipline. The elements of this set of disciplinary goals do not always peacefully coexist in that ideal execution at one level may conflict with the needs of another. These tensions are also discussed in the following chapters.

Suggestions for Further Reading

Helpful volumes outlining methodology are available for each of the three levels of anthropological study:

Ethnography: Robert Aunger, *Reflexive Ethnographic Science* (2004); Charlotte Aull Davies, *Reflexive Ethnography: A Guide to Researching Selves and Others* (1999); Victor C. de Munck and Elisa J. Sobo, eds., *Using Methods in the Field: A Practical Introduction and Casebook* (1998); Scott Grills, ed., *Doing Ethnographic Research: Fieldwork Settings* (1998); Karen O'Reilly, *Ethnographic Methods* (2005); Geoffrey Walford, ed., *Debates and Developments in Ethnographic Methodology* (2002) (although the collection targets educational research settings, its discussions can be useful for broader contexts).

Comparative: Leonore L. Adler, ed., *Issues in Cross-Cultural Research* (1977); H. Russell Bernard, ed., *Handbook of Methods in Cultural Anthropology* (1998); H. Russell Bernard, *Research Methods in Anthropology: Qualitative and Quantitative Approaches* (2002); Ladislav Holý, ed., *Comparative Anthropology* (1987).

Applied: Carole E. Hill and Marietta L. Baba, eds., *The Unity of Theory and Practice in Anthropology: Rebuilding a Fractured Synthesis* (2000); James H. McDonald, ed., *The Applied Anthropology Reader* (2002); Riall W. Nolan, *Anthropology in Practice: Building a Career outside the Academy* (2003).

References

Paul Bohannan, *Justice and Judgment among the Tiv* (1957); Bruce M. Knauft, "Anthropology in the Middle," *Anthropological Theory* 6, no. 4 (2006): 407–30, at 407; Karl N. Llewellyn and E. Adamson Hoebel, *The Cheyenne Way: Conflict and Case Law in Primitive Jurisprudence* (1941), at 19; Fran Mascia-Lees, "Can Biological and Cultural Anthropology Coexist?" *Anthropology News* 47, no. 1 (January 2006): 9, 13.

II

Forerunners

LTHOUGH THE MODERN discipline of legal anthropology dates only from 1926, when Bronislaw Malinowski published the first modern ethnographic treatment of the subject, the study of law in its sociocultural context has been pursued for far longer. The emergence of a distinct field of study can be described as the most recent of three stages. The first, the period of natural law theorizing, has its roots in philosophies that attempted to ground values in facts. Natural law found meaningful and binding obligations of ethics through contemplation of the order observed in the physical world. The earliest discussions of law either advanced this school of natural law theorizing or explicitly reacted against it.

The review of this first stage is the topic of chapter 3, while chapter 4 recounts the major work that emerged in the second phase leading to legal anthropology, the sociology of law. Sociology of law distanced itself from natural law studies by advocating no special evaluative posture about the object of study. Laws were deemed neither good nor bad but instead logical or coherent, flowing not from natural order but from social organization. Sociologies of law share much in common with the anthropology of law, but the former tends—as but two differences—to minimize the significance of the individual and to work predominantly with behavioral rather than cultural explanatory models.

CHAPTER 3

Natural Law

Description and Reactions

Development of Natural Law Theory

The connecting theme of **natural law** theories is that some empirical *fact* (be it nature generally or human nature specifically) determines how people *ought* to live. Because the physical world tangibly expresses the will and desires of a higher order (i.e., often but not always the Christian God), study of that realm will provide insights into how the human moral and legal structures should be ordered.

Normative conclusions are accordingly derived (by reason, intuition, or other processes) from statements of objective facts. This theory is distinguishable from mere claims that the most *efficacious* organization or most *practicable* rule is of a certain type (usually one that matches the status quo) because that approach seems to "work." Natural law goes further: conclusions about preferred arrangements become standards of moral evaluation (they are *good*, not merely effective; they are *just*, not merely pragmatic). Stated in unflattering philosophical terms, natural law performs the core transformation of the **naturalistic fallacy**—a term coined by philosopher G. E. Moore to deny that the "good" can be defined by reference to any natural qualities.

Within most accounts the antithesis of natural law theory is **positive law**, which says that law is not a moral position at all, unless one equates the moral with the legal (i.e., the good is the legal by definition). Law here reflects no fundamental moral order but only the will of the Austinian legislator.

The differences between natural and positive legal theories are fundamental. In the first, social law is purportedly "found" in nature; in the second, it is whatever the sovereign decrees. Within systems of natural law, a law that has been properly enacted can still be unjust, making it moral to disobey it; positive law derives its legitimacy wholly from its genealogy, making any procedurally proper law one that the citizen is morally bound to obey.

The prototypical example of the tension between these two legal positions arose in Nazi Germany. Natural law theorists believe that Germans were bound by a higher duty than the civil law and thus should have refused to comply with certain obligations imposed by the state that made them complicit in the Holocaust. Positive law makes no such demand of citizens. These theorists are left to justify why, no matter how inhumane the law, the German citizen had no ethical duty to refuse to comply. As a result of this historical conflict, natural law thinking would gain in post–World War II a renewed popularity and lead to the creation of today's human rights ethos through the Nuremberg trials.

Despite serving as the basis of human rights, natural law theory has its shortcomings, especially from an anthropological perspective. According to one line of reasoning, because it derives ethical conclusions from physical facts, natural law tends to expect the comparative identity of legal systems. Assuming that all people reason in the same way and that the realities of the natural world are everywhere the same, all societies should in time arrive at roughly similar systems of law. Deviation from this presumed uniformity serves as an indicator of immaturity, lack of a power of rational reflection, or some similarly derogatory assessment. Such societies are ripe for conquest and colonization by a more "civilized" state, an act of aggression routinely justified in the eighteenth century as for the "good" of the colonized given their low condition. Native Americans, for example, were frequently scorned for their failure to elaborate a comprehensive theory of private property, especially of land. Legal deviation from the European model was, in this view, a deficit requiring correction.

Positive law allows for a much wider range of local variation to arise without invidious evaluation. Being based only in the collective will of the legislative authority (whatever that might be), valid law in one context might diverge wildly from that of another, at least in theory, without requiring a judgment that one is better or more just than the other. To the extent such judgments can be made at all, it is only by appeal to standards external to the legal system itself. These were some of the ideas influencing the earliest theorists of the relationship between law and society.

Plato (428–348 B.C.)

Landmarks in the development of natural law theory in Western civilization are outlined in table 3.1. As in all matters of philosophical importance, the ancient Greeks first enunciated for the West the problem to be solved and the principles wherein proper solution would be found. Shirley Letwin offers the following summary of the varied and sometimes contradictory thinking of Plato concerning law:

> In short, Plato presents us with two distinct views of law. One, contained in the *Crito* (and some parts of the *Statesman*), suggests that the law is a set of noninstrumental, general, highly determinate and necessarily somewhat defective written rules, created by an association (a *polis*), purely for the sake of maintaining the association, and which (despite their defects) are to be obeyed by the members for the sake of peaceful coexistence. The second view, which appears most sharply in the *Republic*, the *Gorgias*, and parts of the *Statesman*, suggests on the contrary that the laws are to be obeyed only because (and hence presumably only to the extent that) they are the products of and embody a human wisdom that is the nearest thing in the changing world to the unchanging verities of Reason.

TABLE 3.1 **Landmarks in the Development of Natural Law**

Plato (428–348 B.C.)	Human nature consists of two drives, pleasure and pain. Human law should lead to the greatest pleasure/least pain for the group. Because citizens must learn to find pleasure in virtue and pain in vice, the first duty of the legislator is to provide for the education of society's youth.
	Statesman: Ideal society will be lawless, a condition that grants the ruler needed flexibility to do the best thing in any situation. Lawlessness in nonideal societies, however, invites certain chaos. (See also Plato's *Republic* and *Laws*.)
Aristotle (384–322 B.C.)	Because man is a social animal, one becomes fully human only as a citizen of a state. Thus it is the duty of the state to make people good. Consequently, no aspect of individual thought or action is beyond the purview of state power.
	The ultimate goal for human is happiness. Happiness (*eudaimonia*) is achieved by acting virtuously, which entails choosing the mean between two extremes. A just society is achieved through the knowledge, habituation, and self-discipline of its citizens.

(Continued)

TABLE 3.1 Landmarks in the Development of Natural Law (Continued)

	Justice does not require equality simply but only equal treatment for equal persons. This is a proportionate equality. It is a danger to seek too much equality, treating unlikes as likes. The state must ostracize the clearly superior or subordinate itself to him.
Cicero (106–43 B.C.)	Stoic philosophy originally held that the good life follows from understanding *oikeion,* or natural affinities expressed in the ordered arrangements of the world. Because nature is fundamentally rational, one should live in accord with that nature. Each person has a role in the natural order, and it is the function of education to find that role.
	Neo-Stoicism was less utopian: Perfect compliance to nature was not necessary, but man must still respect nature. Cicero's *Republic* claimed that the best life is to serve the state and to govern (in contrast to the Platonic preference for a life of philosophical contemplation). By the "State," Cicero was referring to "the coming together . . . united by a common agreement about rights and laws and by the desire to participate in mutual advantages," which was essentially an early social contractarian theory.
	Natural law as articulated by Roman law (*ius naturale*) would expand to reflect the standard of the Stoics, that the law-based workings of the universe should be the model on which human society should be structured.
Aquinas (1225–1274)	*Summa Theologia,* prima secundae: Law is "an ordinance of reason for the common good, made by him who has care of the community, and promulgated."
	The "common good," however, does not necessarily refer to the *greatest* good.
	Within Aquinas's scheme, there are four kinds of law:

ETERNAL LAW

NATURAL LAW
General principles;
derived by reason/
intuition

Human law Divine law
Specific principles;
created by positive
enactment

1. Eternal law: Complete set of God's law, known only to him.

2. Natural law: discerned by participation of rational creatures in eternal law, addressing matters of general concern. "Do good and avoid evil." *Natural law gives us our natural inclination to our proper end.* Pleasure and pain guide us in identifying principles of natural law. One could say that we know we are doing the right thing because of the way we feel.

3. Human law (positive law) attempts to derive laws of particular application from the general rules of natural law and should still conform to eternal law. Natural law limits the extent of legislative action: an unjust law is no law at all (after Augustine). Human law should proscribe only the most egregious of vices and promote only the virtues that are public (not private) goods.

4. Divine law (divine positive law, "revelation"): Laws in the Bible and other particular enactments that God has specifically revealed.

While imagining the ideal society and what role law would play in such a society, Plato recognized that law was meant to govern the actions of the ignorant. To truly know what is right and good is necessarily to act in accordance with that knowledge. It is impossible, he argued, to "know" in some abstract sense what is the wise and moral action and still choose to do something different. Proper action from this view is a matter of proper education. Plato accordingly returned often to the problem of how a society should educate and train its youngsters in the ways of virtuous living.

Under the rule of a suitably trained philosopher-king, the ideal society would have no need of law. Plato expected that because the ruler is wise, he could be trusted to do the right thing in any situation. Laws and rules would serve only to restrain him from what may be the correct action. Such restraints, however, are indispensable in any society ruled by imperfectly wise persons (which is to say all real ones). Because such poorly educated rulers *cannot* be trusted to always act wisely, laws are necessary to serve as a moral prosthetic, compensating for the ethical shortfalls of the ruler and his people.

Such laws seek to maximize the pleasure and minimize the pain of the society, evoking principles that would become familiar under the label of **utilitarianism**. Because what causes both pain and pleasure is often rooted in human nature, legitimate laws will reflect the contours of these natural predispositions. The goal of education should be to make the exercise of virtue the greatest pleasure a person can enjoy.

Aristotle (384–322 B.C.)

Of the Greeks, Aristotle would have the greatest influence on later natural law thinking, as it would be his philosophy that would mold the theology of Thomas Aquinas. Aristotle was an early first proponent of the empirical method, contrasting with Plato's purely speculative approach. Whereas some strains of thinking within Plato pitted pure legalism as an inflexible set of rules against considerations of equity, the search for the right thing to do in a specific set of circumstances, Aristotle's significant achievement was to achieve a reconciliation of these two competing interests through the introduction of a distinction between theoretical and practical reason. Theoretical legal reasoning involves the search for first principles, while practical reasoning requires interpreting and applying those first principles to the local circumstances. So, while positing the existence of fundamental and uniform legal principles at the level of first principles (i.e., a natural law), Aristotle also denied that these principles must produce equivalent systems in all societies.

The search for first principles builds on his understanding of the moral purpose of human life (discussed in texts such as the *Nichomachean Ethics*). *Eudaimonia*—variously translated as "happiness" or "flourishing"—was for Aristotle the goal of that life and arises from acting in concert with one's true nature. An important element of human nature, according to Aristotle, one that offered the only way to be truly human, is participation in civil government. When one speaks of the human being as opposed to the animal, one is referring to social ties rather than individual endowments. In his ideal state, the good person and the good citizen will be equivalent, although it is also possible to be a good citizen without being what we might deem a good man.

Turning to the more practical exercise of lawmaking and government, Aristotle in the *Politics* presented ideas on the forms of government and their structures (**tyranny**, with the king at its head; **aristocracy**, governed by an oligarchy; and a constitutional **democracy**). His model included the first statement of a doctrine of separation of powers and discussed what kinds of courts should be available.

Thomas Aquinas (1225–1274)

Thomas Aquinas, the great scholar of the Catholic Church, would latch onto Aristotle's suggestions and develop natural law to its fullest intellectual extent. He incorporated tenets of Stoic philosophy that argued that the good life was one that was lived according to nature. Believing that nature was itself basically rational, Stoics such as Cicero had reasoned that it should serve as the standard for virtuous living, which required each person performing his or her role in the order of things. As ultimately articulated by its later proponents, Stoicism asserted that the law of nature as revealed by reason should serve also as the foundation for the legal enactments of the state.

When Aquinas wrote his *Summa Theologica*, the Greek philosophers had only recently become again available in the West. One of his primary tasks was to reconcile faith with the rational philosophy of Aristotle. As for Aristotle, for Aquinas law presupposes a theory of human nature. The outline of that moral portrait was to be based on idealizing theory and not descriptive psychology, as Aristotle might have preferred. For Aquinas, this obviously meant the model of human flourishing espoused by Catholicism. After deciding on the kind of life humans *should* lead, the role of law is to provide the kind of direction that fully rational beings, if unimpeded, would choose for themselves. But because people are not unimpeded in the use of their rational capabilities but instead distracted by passions and emotions, law works to keep citizens on the proper course. Duties to family and the Church would rise to the top of Aquinas's list of institutions to properly organize human life. Concluding that law (and the state) exist to further the happiness of the citizen, Aquinas defined "law" as "an ordinance of reason for the common good, made by him who has care of the community, and promulgated" (Second Part, Q.90).

Aquinas outlined a hierarchical typology of the kinds of law, with the eternal law of God at the top. Natural law was that part of the eternal law that could be determined by man's powers of rationality. Human, or positive, law consisted of the dictates of practical reason that addressed the needs of ordinary life. These latter were not unrestrained in their content, however. Human law, to be legitimate and therefore binding, was required to be in accord with the general understanding of the broad principles of natural law (which were, in their turn, extracted through our rational participation in the eternal law). One consequence of this system is that natural law did not cover all the details of life but only identified the core values according to which life should be ordered (the "minimalist" view).

State of Nature

Although anthropology had yet to emerge as a separate science, the questions that would serve as its focus—not least being what it means to be "human"—have a history of speculative imaginings. One active discussion concerned the characterization of the "original" condition of mankind and the consequences of that primordial way of living for understanding the ideal social arrangement for present citizens (see this book's introduction).

Over time, natural law philosophy was applied to describe these presocial states of nature. Descriptions supplied a foundation from which to identify the form of the ideal government—which is to say the one that followed most closely from the state of human living when only dictates of godly natural law applied. Society brought its adopted government into existence by an imagined **social contract**. Within these theories, the central issue was not the duties owed by man to the state and its law but what rights the citizens possessed, the protection of which had occasioned the need to move out of the state of nature and to join in the contract to create civilization. This change in focus was one from natural law to the natural rights discussed by Thomas Hobbes and John Locke (see table 3.2).

TABLE 3.2. **Transitional Arguments from Natural Law to Natural Rights**

Hobbes (1588–1679)	His legal positivism imagines a law severable from morality. Denying that human reason was capable of discerning indisputable rules of law, Hobbes found the only basis for orderly social life in a complete acquiescence to an authorized legislator.
	Leviathan: The original state of nature was "a condition of war of every one against every one"; "the life of man [is] solitary, poor, nasty, brutish, and short."
	It is the law of nature for man to seek peace and the right of man to defend himself; thus, he creates society (*Leviathan*). It is the law only that makes something right or wrong. We need terror of a superior power to make the state work. The sovereign, or "mortal god," is both supreme and absolute.
Locke (1632–1704)	Locke emphasizes the shift from natural law, which imposed duties on the individual, to natural rights, which placed constraints on the state and which existed in the state of nature, preceding creation of law and state.
	Second Treatise of Government: The state of nature was one of equality and the rule of natural law, the execution of which is "put into every man's hands"

through a universal right of self-help. War occurs when one man "attempts to get another man into his absolute power." Desire to avoid potential war (rather than the actual war envisioned by Hobbes) constitutes one reason to enter into bonds of society.

Locke places a heavy emphasis on a right of private property and the value-added theory of its creation. For him, the purpose of society is the protection of property through law.

"The liberty of man in society is to be under no other legislative power but that established by consent in the commonwealth, nor under the dominion of any will or restraint of any law but what that legislative shall enact according to the trust put in it. Freedom then is not what Sir Robert Filmer tells us, 'a liberty for every one to do what he lists, to live as he pleases, and not to be tied by any laws'; but freedom of men under government is to have a standing rule to live by, common to every one of that society and made by the legislative power erected in it" (§22).

Critique of Natural Law Theory

Judged on its own terms, natural law theory suffers from several profound weaknesses. While it holds obvious attraction as a possible source of superior claim against the shortcomings of positive law, a particular problem arises in any attempt to assign specific content to the natural law. What part of nature serves as the standard?

An example of the difficulty in using nature to identify rules of conduct would be the arguments that homosexuality is "unnatural," and thus should be criminalized or at least not recognized or tolerated by civil law. At one time, evidence for this natural law argument included conclusions that, because homosexuality was never observed in nature (i.e., among animals), homosexuality was unnatural and therefore unacceptable among humans. However, more attentive observation has revealed that homosexual attachments are surprisingly common in the animal kingdom. Were natural law theorists serious about their arguments, this new evidence would count in favor of the naturalness of same-sex romantic couples. That they have instead tended to move on to other arguments (e.g., based on the complementary design of male and female sex organs) demonstrates that natural law as a school of thought is sufficiently flexible to encompass any desired position. There are not, in other words, predetermined external standards to ascertain what is or is not "natural" that would permit disinterested inquiry to either arrive at the same rational outcome or rebut such a claim. One lesson may be that while there is a sense that some kind of natural law ethos is required for the creation of a human rights category, that same natural law approach is particularly ill suited to populate that category with any specific content meant to function as universal norms.

Aristotle's answer to this conundrum was that what was "natural" was not what happens—whether or not animals formed same-sex bonds or whether male and female genitalia were a "perfect fit"—but only what happens that is in conformance with one's essential nature. Aristotle's **teleological** (future oriented, moving toward a predetermined "end," or *telos*) identification of the natural was essentially an act of definition, explaining the ancients' obsessive interest in clarifying the meanings of categorical terms.

Aquinas's answer—arrived at by combining Aristotelian and Stoic philosophies—was somewhat different. The natural was that which conformed to reason. While identification of natural kinds was also an act of definition, Aquinas did not limit his analysis to defining qualities of the category but expanded it to include the "reasonable" implications thereof.

Does such a strategy render the content of natural law any less variable? What would have been reasonable to Aquinas would not be reasonable to us today. While for us the equality of women would be uncontroversial, for him the female sex is formally to be subordinated to males, whether to fathers, brothers, and husbands, or by exclusion from ministerial authority within his denomination. Both positions can be defended through some form of natural law argument. That natural law supports mutually exclusive positions on a single issue suggests that it provides an insubstantial foundation on which to construct an actual legal system.

Based on this description, natural law positions might be expected to be rare among legal anthropologists. And indeed, few (if any) expressly announce adherence to this theoretical model. A tension can arise, however, in that these same scholars frequently advocate for human rights, which are themselves most commonly justified by appeal to natural law (see chapter 16).

Reactions to Natural Law Theory

Natural law philosophy originally suffered no serious intellectual competitor. It reached a high level of articulation by the Roman Catholic Church, which held uncontested dominance over the intellectual life of Western Europe. As Europeans became more familiar with cultures other than their own, however, they were forced to confront some of the fundamental difficulties hidden within the natural law outlook.

According to the logic of natural law, because physical nature and human rational abilities were similar, all law everywhere should develop toward the same values, if not literal forms. Beginning with the Age of Discovery, however, Europeans encountered cultures sufficiently unlike their own that they were compelled to make some uncomfortable choices. Either physical reality was *not* the same everywhere—supported by fantastic tales of bizarre peoples, creatures, and environments; *or* human rational abilities were *not* similar—leading to derogatory evaluations of the mental capacities of non-Europeans specifically and non-Caucasians generally; *or* natural law premises—and by implication perhaps also the theology it implied—were false.

Perhaps for obvious reasons, the third logical possibility was the last to be seriously considered. Broader contact with non-Europeans had begun to discredit the first two options—no distinctly alien environment was ever found, and the image of the non-European as possessing fundamentally different abilities gradually yielded to the equally disparaging but qualitatively different posture of outsiders as "childlike" in their capabilities. This analogy denied them the mature use of human abilities but was less likely to support a claim that they failed utterly to possess the capacity for such abilities.

The way was thereby cleared to critically evaluate the claims of natural law theory itself. Instead of the more traditional chronological presentation, reactions to natural law reasoning can be instructively arranged according to the number of changes required to describe the new model.

Lewis Henry Morgan (1818–1881)

If one removes the teleological element from natural law but leaves all else untouched, one can easily generate a pattern of unilinear evolution. For Morgan, this was the **savagery–barbarism–civilization** sequence put forward in his classic *Ancient Society* (1877).

Trained as a lawyer, Morgan's initial interests lay in discovering the relation of kinship systems to social and particularly economic conditions. *Ancient Society* emerged out of this early research. Having earlier documented the relationship of kin terms and social structure in *The League of the Iroquois* (1851), in *Systems of Consanguinity and Affinity of the Human Family* (1871) Morgan broadened his inquiry beyond the Iroquois context by soliciting anecdotal information from missionaries and others working in places around the world.

The patterns he discerned motivated Morgan to attempt a kind of universal history of human social development, leading to his three major **ethnical periods** mentioned previously. The criterion for placement within this typology was based on the presence of specific technology ranked according to relative complexity. "Upper savagery" societies, for instance, were those that relied on the bow and arrow, while the next level, "lower barbarism," included pottery.

The second part of *Ancient Society* covers the rise of systems of government, while the fourth emphasized the primacy of property as the genitor of higher levels of society, recalling Locke's emphasis on a need to protect private property as the impetus to move out of nature and to form the state. Morgan deviated from the social contractarians, however, when he allowed the possibility of a tension between the interests of the individual and the state.

Morgan's and similar schemes of unilinear evolution essentially replicate the programmatic unfolding found in natural law theories. The primary theoretical differences are two. First, the *cause* of the change has been secularized and thus no longer contains explicit moral value. Although values are frequently imposed on cultural levels below that of the "civilization," these values are imported into the theory rather than derived from it. More important, the described evolutionary changes no longer moved *toward* a predetermined outcome (as in natural law) but rather *out of* initial conditions. Although the description inevitability remains much the same, the understanding of the process is no longer overtly teleological but is instead historical.

Morgan has a special place among the forerunners to modern legal anthropology in that he was the first who did significant fieldwork. Working among the Iroquois, he brought the cultural study of legal systems closer to modern ethnography than few before him, notwithstanding the fact that the extent of this fieldwork was meager by today's standards.

Of enduring relevance is Morgan's attempt to relate one feature of culture to another in a predictable manner. That he chose property as determinative of kinship would draw his work to the attention of Karl Marx and Frederick Engels (see chapter 4). But heretofore we had rarely seen culture so completely (if exaggeratedly) represented as an integrated whole rather than the mere concatenation of discrete, independent elements.

Montesquieu (1689–1755)

Although writing earlier than Morgan, the refutation of natural law by Charles-Louis de Secondat, Baron de Montesquieu, was more radical. While secularizing natural law Morgan had implicitly retained the theory's premise that there is but one correct script for the development of legal systems. Individual societies might stop at different points along this single line, but the same metric of progress could evaluate them all.

Montesquieu rejected this assumption that law was—or even should be—universally similar. Writing in *The Spirit of the Laws* (1748), he argued for the situational contextualization of law to local variables, including climate. The cross-cultural content of law would no longer be uniform but would be adapted to the "disposition of the people" so that it was "appropriate."

He had previously dramatized the power of viewing customs through the lens of local practices with his anonymously published *Persian Letters* (1721), in which fictional correspondence between foreigners relate their observations of eighteenth-century French culture. The popular work demonstrated that familiar practices can be strange when viewed from the outside and was part of the increased sense of cultural relativity that had grown with European exploration.

The Spirit of the Laws put this cultural and legal relativity on a theoretical foundation. Unlike social contractarians such as Hobbes and Locke, Montesquieu believed that knowledge of the state of nature and of the transition out of that condition did not predetermine the forms of government, much less help identify the best one. Instead, legal traditions grew out of the specific local conditions, including culture, mores, climate, geography, and the like. This locally tailored tradition constituted the "spirit" that molded each example of the legal institution.

Despite the range of local variation, Montesquieu did identify three basic forms of government—the **despotic, republican**, and **monarchical**—that were rooted in fear, virtue, and honor, respectively. The most enduring of Montesquieu's contributions to political philosophy would prove to be his doctrine of the **separation of powers** (which had been suggested earlier in Aristotle's *Politics*), which would exert deep influence over the framers of the American and French constitutions.

Montesquieu's was not, however, a complete renunciation of all the premises of natural law, as he shared with natural law thinkers the belief that law was not sui generis but could be explained by variables outside the institution. Specifically, he argued that given the known local conditions, certain kinds of law would follow. Legal systems, in other words, developed according to "types." Law was no longer held to be uniform across peoples, but it was still expected to be the end result of a process involving extralegal forces. Law remained, as it was in natural law, a dependent variable.

Looking ahead to later discussions, we can begin to see here some of the theoretical dilemmas that would come later to plague anthropology. Montesquieu reasonably argued his thesis of the relativity of legal systems against the sweeping doctrine of natural law, which had begun to crack in the face of encounters with non-European, non-Christian cultures. Yet if law is not bounded in *some* way, if it is in fact truly a response to purely local conditions (i.e., law is, in the words of Clifford Geertz, a "distinctive manner of imaging the real"), what does this imply for the possibility of legally based universal human rights? What would these rights be, and how would we determine their content? In other words, can the cultural particularism that Montesquieu initiated go too far? If, on the other hand, there are to be principled limits, of what do they consist?

Henry Sumner Maine (*1822–1888*)

The reputation of Sir Henry Maine rests on his 1861 book *Ancient Law*. In this classic work, Maine pushed Montesquieu's legal relativity to the next level. Montesquieu had broken the unilinear development of law into more variable local patterns but still left law as the dependent variable to be determined by forces outside the legal system. Maine would argue that law was indeed locally variable but that the path of legal development depended far more on the influence of ideas and strains within law: the ultimate explanation of law should rest in law itself.

Like his fellow forerunners, Maine—a law professor at Cambridge—was concerned with the problem of how law developed and changed. His most famous dictum was that the progress of law was one "from status to contract." The original condition of society, he claimed,

> was not what it is assumed to be at present, a collection of *individuals*. In fact, and in the view of the men who composed it, it was *an aggregation of families*. The contrast may be most forcibly expressed by saying that the *unit* of an ancient society was the Family, of a modern society the Individual.

Over time, contracts between individuals replace "by degrees those forms of reciprocity in rights and duties which have their origin in the Family":

> All the forms of Status taken notice of in the Law of Persons were derived from, and to some extent are still coloured by, the powers and privileges anciently residing in the Family. If then we employ Status, agreeably with the usage of the best writers, to signify these personal conditions only, and avoid applying the term to such conditions as are the immediate or remote result of agreement, we may say that the movement of the progressive societies has hitherto been a movement *from Status to Contract*.

This claim has been vulnerable to misinterpretation. Too often readers assume that Maine was offering his own version of a unilinear evolutionary sequence that differed from Morgan's only in its details. Instead of a development of law through technological and economic-defined stages of savagery, barbarism, and civilization, Maine was read to be presenting a two-stage model from one in which the determinant of the applicable rule was one's status within a kinship network to one where law was characterized as the contracting between discrete individuals.

Reviewing the influence of Maine, Kenneth Bock conceded that

> the boldness of his language often leaves an impression (which has been a lasting one in critical analysis of his work) that he was writing about all

times, all places, all peoples. . . . [However, his] attention was always on a particular time and place set of phenomena—and the object was to explicate that particular "history."

Ancient Law attempted something far more radical than either Morgan or Montesquieu, if also more subtle. Instead of constructing evolutionary sequences from little or no data, Maine's work was excruciatingly dependent on the details of the Roman law and its influence on Western legal forms. He argued that it was the workings of this specifically legal history that determined the form of the observed modern institutions. He was not, in other words, writing a universal legal history (such as Morgan attempted) or, like Montesquieu, isolating forces that would predict the character of legal institutions. On the contrary, as Maine stated forthrightly in a later work, it was not the intention of *Ancient Law* "to determine the absolute origin of human society."

Dante Scala provides an accessible synopsis of how this historical development can be traced in Western civilization and helps explain the influence of natural law theory in our own culture. Maine's argument is that Roman law, which became Europe's standard not only of legal theory but of educated life in general, functioned as the tool of intellectual thought in the West. In contrast, Greek philosophy served a similar role in the East, and this difference explains much of the fundamental divergence between the two civilizations after the split of the Roman Empire. In Maine's words,

> Few things in the history of speculation are more impressive than the fact that no Greek-speaking people has ever felt itself seriously perplexed by the great question of Free-will and Necessity. . . . [Neither] the Greeks, nor any society speaking and thinking in their language, ever allowed the smallest capacity for producing a philosophy of law. Legal science is a Roman creation, and the problem of Free-will arises when we contemplate a metaphysical conception under a legal aspect.

The legal system devised by the Romans was proprietary. Only Roman citizens were bound by the Roman civil law. Disputes involving aliens relied instead on the *ius gentium*, the law purported to be common to all the nations of the world. Originally a disdained "appendix to the civil code," the influence of Greek philosophers such as Plato and Aristotle transformed the *ius gentium* into the *ius naturale*, "the lost code of Nature." In Scala's imagery, what had begun as a peripheral legal necessity, barely tolerated, became in the end the core of Roman jurisprudence. This result reverberated through legal thought in all parts of the former empire, including the Roman Catholic Church, which effected the final elevation of natural law to its premier status.

Maine's method of legal history would evoke little negative reaction today, something that cannot be said for either Morgan's or Montesquieu's more a priori efforts. Maine showed that meaningful patterns could be discerned in historical details of a particular culture. Modern legal forms need not be explained by invocation of universal evolutionary principles or extralegal forces. Instead, law could develop according to its own internal logic in response to the unique demands made on the institution in that place and at that time.

Some have suggested that this idea that legal systems uniquely reflect the history and lifeways of a people has been overly exaggerated. Alan Watson finds that the wholesale borrowing of codes has been an unappreciated method of legal development within states. This was true not only after the fall of Rome, when invaders took back with them Roman law, but also in the efforts of new nations to quickly enact modern systems. Watson does concede that there are limits beyond which the introduction of foreign laws would be unsuccessful because of their inability to find acceptance within the citizenry; a challenge for future work in legal anthropology should be to identify those boundaries.

Summary and Conclusions

Natural law emerged as a means to intellectually account for the broad resemblances of legal systems observed in the ancient world. This theory served as a tool for the efficient government of a multicultural urban environment. Its later elaboration in the Christian tradition reversed this line of analysis: what was once the inductive conclusion of legal comparison became the moral premise by which all law was to be judged. Implicit in this approach is the expectation that human legal systems should converge toward similar standards and practices.

For a variety of reasons, this posture was vulnerable to criticism, as illustrated by Montesquieu, Morgan, and Maine. All three of these scholars, each writing in reaction to natural law theory, had their formative educations in law. With their attentions directed to this institution, each attempted in his own way to answer some of the broader philosophical questions about law, such as why it arose, how it developed through time, and what forces continue to shape its direction today.

As approaches to the study of law multiplied, appraisals of these first writers waxed and waned. Marxists especially appreciated Morgan, while interpretive anthropologists will find some early precursors of their views in the cultural specificity of Montesquieu. Maine has endured particularly well and is recognized by some as the first true legal anthropologist. All deserve praise for working as well as they did with the materials then available. Morgan went so far as to conduct some of his own fieldwork. While both their works and writings fall easily into the category of the old-fashioned, they merit respect and study not only for what they offer today but even more so for the enormous influences they exerted in their own times.

Finally, the point about the explanatory locus for law should not be misunderstood. Before Maine, law tended to be viewed as fully determined by forces external to the legal system. The form of law could be comprehended without study of the law itself or its development but rather through looking at independent variables (most infamously, climate). Maine did not claim to argue the opposite extreme, that law was impervious to its context, but only that a thorough understanding of no legal system is possible without attention to the features of the law itself. This result can sit uncomfortably with Laura Nader's observation that for students of law and society "law is not autonomous but embedded in society and explained by forces outside the law." If Maine is correct, these forces influence but do not fully explain. The possibility remains, therefore, that contemporary legal anthropologists fail to give sufficient attention to the dynamism of law itself, which can make it a moving force rather than a mere reaction to other pressures.

Suggestions for Further Reading

Natural Law: John Finnis, *Natural Law and Natural Rights* (1980); Robert P. George, *In Defense of Natural Law* (2001); Howard P. Kainz, *Natural Law: An Introduction and Re-Examination* (2004); Anthony J. Lisska, *Aquinas's Theory of Natural Law: An Analytic Reconstruction* (1997); Pauline C. Westerman, *The Disintegration of Natural Law Theory: Aquinas to Finnis* (1998); see also Matthew H. Kramer, *In Defense of Legal Positivism: Law without Trimmings* (1999).

Montesquieu: Robert Shackleton, *Montesquieu: A Critical Biography* (1961); Mark H. Waddicor, *Montesquieu and the Philosophy of Natural Law* (1970).

Morgan: Bernard Stern, *Lewis Henry Morgan, Social Evolutionist* (1967).

Maine: R. C. J. Cooks, *Sir Henry Maine: A Study in Victorian Jurisprudence* (1988).

Martha Nussbaum's *Frontiers of Justice* (2006) offers the reader a complete review and critique of the tradition of social contractarianism from Hobbes through John Rawls.

References

Kenneth E. Bock, "Comparison of Histories: The Contribution of Henry Maine," *Comparative Studies in Society and History* 16, no. 2 (1974): 232–62, at 244; Clifford Geertz, *Local Knowledge* (1989); Shirley Robin Letwin, *On the History of the Idea of Law* (2005), at 17; G. E. Moore, *Principia Ethica* (1903); Laura Nader, *The Life of the Law: Anthropological Projects* (2002), at 104; Dante J. Scala, "Henry Sumner Maine's *Ancient Law*," *Society* 39, no. 4 (May/June 2002): 46–54; Alan Watson, *Legal Transplants: An Approach to Comparative Law* (2nd ed., 1993).

CHAPTER 4

Sociology of Law

NATURAL LAW THEORY, rising and falling in popularity, has never completely disappeared from the intellectual stage. The most authoritative formulations attempt to preserve the perceived benefits of the philosophical school while offering solutions to some of its more intractable shortcomings. Among natural law theorists, John Finnis has earned special esteem for his attempted revivification of the school by arguing that anthropological data could be used to identify core components of what constitutes the *human* (and thereby universal) "good." This methodology converges with that practiced in international law when it rules that the customary practice of most nations—an empirical as opposed to an abstract or theological standard—becomes binding on all nations.

Even critics of natural law tend to support its most prominent descendant, human rights, which were explicitly conceived as a secular version of natural rights that, as we have seen, were little more than a shift in emphasis in the focus in natural law from duties owed to the state. The troubling conundrum for those who value intellectual consistency remains whether one can reject natural law while still supporting the existence of human rights (see chapter 16).

For most social scientists focusing on law, however, natural law recedes into the background. Because of the theological foundation of the theory, it cannot be invoked to explain observed phenomena without accusation of resorting to a literal deus ex machina. The sociologists of law discussed here believed that legal institutions incorporated and advanced wider social objectives and were not simply the expressions of either divine will, historical accidents, or inherent tendencies. The questions of interest to the sociologists of law include the following: What was the relationship of law to the other norms, institutions, and structures of society? By what processes were legal norms institutionalized?

These sociologists of law stand midway between natural law scholars on the one hand and legal anthropologists on the other. They moved the academic study of law out of the realm of philosophy and theology and began the search for empirical regularities between legal institutions and social forms.

Pioneers in the Sociology of Law

Karl Marx (1818–1883)

Even when their theoretical interests diverged, sociologists of law drew profound inspiration from writings out of the natural law tradition. It has already been mentioned that Karl Marx (along with **Frederick Engels**) was much enamored of Morgan's identification of the technological determinants of the forms of law.

As part of his theory of **historical materialism**, Marx strove to identify the economic factors that influence or even determine political and legal institutions—the **superstructure** of societies. For him, law was the expression of the interests of the ruling class, which in turn are rooted in the economic means of production. Central to Marx's theory—articulated in the multivolume classic *Das Kapital* (1867–1895)—is the assumption that law does not have an independent history of development but rather is dependent on the evolution of property. In keeping with the discussion of the preceding chapter, Marx treated law as a dependent variable in his social explanations. Law *follows* changes in economic development rather than leads that social change.

Marx identified three functions of law: ideological, political, and economic. As presented by Katherine Newman, while ideologies function to "describe and explain the world" generally, the ideological function of law "describes social relationships and expresses a social morality." Law also serves as a tool of the political system, to further the interests (usually but imperfectly) of the ruling classes: law is "but the will of your class made into law for all, a will, whose essential character and direction are determined by the economical conditions of existence of your class" (*Communist Manifesto* [1848]). Finally, the economic dimension of law becomes manifest in the property laws that maintain the unequal access to basic resources that is the source of social inequalities.

Whether this tripartite dissection of the functions of law is ultimately helpful can be questioned. As explained by Newman, the political and economic are less functions of law than applications of law to achieve nonlegal ends. Within this description, only the ideological function of law—to provide a way to construct and interpret social relationships and assign meanings thereto—rises to the level of what is typically expected of a "function," and thus there seems here to be a reason to privilege ideological (i.e., normative) functions of law over the remaining alternatives.

Crime he defined as "the struggle of the isolated individual against the prevailing conditions" (*The German Ideology* [1845–1846]). In this formula, he focuses entirely on the retributive, penal dimension of law. A crime occurs when the individual rejects the "social relationships" and "social morality" that law is meant to express. Interestingly, not all violations of formal laws rise, in his opinion, to the level of crime, as indicated by Marx's distinction between "offences" and true crimes. An offense is a "breach of regulation" that should not be criminalized: "If popular customary rights are suppressed, the attempt to exercise them can only be treated as the simple *contravention of a police regulation*, but never punished as a crime" (*Debates on the Law on Thefts of Wood* [1842]). Paul Philips explains that, within this view, "any regular pattern of behavior (other than at the purely individual level) is an expression of the social instinct and therefore cannot be a 'crime,' since the essence of 'crime' is its *anti*-social nature." By definition, anything most people are doing cannot be criminal.

The need for this distinction underscores some of the difficulties with Marx's treatment of law. Although his system captures the interesting features of some components of law, strictly applied they fail to account for the full complexity of many modern legal systems—which is to say, those societies that Marx was especially concerned to explain.

At most points, his emphasis falls to law as enactments of politically controlled legislative bodies. These are the rules that embody the economic interests of the propertied classes. Yet at the same time, his characterization of the nature of the noncriminal offense portrays codified law in conflict with another level of regulatory force, "popular customary rights." The conclusion must be that Marx's model leaves unaccounted for significant dimensions of legal phenomena while perhaps counting as an early unintended description of the phenomenon of legal pluralism (see chapter 15).

In contrast to Marx's unilinear determinism, his longtime collaborator Engels displayed an openness to the possibility of a more complex relation between law and society's economic base:

> Political, legal, philosophical, religious, literary, artistic, etc., development is based on economic development. But all these react upon one another and also upon the economic basis. One must not think that the economic situation is *cause, and solely active* whereas everything else is only a passive effect. . . . The economic situation does not therefore produce an automatic effect as people try here and there conveniently to imagine, but men make their history themselves, they do so, however, in a given environment, which conditions them, and on the basis of actual, already existing relations, among which the economic relations—however much they

may be influenced by other, political and ideological relations—are still ultimately the decisive ones. (*Letter to Borgius, Jan. 25, 1894*, quoted by Phillips 1980)

Émile Durkheim (1858–1917)

Durkheim placed special emphasis on the variable of **social solidarity** and very early in his thinking carved out a privileged place for law in his analysis. As explained in his first and arguably most influential text, *Division of Labor in Society* (1893), because solidarity is a "wholly moral phenomenon" and therefore not directly observable, a proxy measure was required to study it. For Durkheim, law served this role of the ideal "visible symbol." He reasoned that the amount of solidarity existing in a group "is necessarily proportioned to the sum of legal rules which determine" it. As law is "nothing more than the most stable and precise element in this very organization . . . we may be sure to find reflected in law all the essential varieties of social solidarity." If true, a classification of the types of law should correspond to the "species of social solidarity" present in human societies.

He chooses to classify law according to the kinds of sanctions the law imposes. Durkheim then identifies two types of law—that based in **repressive** sanctions and that in **restitutory** sanctions. Repressive sanctions seek to *punish* the transgressor, while the latter intends only to *restore* the previolation status quo. These two types of law in their turn correlate with the two kinds of social solidarity he identifies: **mechanical** and **organic**.

Durkheim's category of crime appears to be broader than Marx's. Whereas crime for Marx was that subset of legal violations that were also antisocial, Durkheim defines as criminal "any act which, regardless of degree, provokes against the perpetrator the characteristic reaction known as punishment." He later offers a slightly different definition, one that shifts attention away from the sanction element and onto the antisocial: an act is a crime "when it offends the strong, well defined states of the collective consciousness." This conceptual slippage between the two definitions of "crime" suggest that the intersection of his division of law into two types based on sanctions (an imperfect scheme, at best), with his intention to use the legal typology to map the species of social solidarity, may not be completely effective.

Durkheim insisted that "we should not say that an act offends the common consciousness because it is criminal, but that it is criminal because it offends that consciousness. We do not condemn it because it is a crime, but it is a crime because we condemn it."

Following from his theory is the conclusion that mechanical solidarity and repressive law characterize "primitive" societies, while modern societies enjoy organic solidarity and a restitutory legal system. This outcome may strike the reader as counterintuitive. It seems as likely that traditional cultures will be based on a restitutory system that sought to keep the peace within a relatively small, close-knit group in which more informal regulatory norms could also operative. Large societies would lack those means of informal censure, requiring the imposition of more draconian penalties in order to maintain a working social structure.

Durkheim, however, sees the matter differently. For him, restitutory sanctions evoke only shallow reactions from the collective consciousness and thus refer to transgressions that involve individuals rather than society at large. That condition emerges only in complex societies that have developed a division of labor and its correlative organic solidarity. On the other hand, because traditional societies are more homogeneously mechanical, infractions strike more readily at the collective consciousness, provoking an aggressive, repressive reaction.

Critics have not been kind to the specifics of Durkheim's theory. His "whole line of argument rests exclusively on bluster and *a priori* assertion," conclude Steven Lukes and Andrew Scull. They cite literature documenting that, contrary to expectations, "'the ethnographic evidence shows that, in general, primitive societies are not characterized by repressive laws' and that 'it is governmental action that is typically repressive.'" Karl Llewellyn and E. Adamson Hoebel, classic legal ethnographers who are the subjects of chapter 7, reverse the alleged associations. They observed that "there is, for instance, the conception that primitive law runs much more heavily to 'tort,' that is, private wrong, than to 'crime,' or public wrong," a belief they then proceed to rebut. Finally, Lukes and Scull marvel at "Durkheim's own extraordinary neglect of the phenomenon of power":

> Law, after all, is one of the focal points of conflict and struggle in modern societies, a major means by which power is legitimized, and the form in which coercion is most routinely exercised. Durkheim's insistence on viewing law and its associated penal systems as straightforward expressions of a unitary *conscience collective* effectively precludes any serious attempt to grapple with these issues.

Max Weber (1864–1920)

Like Marx, Weber's original training anticipated a career of legal practice. Perhaps oddly in light of this education and also like Marx, he devoted little specific attention to the question of law, instead preferring to discuss law primarily in the context of other issues. Consequently, Weber's only dedicated exposition on law is one chapter in his posthumously published *Economy and Society* (1922).

Weber's sociology of law launches from Plato's position discussed in chapter 3. That philosophy argued that true knowledge necessarily results in correct action (and, thereby, happiness). Anthony Kronman, in his classic analysis of Weberian sociology, observes that "Weber strenuously denies the stronger claim, associated with the Socratic view, that a person's knowledge is also a *sufficient condition* for his having a particular value or set of values. According to Weber, a person *chooses* his values," a choice exemplified in an act of **will**.

Placing the individual's conscious will at the center of his legal theory renders Weber's approach qualitatively different from that of either Marx or Durkheim. For these latter, the locus of criminality rests in the *effect* of an act upon society, that is, its antisocial impact. In an important sense, Weber introduces the element of the mens rea, or "guilty mind," into this discussion (although it could perhaps be argued that intentionality is implicit within the evaluation of an act as antisocial). For an act to be immoral, the perpetrator must will the deed and presumably also the effects that flow from it. To convict him of a crime, therefore, requires an investigation less into the level of revulsion in society and more into the intention of the defendant. An unintended yet utterly repulsive act could, in Weber's view, be less of a crime than one that is socially unremarkable yet freely willed.

Weber's formal definition of law was recited earlier as an order "externally guaranteed by the probability of coercion [physical or psychological] to bring about conformity or avenge violation, and is applied by a staff of people holding themselves specially ready for that purpose." This definition puts no obvious limitation on the content of legal rules, focusing instead on the social structures activated in the task of law enforcement. The essential quality of law for Weber was not the nature of the sanction but the manner of its administration. Law requires a specialized entity to enforce compliance and impose sanctions.

People commit to a given legal order because they perceive it as being legitimate, by whatever standard such determinations are made in that setting. Processes of legitimation therefore become a significant issue for Weber, one that he seeks to explain through his theory of **authority**, defined as

> the situation in which the manifested will (*command*) of the *ruler* or rulers is meant to influence the conduct of one or more others (*the ruled*) and actually does influence it in such a way that their conduct to a socially relevant degree occurs as if the ruled had made the content of the command the maxim of their conduct for its very own sake. Looked upon from the other end, this situation will be called *obedience*. (quoted by Kronman 1983)

Authority is a species of power but not one necessarily rooted in violence. Instead of naked force, authority acquires its power through normative legitimacy. Illegitimate leaders may impose their will through force, but they lack authority—that is, they are not due obedience—because they lack that legitimacy.

Weber deconstructs authority into three types. Each of the three kinds had its own standard to test for a leader's legitimacy: **traditional**, or patriarchal, which values the established status quo—legitimacy here was linked to conformity with a preexisting social order; **charismatic**, basing authority on the personality of the leader; and the **bureaucratic**, or legal-rational, grounded in the logic of organization and conformity to its rules and regulations. Charismatic authority is inevitably short lived and transforms (often after the death of the original founder) into one of the other two types through a process of **routinization**.

In addition to this typology of authority, Weber constructed another for the kinds of legal thought. He identified two dimensions—substantive/formal and rational/irrational—and matched each of the four logical combinations with a particular style of jurisprudence (see table 4.1).

To some readers, Weber, while offering powerful theoretical glimmerings, never succeeded in synthesizing his model into a coherent whole. The relationships between this several typologies, for example, are not always clear. One explanation for this perceived shortcoming may be that Weber died before the primary exposition of his ideas on law was completed, and thus his writings were not given the opportunity to sort out some of their troubling incompleteness.

TABLE 4.1 **Weber's Four Types of Legal Thought**

Formal rational	Considers only unambiguous general characteristics to determine the appropriate outcome, such as whether the proper procedures have been followed, or through analysis of applicable abstract legal concepts. Ideally a "gapless" system, the prototypical example of this category was, for Weber, represented by Roman law.
Formal irrational	The case is decided by factions not controlled by the intellect, such as oracles.
Substantive rational	Decisions for disputes are influenced by norms different from and external to those of the legal system, such as religion within theocratic states.
Substantive irrational	The judge settles the complaint based not by referral to norms but according to the concrete factors of the particular case. Weber called this "Khadi justice," evoking the image of the (allegedly) ad hoc hearings held under a tree by Muslim clerics.

Summary and Conclusions

At the disciplinary level, little distinguishes sociology from anthropology. Both claim Durkheim and Weber as early influences, if not contributing founders. Once one begins to consider specialized studies, the line can blur to vanishing between a work in cross-cultural sociology and one in social anthropology. The few enduring differences pertain more to method and unit of study than to the questions the investigator hopes to answer.

For present purposes, the sociologists of law offer a transitional perspective between the natural law theorists who preceded them and the legal anthropologists to follow. On the one hand, they helped secularize the study of law, no longer presuming that it encapsulates the mysteries of a deity, or displays an inevitable form resulting from a predetermined developmental path. Instead, they looked to the structure of society in order to glean an understanding about the observed variability of legal forms.

Their answers to this problem varied considerably. For Marx, law represented the economic interests of the ruling class, while for Durkheim it followed from the type of solidarity binding the members of society together. Weber rooted law in the types of legitimate authority recognized by the relevant group and the grounds used to settle disputes.

None of these early models has fared well in its specifics. One flaw that plagued all three was the dearth of reliable cross-cultural data on which to build their grand theories. Filling this need would be but one purpose of the soon-to-emerge specialty of legal anthropology.

BOX 4.1

Law, Politics, and Power

Law and politics are two distinct sociocultural dimensions that are often confused. While related, they are not synonyms despite some intellectual traditions that insist on construing "law" as the output of a political process. The presumed equivalency perhaps arises because the two variables are more intimately entwined in some cultural settings than in others, most particularly in the Western societies that have produced the theorists. Scholars from those backgrounds have tended to elevate their own experiences out of the particular and into the universal.

Politics, like law, refers to an inherently social process, one concerned with the way in which groups resolve issues and render

(Continued)

BOX 4.1
Law, Politics, and Power (Continued)

decisions. In a broad sense, politics concerns the techniques by which one party imposes its will on others. Because law is one method of regulating social behaviors, legal maneuvering may well be the method employed in a political exercise. The difficulty in legal anthropology is remembering that this is only one method that can produce law.

The key component of most political studies concerns the variable of **power**. While power may be as obvious as a resort to violent force, more subtle means also fall within its purview. Again, the overlap with law can be found in the element of legal process that includes the ability to sanction, or punish, those who transgress the legal norm. Politics can not only determine the nature of the infractions but also legitimate who may impose the sanction and stipulate who should write the laws in the first place.

The perfect equivalence between law and politics perhaps occurs when law is reduced to a study of the exercise of power relationships (as some readings of Marx might suggest). In that view, law reflects simply the will of the individual or group with the most power as embodied in the formal code, with a legitimized ability to inflict violence on dissenters.

Few today would agree that law could be profitably reduced to this description. Even when those holding political power intend the system to work in that way, it rarely is so simple. However, the opposite extreme should also be avoided, one that characterizes law as emerging from an apolitical, atemporal custom. As is typical in such matters, most cases will lie somewhere in between.

Suggestions for Further Reading

Sociology of Law: Donald Black ranks as especially influential among today's sociologists of law: see especially *The Behavior of Law* (1976) and *Sociological Justice* (1989). A classic in the field that still provokes comment is Eugen Ehrlich's *Fundamental Principles of the Sociology of Law* (1936), known for its evocation of the concept of the "living law."

Marx: Csaba Varga, ed., *Marxian Legal Theory* (1993).

Durkheim: Anthony Giddens, *Capitalism and Modern Social Theory: An Analysis of the Writings of Marx, Durkheim and Max Weber* (1971).

Weber: Dragan Milovanovic, *Weberian and Marxian Analysis of Law: Development and Functions of Law in a Capitalist Mode of Production* (1989); Fritz Ringer, *Max Weber: An Intellectual Biography* (2004).

References

Anthony T. Kronman, *Max Weber* (1983), at 19; Karl N. Llewellyn and E. Adamson Hoebel, *The Cheyenne Way: Conflict and Case Law in Primitive Jurisprudence* (1941), at 47–48; Steven Lukes and Andrew Scull, *Durkheim and the Law* (1983), at 6, 11, 24; Katherine Newman, *Law and Economic Organization* (1983, extracted in Sally Falk Moore, ed., *Law and Anthropology: A Reader* [2005], at 32–39); Paul Philips, *Marx and Engels on Law and Laws* (1980), at 160–61.

p a r t

III

Ethnographic Foundations

THE STUDY OF the major ethnographies of legal anthropology contained in this section represents the core of this textbook. Chapters 5 through 10 ("The Classic Period") examine classic ethnographies in the field of legal anthropology, from Malinowski through Pospisil, while chapters 11 and 12 ("Postclassic Ethnography") sample representative contemporary practitioners in the field. Each of these workers is seen through the lens of the attempt to address an especially important problem.

Whereas other sections are primarily idea or theory driven, part III concentrates on specific monographic texts and the ethnographic fieldwork that produced them. By the end of these chapters, the reader will control not only the history of the field's fundamental writings and personalities but also the broad outlines of its basic categories of discourse.

The Classic Period

A S BROAD INTELLECTUAL trends, the period of classic ethnography took as its topics such questions as whether law was a cultural universal and thus worked primarily with "primitive" societies. Many of the efforts during this period were directly associated with the British colonial projects in Africa and the world and were designed to improve administrative control over the local populations.

The following nonexhaustive sampling of ethnographies hints at the rich scope of the work that has been conducted in the discipline on social units below the level of the state. As a rule, selection favored works with *substantive depth* (monographs, not journal articles), *ready availability* (English language; commercially published, not dissertations), and *fieldwork methodology* (participant observation, not historical reconstruction). These criteria have been interpreted expansively; if a report fell below these thresholds yet described an underrepresented area or seemed otherwise useful, it has been included nonetheless. The limitation to monographs does not minimize the importance of the periodical literature; an annotated bibliography including this genre has been compiled by Laura Nader, Klaus F. Koch, and Bruce Cox, "The Ethnography of Law: A Bibliographical Survey," *Current Anthropology* 7 (1966): 267–94.

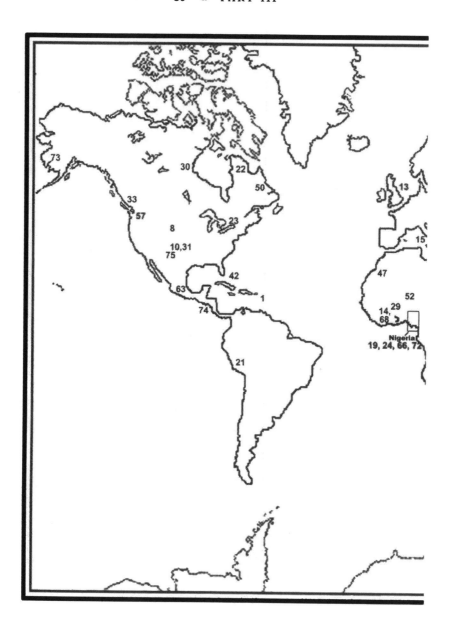

73

30

22

13

33

57

50

8

10,31
75

47

42

52

63

1

14, 29
68 3

74

Nigeria
19, 24, 66, 72

21

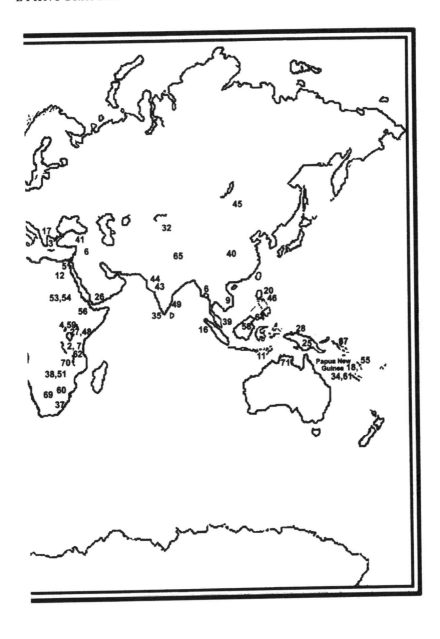

TABLE III.1 Representative Legal Ethnographies

Map Key	People	Location	Ethnographic Source
1	Antiguans	Antigua and Barbuda (eastern Caribbean)	Mindie Lazarus-Black, *Legitimate Acts and Illegal Encounters: Law and Society in Barbuda and Antigua* (1994)
2	Arusha	Tanzania (formerly Tanganyika)	Philip H. Gulliver, *Social Control in an African Society* (1963)
3	Athenians (ancient)	Greece	Adriaan Lanni, *Law and Justice in the Courts of Classical Athens* (2006)
4	Basoga	Uganda	Lloyd A. Fallers, *Law without Precedent: Legal Ideas in Action in the Courts of Colonial Busoga* (1969)
5	Bedouin, western	Egypt	Austin Kennett, *Bedouin Justice: Laws and Customs among the Egyptian Bedouin* (1925)
6	Burmese (formerly Burma)	Myanmar	Maung Maung, *Law and Custom in Burma and the Burmese Family* (1963)
7	Chagga	Tanzania	Sally Falk Moore, *Social Facts and Fabrications* (1986)
8	Cheyenne	Montana (United States)	Karl N. Llewellyn and E. Adamson Hoebel, *The Cheyenne Way* (1941)
9	Chiangmai province	Thailand	David M. Engel, *Code and Custom in a Thai Provincial Court* (1978)
10	Comanche	Oklahoma (United States)	E. Adamson Hoebel, *The Political Organization and Law-Ways of the Comanche Indians* (1940)
11	Dou Donggo	Sumbawa Island (Malay Archipelago)	Peter Just, *Dou Donggo Justice: Conflict and Morality in an Indonesian Society* (2001)

12	Egyptians (ancient)	Egypt	Traianos Gagos, *Settling a Dispute: Toward a Legal Anthropology of Late Antique Egypt* (1994)
13	English	England	George Lawrence Gomme, *Primitive Folk-Moots: Open-Air Assemblies in Britain* (1880)
14	Fanti	Ghana	John Mensah Sarbah, *Fanti Customary Laws* (1897)
15	Florence	Italy	Thomas Kuehn, *Law, Family, and Women: Toward a Legal Anthropology of Renaissance Italy* (1991)
16	Gayo Highlands	Sumatra (Indonesia)	John R. Bowen, *Islam, Law and Equality in Indonesia: An Anthropology of Public Reasoning* (2003)
17	Ghegs	Albania	Margaret Hasluck, *The Unwritten Law in Albania* (1954)
18	Hageners	Papua New Guinea	Marilyn Strathern, *Official and Unofficial Courts: Legal Assumptions and Expectations in a Highlands Community* (1972)
19	Ibo	Nigeria	Charles K. Meek, *Law and Authority in a Nigerian Tribe* (1937)
20	Ifugao	Philippines	Roy Franklin Barton, *Ifugao Law* (1919)
21	Incans	Peru	Sally Falk Moore, *Power and Property in Inca Peru* (1958)
22	Inuit	Nunavik (Canada)	Susan G. Drummond, *Incorporating the Familiar: An Investigation into Legal Sensibilities in Nunavik* (1997)
23	Iroquois	Ontario (Canada)	John A. Noon, *Law and Government of the Grand River Iroquois* (1949)

(Continued)

TABLE III.1 Representative Legal Ethnographies (Continued)

24	Ishan [Esan]	Nigeria	Christopher Gbelokoto Okojie, *Ishan Native Laws and Customs* (1960)
25	Jalémó	West Irian Jaya	Klaus-Friedrich Koch, *War and Peace in Jalémó: The Management of Conflict in Highland New Guinea* (1974)
26	Jabal Razih	Yemen	Shelagh Weir, *Tribal Order: Politics and Law in the Mountains of Yemen* (2007)
27	Kamba	Kenya	D. J. Penwill, *Kamba Customary Law* (1951)
28	Kapauku Papuans	Papua (formerly Netherlands New Guinea)	Leopold Pospisil, *Kapauku Papuans and Their Law* (1958)
29	Karaboro	Burkina Faso	Sten Hagberg, *Between Peace and Justice: Dispute Settlement between Karaboro Agriculturalists and Fulbe Agro-Pastoralists in Burkina Faso* (1998)
30	Keewatin	Nunavut (formerly Northwest Territories, Canada)	G. Van Den Steenhoven, *Leadership and Law among the Eskimos of the Keewatin District, Northwest Territories* (1962)
31	Kiowa	Oklahoma (United States)	Jane Richardson, *Law and Status among the Kiowa Indians* (1940)
32	Kirghiz	Kyrgyzstan	Valentin A. Riasanovsky, *Customary Law of the Nomadic Tribes of Siberia* (1938)
33	Kitwancool	British Columbia (Canada)	Wilson Duff, *Histories, Territories, and Laws of the Kitwancool* (1959)
34	Kuma	Western Highlands (Papua New Guinea)	Marie Reay, *The Kuma: Freedom and Conformity in the New Guinea Highlands* (1959)

35	Lakshadweep Islanders	India	V. Vijayakumar, *Traditional Futures: Law and Custom in India's Lakshadweep Islands* (2006)
36	Lebanese	Lebanon	Cathie J. Witty, *Mediation and Society: Conflict Management in Lebanon* (1980)
37	Lesotho	Lesotho (Africa)	Ian Hamnett, *Chieftainship and Legitimacy: An Anthropological Study of Executive Law in Lesotho* (1975)
38	Lozi	Zambia (formerly Rhodesia)	Max Gluckman, *The Judicial Process among the Barotse of Northern Rhodesia* (1955)
39	Malay	Malaysia	M. B. Hooker, *Adat Laws in Modern Malaya: Land Tenure, Traditional Government, and Religion* (1972)
40	Manchu	China	Sybille Van der Sprenkel, *Legal Institutions of Manchu China: A Sociological Analysis* (1966)
41	Mandalinci	Turkey	June Starr, *Dispute and Settlement in Rural Turkey* (1978)
42	Mayaguana	Mayaguana Islands (Bahamas)	Jerome Lurry-Wright, *Custom and Conflict on a Bahamian Out-Island* (1987)
43	Meos	Mewat (India)	Shamsuddin Shamsh, *Meos of India: Their Customs and Laws* (1983)
44	Misalpur	Pakistan	Muhammad Azam Chaudhary, *Justice in Practice* (1999)
45	Mongol	Mongolia (China)	Valentin A. Riasanovsky, *Customary Law of the Mongol Tribes* (1929)

(Continued)

TABLE III.1 Representative Legal Ethnographies (Continued)

46	Moro	Bangsamoro (Philippines)	Najeeb M. Saleeby, *Studies in Moro History, Law, and Religion* (1905)
47	Moroccans	Morocco	Lawrence Rosen, *The Anthropology of Justice* (1989)
48	Nandi	Kenya	Geoffrey Stuart Snell, *Nandi Customary Law* (1954)
49	Nandiwallas	Maharashtra (India)	Robert M. Hayden, *Disputes and Arguments amongst Nomads* (1999)
50	Naskapi (Kawawachi-kamach)	Quebec (Canada)	Julius E. Lips, "Naskapi Law: Lake St. John and Lake Mistassini Bands—Law and Order in a Hunting Society," *Transactions of the American Philosophical Society* 37, no. 2 (1947): 378–492
51	Ndembu	Zambia (formerly Rhodesia)	Victor W. Turner, *Schism and Continuity in an African Society* (1957)
52	Nigerien	Niger	Christian Lund, *Law, Power and Politics in Niger: Land Struggles and the Rural Code* (1998)
53	Nuba	Sudan	S. F. Nadel, *The Nuba* (1947)
54	Nuer	Sudan	Paul P. Howell, *A Manual of Nuer Law* (1954)
55	Ontong Java	Solomon Islands	H. Ian Hogbin, *Law and Order in Polynesia* (1934)
56	Oromo-Borana	Ethiopia, Kenya	Marco Bassi, *Decisions in the Shade: Political and Juridical Processes among the Oromo-Borana* (2005)
57	Salish (Coast)	Vancouver (Canada)	Bruce G. Miller, *The Problem of Justice: Tradition and Law in the Coast Salish World* (2001)

58	Sarawak	Borneo	A. J. N. Richards, *Sarawak, Land Law and Adat* (1961)
59	Sebei	Uganda	Walter Goldschmidt, *Sebei Law* (1967)
60	Shona	Zimbabwe	J. F. Holleman, *Shona Customary Law* (1952)
61	Simbu	Papua New Guinea	Aaron Podolefsky, *Simbu Law* (1992)
62	Sukuma	Tanzania (formerly Tanganyika)	Hans Cory, *Sukuma Law and Custom* (1953)
63	Taleans	Oaxaca (Mexico)	Laura Nader, *Harmony Ideology* (1990)
64	Tausug	Jolo (Philippines)	Thomas M. Kiefer, *The Tausug: Violence and Law in a Philippine Moslem Society* (1972)
65	Tibetans	Tibet (China)	Rebecca French, *The Golden Yoke: The Legal Cosmology of Buddhist Tibet* (1995)
66	Tiv	Nigeria	Paul Bohannan, *Justice and Judgment among the Tiv* (1957)
67	Trobriand Islanders	Papua New Guinea	Bronislaw Malinowski, *Crime and Custom in Savage Society* (1926)
68	Tshi	Ghana	Alfred B. Ellis, *The Tshi-Speaking Peoples of the Gold Coast of West Africa* (1970)
69	Tswana	Botswana (formerly the Bechuanaland Protectorate)	Isaac Schapera, *A Handbook of Tswana Law and Custom* (1938)
70	Yao	Malawi (formerly Nyasaland)	J. Clyde Mitchell, *The Yao Village: A Study on the Social Structure of a Nyasaland Tribe* (1956)
71	Yolngu	Arnhem Land (Australia)	Nancy W. Williams, *Two Laws* (1987)
72	Yoruba	Nigeria	A. K. Ajisafe, *The Laws and Customs of the Yoruba People* (1924)

(Continued)

TABLE III.1 **Representative Legal Ethnographies (Continued)**

73	Yup'ik	Alaska (United States)	Nella Lee, *Crime and Culture in Yup'ik Villages* (2000)
74	[Mayan] Zinacantecos	Chiapas (Mexico)	Jane Fishburne Collier, *Law and Social Change in Zinacantan* (1973)
75	Zuni	New Mexico (United States)	Watson Smith and John M. Roberts, *Zuni Law: A Field of Values* (1954)

Malinowski and
Reciprocity-Based Law

THE FIRST CHALLENGE for the nascent legal anthropologists was to determine the extension of the "law." Was law the achievement of select and privileged societies, or was it part of every stable human group, regardless of its technological accomplishments? Resolution of this question remains essentially one of definition (see chapter 1) since "law" could, either openly or implicitly, be simply stipulated to favor one view over the other. Bronislaw Malinowski's seminal work among the Trobriand Islanders urged the recognition of law as a universal of human culture and in the process created the specialty of legal anthropology.

Inception of the field of modern legal anthropology has therefore been dated from the 1926 appearance of Malinowski's *Crime and Custom in Savage Society*. As elaborated in earlier chapters, this short monograph does not represent the first exploration of legal topics from the perspective of social science. What makes *Crime and Custom* special, however, is that it marks one of the first (if not *the* first) legal anthropological texts based on in-depth ethnography. Earlier works do exist that draw on the authors' extensive familiarity as missionaries or travelers with local cultures. However insightful, these documents lack the well-rounded theoretical execution of the trained fieldworker.

Malinowski self-consciously saw himself as striking into untrod territory, culminating in his call for "a new line of anthropological field-work: the study by direct observation of the rules of custom as they function in actual life." His work also occurred in a context lacking what westerners then considered the required accoutrement of law—courts, legislatures, and police forces: if law could be found in the Trobriand Islands, it could perhaps be found anywhere. Moreover, Malinowski is the first of the social sci-

---

BOX 5.1
Malinowski Highlights

Born: 1884, Poland
Died: 1942, New Haven, Connecticut
Relevant Fieldwork: Trobriand Islands, between 1915 and 1918
Teaching Appointments: London School of Economics, 1913–1939;
    Yale University, 1939–1942
Significant Publications: *Argonauts of the Western Pacific* (1922, fore-
    word by Sir James Frazer); *Crime and Custom in Savage Society*
    (1926); *Sex and Repression in Savage Society* (1927)
Law-Related Conclusions: Law, especially civil law, based in binding
    reciprocal obligations; no society is without law

---

entists discussed who focused on law as the primary theoretical problem
rather than as a peripheral sidebar connected to broader themes.

Malinowski's Reciprocity-Based Law

The central problem Malinowski addressed was whether Trobriand
Islanders, among whom he worked for many years, could have "law" even
while lacking what many deemed the definitional requirements thereof.

Under prevailing assumptions, people obeyed the law only because they
were compelled to do so by powerful authorities. According to Shirley
Letwin, while Aristotle and Cicero had commented in passing on a correlation between law and the power of coercion, this equation gained commonsense status only after the elaborations of Augustine and Aquinas:
"What distinguishes the law from the commands of the father is not then,
as Aristotle holds, that law rules a *polis* rather than a household, but that the
law has 'coercive power' and can inflict penalties. Aquinas, like Augustine,
thus considers punishment intrinsic to the idea of law." Commitment to
such a relationship between law and the power to punish leads to the expectation that law can exist only where mechanisms work to effectuate that kind
of coercion. And indeed, that became the standard definition of law among
Western intellectuals.

Societies that lacked such mechanisms, therefore, could not have law
but might still be able to maintain order because "savages" dwelled in a psychological state of utter submission to custom and tradition. Malinowski
likened this alleged state to Durkheim's theory of "extreme" collectivism
that located "responsibility, revenge, in fact all legal reactions" in the "psy-

chology of the group and not of the individual." These early models could admit that both "primitive" and modern societies were ordered, but the explanations for that order differed according to the degree of institutional elaboration and formal sanctioning.

Malinowski saw at least two problems with this approach. First, it made the "savage" a qualitatively different kind of human being from those who lived in societies maintained under Western-type legal systems: whereas "primitives" slavishly followed ritual and custom, "civilized" people could decide for themselves what actions to take. The power of free will was apparently limited to westerners.

This traditional position raised innumerable issues regarding the status of human nature that is, as mentioned earlier, an important focus of anthropological inquiry. In essence, it said that there was no "human" nature but at least two natures in the species *Homo sapiens*: "savage" and "civilized," one innately enthralled to custom, the other able to build a civilization based on rational choice.

At the level of logical inquiry, though, the prevailing attitude presented a still different problem: it begged the question about why rules of conduct are obeyed. Even assuming that "savage" psychology was such that persons were compelled to conform blindly to traditional practices, that reason did not actually explain why they did so. Description should never be conflated with explanation. Malinowski sought to place the phenomenology of the obligation to conform on firmer empirical ground.

To isolate the variables that would explain conformity to social rules, he began by looking at *all* the "rules conceived and acted upon as binding obligations" (i.e., all the norms of social regulation). Malinowski employed an **inductive** methodology: by listing every instance of the phenomena, he hoped to find a pattern that would account for the data. This innovative approach should not be underestimated.

Contrasting with Malinowski's novel inductive method would be those styles of exposition that employed ethnographic data selectively to illustrate preconceived ideas or that insisted on interpreting foreign practices by forcing them to fit into the conceptual categories of the observer's own culture. In both approaches, the writer's own cultural assumptions become the interpretive standard against which the new information is compared. The likelihood of recognizing something genuinely new is accordingly diminished. Strictly applied, Malinowski's method allowed for the possibility of observations of novel and unexpected patterns. To the greatest extent possible, the data would be allowed to speak for themselves rather than merely provide exotic illustrations to the writer's preconceptions. Inductive methodology would become the standard for ethnographic fieldwork.

From this process, Malinowski isolated occurrences of the "binding force of economic obligations." He concluded that **reciprocity** between trading partners was the common theme that enforced conformity to social expectation even in the absence of official sanctioning agents. Because each person depends on an economic partner for both essential and prestige goods, flagrant violation of behavioral norms risked severing these essential bonds:

> The real reason why all these economic obligations are normally kept, and kept very scrupulously, is that failure to comply places a man in an intolerable position, while slackness in fulfillment covers him with opprobrium. The man who would persistently disobey the rulings of law in his economic dealings would soon find himself outside the social and economic order—and he is perfectly well aware of it.

That fear served to keep ill-considered antisocial actions to a minimum. An attractive aspect to this theory is that the enforcement component of law was contained within the relationship itself rather than imposed by outside agencies. No policing is required; the rules are self-enforcing.

Reciprocity did not preclude additional motivations for conforming to norms of social regulation. Malinowski differentiated law from these other norms based in part on the "psychological" forces that motivated compliance, such as social ambition and self-interest. Law, in contrast, stands out

> from the rest in that they are felt and regarded as the obligations of one person and the rightful claims of another. They are sanctioned not by a mere psychological motive, but by a definite social machinery of binding force, based, as we know, upon mutual dependence, and realized in the equivalent arrangement of reciprocal services, as well as in the combination of such claims into strands of multiple relationships.

This distinction ultimately appeared in his definitions of both law and custom. Malinowski defined law functionally as norms of rights and duties enforced by pressures of reciprocal obligations:

> There must be in all societies a class of rules too practical to be backed up by religious sanctions, too burdensome to be.left to mere goodwill, too personally vital to individuals to be enforced by any abstract agency. This is the domain of legal rules, and I venture to foretell that reciprocity, systematic incidence, publicity and ambition will be found to be the main factors in the binding machinery of primitive law.

Custom he defined as those norms enforced by means *other* than reciprocal obligation, such as habit, imitation, utility, and sanction. A person can feel customary practices as a duty even where there exists no reciprocal claim of a right by any other person.

Critique of Malinowski's Theory of Law

Malinowski's prediction on the fate of this theory fared no better than the theory itself. The strength of Malinowski's theory is that it appears to account for conformity to social norms in the absence of external policing authorities due to the balance of social ties themselves rather than by invoking nonhuman psychologies or by failing to see the "savage" society as regulated at all. His thesis, however, contains several shortcomings that severely limited its long-term viability.

The text of *Crime and Custom* does not treat civil and criminal law equally (for details about civil and criminal law, see box 5.2). The first section of the book reports a case of civil law and seems to be the context in which Malinowski's theory works best. The second, final section on criminal law is noticeably less successful.

Assume for the moment that Malinowski's theory works very well in explaining civil law situations but less well at criminal law. What conclusions should be drawn from that result? Does the inability of reciprocity to account for criminal law indicate that the theory is wrong? Or does it suggest that civil law and criminal law require discrete explanatory theories? How should we decide between these two alternatives? The theoretical implications of the latter approach are not insignificant, perhaps explaining why the former is the stance most often adopted. And these are the problems raised before questioning the meaningfulness of the very distinction between "civil" and "criminal" law.

One reason why this problem has not been faced more directly is that the initial condition for it to arise has not been satisfied. Few would agree that Malinowski's theory does, in fact, succeed at explaining even civil law, much less both civil and criminal law. Malinowski's explanation for civil law—which he had defined as "the positive law governing all the phases of tribal life"—suffered from the shortcomings contained within all classical functionalist models.

Malinowski prided himself on formulating a new theory of anthropology, **functionalism**. As he explained in "The Group and the Individual in Functional Analysis" (*American Journal of Sociology* 44 [1939]: 938–64), before his innovations anthropological analysis suffered from a piecemeal approach. Each chapter devoted its attention to one aspect of life, followed by the next offering its own disconnected description of yet another theme. Lacking was a perspective that melded these individual elements into a coherent description of the social structure. The method to obtain that portrait would be functionalism.

Malinowski's functionalism accorded privileged position to the individual, a focus that can be contrasted with that of another prominent founder of functionalist thinking, Radcliffe-Brown. Radcliffe-Brown believed that science (as distinguished from history or biography) is not concerned with the particular, the unique, but only with the general, with kinds, with events which recur. The actual relations of Tom, Dick and Harry or the behaviour of Jack and Jill may go down in our field note-books and may provide illustrations for a general description. But what we need for scientific purposes is an account of the form of the structure.

Far from relegating the individual person to the unreported pages of field notes, Malinowski begins with the individual as a biological entity preceding his emergence as a social actor. In his approach, the biological needs of the individual serve as the initial impetus for the creation of cultural solutions to meet those needs: "Functionalism is, in its essence, the theory of transformation of organic—that is, individual—needs into derived cultural necessities and imperatives." These solutions would, in turn, generate their own "secondary or derived imperatives," which were then addressed by their own set of institutional responses. Complete understanding of any one component required a grasp of its place within this interlocking scheme of needs and responses, explaining why any anthropological description worth the title seeks a holistic account. Gone was an artificial, misleading contrast between "the individual" and "the group." One is incomprehensible without the other:

> [At] every step we had to study, in a parallel and co-ordinated manner, the individual and the group, as well as their relations. The understanding of both these entities, however, must be supplemented by including the reality of environment and material culture, The problem of the relation between group and individual is so pervading and ubiquitous that it cannot be treated detached from any question of culture and of social or psychological process. A theory which does not present and include at every step the definitions of individual contributions and of their integration into collective action stands condemned. (Malinowski 1939)

For perhaps obvious reasons, functionalist explanations serve as models of stability, with no easy way to account for change or *dys*function. The imperfectly working social system necessarily becomes viewed as one that is *mal*functioning, sick, disintegrating, or some other pejorative. This position could be contrasted with that of Marx, who believed that conflict and revolution was a progressive inevitability rather than a sign of disintegration, or with Durkheim, who suggested that a certain level of crime—and thereby of antisocial activity—was necessary for the normal operation of society and may even serve as a source of moral innovation as one-time criminals initiate new standards of social norms. The shortcoming of functionalism was that it made stability the norm, when in fact conflict and change is more the usual experience of daily life. Only later, when processual perspectives had replaced classic functionalist theories, could tension and conflict be viewed as potentially healthy and adaptive.

Despite the established pitfalls of the theory's details, however, in the end all anthropologists remain functionalists. While no longer making any necessary assertions about the goodness of fit between the cultural slices, few anthropologists seriously argue that they should not be studied contextualized within the overall setting, including the biological and individual.

The civil law, according to Malinowski's model, was just such a tightly packed network of mutually binding obligations that functionalism expected. Little room existed in such a description for discrepancies between norms and practices. Nor could it easily allow for the extinguishing of a normative obligation through social changes, although such could easily be observed to occur. In short, functionalism was not an unmixed blessing. Granting that it was an advance over the method that preceded it, functionalism clearly required either supplementation or replacement. Because Malinowski's model of law in general and civil law especially was utterly dependent on the functionalist perspective, it could not endure.

Summary and Conclusions

Even in light of the difficulties with the details of Malinowski's solution, his critique of the conventional equation between law and organized agents of coercion proved compelling. While it is not the case that this view has been completely abandoned—individuals can still be found who advocate a firm delimitation of the honorific "law" to only state-level machinery—Malinowski's work made it reasonable to imagine a more complicated picture of how law operates in society. That new model did not begin with an assumption that the more technologically "primitive" were inherently incapable of producing true legal process.

Malinowski's scholarship instructs us as well on a much broader array of issues. *Crime and Custom* is a book about social cohesion. Any doubt on this point should be removed by the title of the last chapter, "The Factors of Social Cohesion in a Primitive Tribe." Malinowski, in this paradigm work for legal anthropology, eschewed social control—defined as social regulation through external enforcement—in favor of social cohesion, or social regulation by internalized norms, as the most productive view of the function of law in group life. As we shall see, subsequent workers would gradually reverse this opinion.

Malinowski highlights the qualitative difference between the then-prevailing concept of law as "the machinery of carrying out justice in cases of trespass"—a unilateral view limited to forcing compliance in order to avoid punishment—and the native bilateral view of law as deserving obedience as one part of a larger, personally beneficial chain of binding relationships. Social bonds are formed through the intertwining of reciprocal obligations; a network of individual obligations creates the higher organization of the social structure.

Whatever the shortfalls of his text, Malinowski merits highest respect for his vision of what the task of legal anthropology should be ever after: "The true problem is not to study how human life submits to rules—it simply does not; the real problem is how the rules become adapted to life."

BOX 5.2
Civil and Criminal Law

Malinowski's work incorporates a classic distinction between the "civil law" and the "criminal law." Civil law he defined as "the positive law governing all the phases of tribal life." This definition seems all-encompassing, leaving him little room to distinguish it from criminal law, about which he can only sigh that "crime in the Trobriand society can be but vaguely defined," followed by a list of what acts rose to the level of crime rather than a helpful definition of the category itself. From the case study he offered, John Conley and William O'Barr summarize Malinowski's implicit definition of crime "as an act that (1) violates a fundamental social norm, (2) is not deterred by the ordinary incentives of reciprocity, (3) is made public, and (4) because of these other attributes, cannot be either ignored or resolved between individuals." They see in this idea a Trobriand analogue to the English common law's view of crime as "an offense against the peace and dignity of the state."

Durkheim also worked this dichotomy into his model. Repressive laws "covers all penal law; the second [restitutory law], civil law, commercial law, procedural law, administrative and constitutional law." The distinction between civil and criminal law, therefore, is well entrenched. The question that must be asked is whether it falls along natural fault lines in legal phenomena or whether it is utterly arbitrary. Added to the mix must be contexts when a single act falls into multiple categories. Murder, according to Karl Llewellyn and E. Adamson Hoebel, "was crime, sin, and tort to the Cheyennes: sin first, crime second, and private wrong, third."

Any conclusion will rest in part on what one believes separates the two categories. According to some models, what distinguishes civil from criminal law is the nature of the possible **sanction**: criminal law imposes imprisonment and death; civil law exacts lesser punishments, such as fines, restitution, and required public service. Life and liberty concerns, then, are the essential question.

By another standard, civil and criminal law belong in different classes of social data because of the locus of the **injury**: criminal law punishes injuries to the social welfare and the state, while civil law addresses those between private parties. Whatever importance the conflict might assume in the lives of the specific parties, the issues in civil law (breaches of contract, fender-benders, and so on) concern only those few people. Murder, on the other hand, threatens society as a whole not because of the individual killed but because unchecked violence unravels the bonds holding the group together and thus should be punished more severely. Because of the severe penalty risked, Western criminal procedure demands a higher burden of proof ("beyond a reasonable doubt") than that required during civil proceedings ("preponderance of the evidence").

The distinction, even in legal systems recognizing it, is certainly far from inevitable, and allows for broad overlap (see, e.g., Ellis-Jones [1985]). Perusal of the debates concerning the appropriateness of **hate crime** laws shows this shifting line. Those favoring hate crime laws with criminal penalties argue that the true victim is society; dissenters often view the matter as a private disagreement between individuals, and thus only civil penalties (if any at all) are the appropriate sanction.

For anthropologists, the primary question should be whether the distinction is meaningful cross-culturally or limited to certain local contexts such as Western jurisprudence. Is the divide recognized in the field setting, or is it an analytical device imposed by the scholar? Conley and O'Barr's summary of Malinowski's position would seem to suggest the former, but interestingly theirs is not the only view. Norbert Rouland's glosses the same topic from *Crime and Custom* as "norms which are likely to be infringed," which yields a starkly different set of behaviors than does Conley and O'Barr's formulation. Given the distinction operable in the backgrounds of Western anthropologists, is it wise to refer to an event as a "crime" without specific clarification of why the observer categorizes the event in this way? Laura Nader, finally, insists that "the existence of different native categories of law forces us to question the two powerful categories of Western law—'civil' and 'criminal'—as cultural constructs that are the legacy of a specific Western lawyering tradition."

Even granting the meaningfulness of the distinction, either generally or specifically, the problem remains what kind of explanation each type requires. Does criminal law require one kind of account while civil law another, or should one model of law apply equally well to both? One possibility to entertain is that disparate phenomena can nonetheless result in convergent behaviors. The observed similarities of civil and criminal laws do not require a unitary explanation if the underlying distinction between the two types is found to be valid.

Suggestions for Further Reading

Malinowski: Max Gluckman, *An Analysis of the Sociological Theories of Bronislaw Malinowski* (1949); Isaac Schapera, "Malinowski's Theories of Law," *Man and Culture: An Evaluation of the Work of Bronislaw Malinowski* (1957), 139–55; Michael W. Young, *Malinowski: Odyssey of an Anthropologist, 1884–1920* (2004).

Functionalism: David Goddard, "Anthropology: The Limits of Functionalism," *Ideology in Social Science* (Robin Blackburn, ed., 1972), 61–75; George W. Stocking Jr., ed., *Functionalism Historicized: Essays on British Social Anthropology* (1984).

References

John M. Conley and William M. O'Barr, "Back to the Trobriands: The Enduring Influence of Malinowski's *Crime and Custom in Savage Society*," *Law and Social Inquiry* 27 (2002): 847–74, at 869; Émile Durkheim, *The Division of Labor in Society* (1947), at 24; Angela Ellis-Jones, "Criminal and Civil—Towards a 'Unified Field'?" *Cambrian Law Review* 16 (1985): 42–51; Shirley Robin Letwin, *On the History of the Idea of Law* (2005), at 70; Karl N. Llewellyn and E. Adamson Hoebel, *The Cheyenne Way: Conflict and Case Law in Primitive Jurisprudence* (1941), at 118; Laura Nader, *The Life of the Law: Anthropological Projects* (2002), at 8; A. R. Radcliffe-Brown, *Structure and Function in Primitive Society* (1952), at 192; Norbert Rouland, *Legal Anthropology* (1994), at 70.

CHAPTER 6

Schapera and Codification of Indigenous Law

IF ONE GRANTS that even "primitive" societies can have their own rules of law—which, after Malinowski, few would disagree with—the obvious next step is to isolate that aspect of the mechanisms for social regulation. While of intrinsic interest to the legal anthropologist, historically the motivations for this undertaking were often less noble. In this classic phase, the major funding for the necessary fieldwork came from government agencies intending to use that information to better govern their colonies. This most typically meant the British colonies in Africa, explaining the disproportionate number of mapped ethnographies appearing on that continent.

From almost any perspective, such a project invites innumerable questions. Not least must be whether support of a colonial administration is an appropriate end for data gathered from the dominated peoples by an anthropologist who must rely on their goodwill and confidence. Today fieldwork is expected to be primarily a benefit to the members of the community that has welcomed the researcher and not to those who wish to exploit them.

More theoretical questions arise as well. Is there something essentially problematic in the reduction of a fluid, often orally based legal tradition to the unchanging text of an anthropological report? The work of Isaac Schapera provides an example both of this type of work by legal anthropology and of its more ironic consequences.

Switching his studies from law to anthropology, Schapera studied under both Radcliffe-Brown and Malinowski. Given that intellectual genealogy, he could have been expected to pursue some form of the functionalist perspectives advocated by these anthropologists. Instead, to the extent Schapera may be said to have held any consistent theoretical position, it would be some variety of *anti*functionalism. Schapera rejected the atemporality of functionalism and its descriptions of pristine, reconstructed original societies. His ethnographic vision includes the full range of elements actually encountered, such as the influencing presence of missionaries and colonial administrators. Schapera's published research, enormously influential both in the nation in which he worked and among his students, therefore provides a vivid contrast with that of Malinowski in the previous chapter.

BOX 6.1
Schapera Highlights

Born: 1905, South Africa
Died: 2003, London
Relevant Fieldwork: Bechuanaland Protectorate (Botswana), 1929–1943
Teaching Appointments: University of Capetown, 1935–1949; London School of Economics, 1949–1969
Significant Publications: *The Khoisan Peoples of South Africa* (1930); *A Handbook of Tswana Law and Custom* (1938); *Married Life in an African Tribe* (1940); *Government and Politics in Tribal Societies* (1956)
Law-Related Conclusions: Denied the usefulness of the cross-cultural comparison of legal systems

---

Schapera's Antifunctionalist Ethnography

Depending on the emphasis given, Isaac Schapera can be seen as both a retreat from and an advance over Malinowski's functionalist ethnography. Schapera's work almost immediately addressed some of the recognized weaknesses of functionalism. As then practiced, the effort to describe the interconnections within traditional cultural life necessarily hid from view those elements that were present at the moment but also "alien" to the original lifeways of the group. For example, although the impact of the Christian missionary or colonial administrator was unquestionably extensive, one would be hard pressed to find a detailed examination of such influences within Malinowski's corpus. In an important sense, classic functionalists worked more with the group as it existed idealized in their minds than with the actual communities in the field.

Schapera avoided this particular trap. From another perspective, however, the ethnographic descriptions he created were more truly functional than those of the functionalists. He took to heart the theory's demand that the fieldworker consider the society simultaneously in all its interacting parts. As Schapera has commented, "What we learnt from Malinowski was to study the people as they are, which he didn't do, and to study the whole of the culture, which he didn't do." As functionalists practiced their theory of descriptive holism, they felt they had to omit some disagreeable bits that sullied their portrait of the traditional existence; Schapera included them, creating a realistic description of extant communities.

To include the contemporary aspects of group life necessarily introduces themes of culture change and dynamic unity, concepts that classic functionalism could not deal with. Why were the colonial administrators there? When did the missionaries arrive, and what did they do? It is at this point that his work turns functionalism on its head. Schapera described his method in this way:

> Look, you start off by studying a thing as you find it. Then you ask why is it like this, and that's where the social change comes in. In other words it becomes historical because things aren't like they were . . . a hundred years ago, when David Livingstone and people like that were there.

Adam Kuper, Schapera's interviewer, notes the theoretical innovation this move represented:

> Now that's exactly the opposite to what most of the functionalists were doing. Because they would provide a description of a so-called traditional system and they would tag on a chapter at the end saying that of course it is all completely different now. You started the other way round. You gave a description of what you saw, the reality, all the complexities of Christianity, and education, and migrant labour, and then you asked: How did it come about? What processes led to the present situation? So it was a reversal, it was a revolutionary reversal of the classic functionalist monograph.

From this perspective Schapera's work becomes something altogether different from and an improvement over Malinowski's. Schapera successfully applied the theory that Malinowski had articulated but never *actually* applied. Ethnographies should describe the *real* people and their life practices and not the imagined world of, as Malinowski's book titles frequently reminded the reader, "the savage."

Schapera also did not reject Malinowski's attention to the role of the individual in cultural life although his concerns were discernibly less interested in the biology of the person. Culture, he reminded us, "is not merely a system of formal practices and beliefs. It is made up essentially of individual reactions to and variations from a traditionally standardized pattern; and indeed no culture can ever be understood unless special attention is paid to this range of individual manifestations" ("Contact between European and Native in South Africa in Bechuanaland," in *Methods of Study of*

Culture Contact in Africa [1938]). At this point, anthropology was still looking at how individual variation produced "culture"; later the problem would reverse and become how individuals negotiated among the different cultural options available to them.

Schapera explored the degree to which an influential individual could introduce variations that reverberated through the whole of society, an interest reflected in "Uniformity and Variation in Chief-Made Law: A Tswana Case Study" (in *Law in Culture and Society* [1969]). His reasonable hypothesis is "merely that in a political system like that of the Tswana, where 'the chief's word is law,' his special characteristics as an individual may have much to do with the nature of his legislation," leading to tribal variations within an otherwise coherent culture group.

Critique of Schapera's *Handbook*

If his innovations in field methods deserve our praise, Schapera's specific contributions to the field of law may be viewed with ambivalence. The most well known of his works on this topic is *A Handbook of Tswana Law and Custom* (1938). The book was commissioned by the Administration of the Protectorate "to place on record, for the information and guidance of Government officials and of the Tswana themselves, the traditional and modern laws and related customs of the Tswana tribes of the Bechuanaland Protectorate." Given such a practical goal, the book understandably made no attempt "to discuss anthropological or other theories of primitive law in the light of the information set forth. I have also had to resist the temptation to deal with what may be termed the 'spirit' as opposed to the 'letter' of the law."

The *Handbook* represents an early foray into the practice of applied anthropology (see part V). The text follows a pattern one might expect from a work meant to guide colonial law enforcement officers in their settlement of disputes among members of the indigenous group. Schapera begins with an overview of the social structure of the Tswana tribes, followed by a description of the source of Tswana law. He then categorizes his topics into sections familiar to any Anglo-American lawyer: a description of the Tswana "constitution," followed by topical sections such as family law, property law, and contract law, concluding with a sketch of local legal procedure. The flavor of this technical content can be gleaned, for those not eager to read the full law treatise, in the shorter presentation within his chapter, "Law and Justice" (in *The Bantu-Speaking Tribes of South Africa: An Ethnographical Survey* [1946]).

Whereas Malinowski had endeavored to explore law as a category of social force binding the group together—thereby elucidating the category itself—Schapera lists only the empirical rules of law he found operating among the Tswana. This is a lesser theoretical project, despite its greater practical utility.

The presentation of rules need not in itself constitute a shortcoming of an ethnographer's body of work, however much it can lead to a disappointing monograph. In theory, the rules can themselves serve as the basis for a more theoretical analysis, either by the ethnographer himself or by subsequent researchers. The *Handbook* can be criticized on this view as well, however, because the methodology employed in its construction limits any application of its contents beyond its intended audience of governmental administrators.

Schapera derives his rules of Tswana law from both observation and informants. He does not, however, allow the reader to identify the source for any specific content. The methodological implication is that one source is as good as or as reliable as the other and that to distinguish one from the other would be pointlessly pedantic.

Schapera also treats too dismissively disagreement among his sources about the precise content of a rule. Although he recognizes when such disagreement arises, he does not elaborate how such disputes were settled, for either his own purposes or those of any official charged to apply such rules. When discussing the estate of married women, he states several rules but concludes by observing, "There seems, however, to be much uncertainty and variety of opinion regarding this whole topic." For the anthropologist, identifying such confusion would be a welcome puzzle by which to investigate some of the society's attitudes toward women or how it resolves disagreements between equally pertinent norms. Even for the administrator, it takes with one hand what the earlier paragraphs had given in the way of concise clarity on how to handle such probates.

He fails to follow through on other similarly suggestive observations. For example, he describes the common practice of a man, experiencing bad luck, to transfer nominal ownership of his property to one of his children. The cultural logic was that the property—now removed from the father— would begin to experience good fortune. Schapera comments,

> At no time in the olden days did the practice of this custom mean that the father had donated the property concerned to the child. He retained full right of control over it, and could do with it as he pleased. On his death it formed part of his general estate, to be handed on according to the customary rules of inheritance, and the child after whom it had been "named" had no special claim over it. *But nowadays,* children have begun to claim such property as theirs by right, maintaining that the "naming" is equivalent to a donation. In several cases of inheritance, disputes have arisen over the ownership of such property. The old custom of "naming" is therefore being abandoned. (emphasis added)

We are unfortunately given no account of any such disputed inheritance claims, despite their potential promise to enlighten us about a significant change in traditional practice. So while Schapera records the fact of the change—which Malinowski probably would have not—the *Handbook* is full of frustrating failures to go as far as the modern anthropologist might wish.

We should also ask to what degree Schapera is here *creating* the law as much as *recording* it when he crafts these topical resumes for use by British officers. The project necessarily freezes what had to that point been a fluid legal context. While memories and understandings of what is the proper way to do things can change surprisingly quickly under the right circumstances, the text on a page does not. The anthropologist in such situations does not record the legal traditions of a group so much as transmute them into a form digestible to powerful outsiders, in the process fundamentally restructuring the relations on the ground. In this important sense, much of early legal anthropology was complicit in the domination of indigenous peoples by providing tools to help the foreign power more efficiently impose its will.

Summary and Conclusions

Of all the legal anthropologists studied in this section, Isaac Schapera is perhaps the most obscure. His treatment in Sally Falk Moore's *Law and Anthropology: A Reader*, for example, is noticeably more terse than that of any of the other classic legal ethnographers considered in part III. John Conley and William O'Barr expressed their opinion that, as concerns the literary canon of legal anthropology, "nothing memorable" appeared in the interim between Malinowski's *Crime and Custom* and Hoebel and Llewellyn's *The Cheyenne Way* in 1941.

Explanations for Schapera's diminished visibility are not readily imagined. The *Handbook* achieved a level of real-world significance rarely enjoyed by a work of anthropology. Despite its ethically ambiguous origins as a work of colonial administration, it continues to be consulted by courts of an independent Botswana and has been cited as a source of binding legal precedence in that jurisdiction as recently as 2000. According to Suzette Heald, "It is ironic that Schapera, so concerned to document changing usage and variation, should have his text turned into a frozen repository of custom."

One possibility lies in his complete dissociation from any aspiration to arrive at anthropological generalizations. Whatever the value of his work at the level of ethnography—and by all estimations it is considerable—he did not believe comparative work was either possible or useful. When asked what has been the "lasting value of such comparative exercises," he replied, "None."

BOX 6.2

Custom, Law, and Customary Law

Compilations of local legal rules such as Schapera's *Handbook* introduce a complicating dimension as to just what it is that is being observed and consequently recorded. The problem centers on the distinction between law and custom.

A sizable literature in legal anthropology devotes its pages to the specification of this relationship between law and custom. Karl Llewellyn and E. Adamson Hoebel refer to custom as "a fused, confused word suggesting at once a very general practice and a felt sense of its rightness." For Schapera, the Tswana distinction mirrors the standard of legal realism: law (*molao*) is what the courts are prepared to enforce; custom (*mokgwa*), on the other hand, they will not ("Tswana Concepts of Custom and Law" [1983]). The distinction, therefore, is wholly one based on enforcement procedures rather than other criteria, such as longevity of the standard or any specific content. As the *Handbook* clarifies, "Tswana law must accordingly be taken to embrace all rules of conduct."

Some have attempted to construe law as a special subset of customary practices (as some of Malinowski's language appears to do) or vice versa, arguing custom to be a kind of legal rule. Alternatively, custom and law could be understood to be hierarchically equivalent normative categories, each covering an identifiably disparate realm of social regulatory norms. Finally, it has been argued that custom and law occupy the same normative field and that as one advances, the other recedes even unto extinguishment (see Diamond 1971).

We must then note the added difficulty of the conjunction of the two problematic categories, **customary law**. At least one anthropologist has urged that the term be abolished (de Josselin de Jong 1960). Contributing to the confusion is that "customary law" carries opposite meanings for legal anthropologists and lawyers.

To anthropologists, customary law is an artificial construction by colonial administrators to rule according to the practices of the subjugated peoples. These reconstructed "customary laws" then serve as a mythical, crystallized set of legal norms to which the contemporary indigenes are expected to happily conform. The "notion of 'customary law' was an ideology of colonial domination. The concept of 'customary law' itself manifested an attempt to reinterpret African legal

(Continued)

BOX 6.2
Custom, Law, and Customary Law (Continued)

forms in terms of European legal categories" (Snyder 1981). It was the perhaps unintentional task of projects like the *Handbook* to create this body of customary law rather than, as the workers probably believed, to simply record the legal traditions of the local community. **Indigenous law**, not customary law, is the preferred term when referring to the traditional (precontact) legal systems, although **folk law** has also been used with this meaning. Another term sometimes heard in this context for areas of Indonesia is **adat**.

This anthropological gloss of the term is exactly the opposite of how the term is used in law. Customary law is one of the recognized sources of international law and has two aspects: state practice (what states do officially) and *opinio juris*, which refers to the belief that a state action is required by the rule of law. Not ticketing the cars of diplomats is *not* customary law because this is a discretionary usage, but diplomatic immunity *is* customary law because it is believed to be obligatory. In contrast to the anthropological term, customary law here has content that is specific and dynamic and perhaps accords with what some laypersons might assume the term to mean: actions that have assumed the force of law through practices intended to fulfill perceived if not necessarily formal obligations.

Suggestions for Further Reading

Schapera: Jane Erica Archibald, *The Works of Isaac Schapera: A Selective Bibliography* (1969).

Customary Law: Melissa Demian, "Custom in the Courtroom, Law in the Village: Legal Transformations in Papua New Guinea," *Journal of the Royal Anthropological Institute* 9 (2003): 97–115; A. L. Epstein, *Juridical Techniques and the Judicial Process: A Study in African Customary Law* (1954); Peter Karsten, *Between Law and Custom: "High" and "Low" Legal Cultures in the Lands of the British Diaspora—The United States, Canada, Australia, and New Zealand, 1600–1900* (2002); Alison Dundes Renteln and Alan Dundes, eds., *Folk Law: Essays in the Theory and Practice of Lex Non Scripta* (1995); Rachel Sieder, *Customary Law and Democratic Transition in Guatemala* (1997).

References

Jean Comaroff and John L. Comaroff, "On the Founding Fathers, Fieldwork and Functionalism: A Conversation with Isaac Schapera," *American*

Ethnologist 15 (1988): 554–65; John M. Conley and William M. O'Barr, "A Classic in Spite of Itself: THE CHEYENNE WAY and the Case Method in Legal Anthropology," *Law and Social Inquiry* 29 (2004): 179–217; Stanley Diamond, "The Rule of Law versus the Order of Custom," *Social Research* 38 (1971): 42–72; Suzette Heald, "The Legacy of Isaac Schapera," *Anthropology Today* 19, no. 6 (December 2003): 18–19; Jan Petrus Benjamin de Josselin de Jong, "Customary Law: A Confusing Fiction," *International Congress of Anthropological and Ethnological Sciences, 3rd, Brussels, 1948: Compte-Rendu* (1960), 67–68; Adam Kuper, "Isaac Schapera—A Conversation: Part I: South African Beginnings," *Anthropology Today* 17, no. 6 (December 2001): 3–7; Karl N. Llewellyn and E. Adamson Hoebel, *The Cheyenne Way: Conflict and Case Law in Primitive Jurisprudence* (1941); Francis G. Snyder, "Colonialism and Legal Form: The Creation of 'Customary Law' in Senegal," *Journal of Legal Pluralism* 19 (1981): 49–90.

CHAPTER 7

Hoebel and the Rise of Legal Realism

DESPITE THEIR fundamental theoretical differences, both Malinowski and Schapera adopted broad understandings of what counted as "law." For Malinowski, law exists wherever reciprocal rights and duties are found; Schapera, on the other hand, expanded the scope of the category to reach all rules of conduct. His sense was that, by being rules, they were standards that the Tswana society was prepared to enforce and that it was this criterion of enforcement that demarcated the category of law.

Legal realists would take this argument to the next level. The critical enforcement that characterized law was not formal but real (hence the name). This theory of jurisprudence proved overwhelming in its influence on both how law was conceptualized within anthropology and the methods thought best to study it in the field. The original spokesman for the new model within legal anthropology was Edward Adamson Hoebel.

Law has not always excited the imaginations of anthropologists. When Hoebel consulted his Columbia department faculty—including Franz Boas, the founder of American anthropology, and Ruth Benedict—for guidance on a law-related dissertation, he was told that Native American tribes had no law. Rather than dissuading his interest, however, they directed Hoebel to the law school where Karl Llewellyn agreed to advise the project. The collaboration proved to be uniquely productive, culminating in one of the true classics of legal anthropology, *The Cheyenne Way* (1941). The methodological innovations advanced by *The Cheyenne Way* reverberate throughout the specialty even today, for better or worse.

The Trouble Case as the Royal Road

Perhaps reminiscent of Malinowski, Hoebel and Llewellyn may be better honored by their fellow legal anthropologists for their method of study than

BOX 7.1

Hoebel Highlights

Born: 1906, Madison, Wisconsin
Died: 1993, St. Paul, Minnesota
Relevant Fieldwork: Cheyenne, Comanche, and Shoshone Native
Americans
Teaching Appointments: New York University, 1934–1941; University of Utah, 1941–1954; University of Minnesota, 1954–1972
Significant Publications: *The Political Organization and Law-Ways of the Comanche Indians* (1940); *The Cheyenne Way: Conflict and Case Law in Primitive Jurisprudence* (1941, with Karl N. Llewellyn); *The Law of Primitive Man: A Study in Comparative Legal Dynamics* (1954)
Law-Related Conclusions: Advocated, with Llewellyn, the "trouble-case method" as a means to access the unarticulated norms governing societal regulation and that was grounded in the philosophy of legal realism

for any particular results that they produced. Their innovations can be parsed into the two problems they addressed. First, where does the anthropologist look to find law-related data, and, second, what is the best means to record, present, and analyze those data? Their solution to these questions was that law best revealed itself in the adjudicated case, and thus the **trouble-case method** provided the most sensible entry point. Taking as their unit the legal case (or its local equivalent), they naturally looked to the law school casebook as a model of presentation (see box 7.2).

Hoebel and Llewellyn began from the position that "law purposes [*sic*] to channel behavior in such manner as to prevent or avoid conflict. . . . But there is more to law than intended and largely effective regulation and prevention. Law has the peculiar job of cleaning up social messes when they have been made." They then offer a squarely functional definition of law: "By its fruits is it to be known; indeed, if it fails to bear fruit on proper occasion, its very existence is drawn into question." Anything, in other words, that accomplishes the work of "cleaning up social messes" should be presumptively considered to be "law," regardless of its external features; conversely, anything that fails to achieve that outcome should *not* be treated as law, even if it has all the expected accoutrement thought necessary and sufficient for the category.

Conceptually, this conclusion fails to respect their starting premise that law is *more* than "regulation and prevention." At the end of their development, law is *not even* that but *only* dispute resolution with no room left for these more positive functions or even other ways of confronting the trouble case that fell outside the legal. Because the successful prevention of dispute will generate no "trouble cases," Hoebel and Llewellyn would "question" the "very existence" of such rules as belonging to law at all. This limitation of law to only the work of "cleaning up social messes," with its emphasis on dispute resolution, would shape legal anthropology throughout its historical development.

Hoebel and Llewellyn rehearse the "three roads into exploration of the law stuff of a culture":

1. **Ideological**, referring to the rules or abstract norms people hold up as the *ideal* of behavior. Falling into the category are those who purport to study law when they study codes and statutes. Of the works seen thus far, Schapera comes closest to this method, given his goal to construct a codebook to govern the Tswana drawing largely on verbal reports to identify social norms.
2. **Descriptive**, by which the researcher endeavors to extract norms from what people *do*, which was Malinowski's approach. From the interactions among partners, he distilled his legal principle of binding reciprocity.
3. "A search for instances of hitch, dispute, grievance, trouble; and inquiry into what the trouble was and what was done about it," which is a method to identify norms by analyzing the means by which social disruptions are resolved. This was their "trouble-case method," which would become the standard of legal anthropology. The choice of method is critical since the alternatives are unlikely to generate the same results.

While all three methods can be productive, the inherent weaknesses of the first two make the third the preferred technique to study law:

The case of trouble, again, is the case of doubt, or is that in which discipline has failed, or is that in which unruly personality is breaking through into new paths of action or of leadership, or is that in which an ancient institution is being tried against emergent forces. It is the case of trouble which makes, breaks, twists, or flatly establishes a rule, an institution, an authority. Not all such cases do so. There are also petty rows, the routine of law-stuff which exists among primitives as well as among moderns. For all that, if there be a portion of a society's life in which tensions of the culture come to expression, in which the play of variant urges can be felt and seen, in which emergent power-patterns, ancient security-drives, religion, politics, personality, and cross-purposed views of justice tangle in the open, that portion of the life will concentrate in the case of trouble or disturbance. Not only the making of new law and the effect of old, but the hold and the thrust of all other vital aspects of the culture, shine clear in the crucible of conflict.

The trouble-cases, sought out and examined with care, are thus the safest main road into the discovery of law. Their data are most certain. Their yield is richest. They are the most revealing.

The background for this claim was Llewellyn's legal realism. Prior to the 1930s, legal philosophy had adopted a posture based on precepts of legal formalism. Legal formalism (briefly discussed in chapter 1) held that law was found or discovered, not made by judges. The role of the judge was merely to apply the law mechanically to specific facts, pronouncing the inevitable outcome demanded by the rules.

Contrary to this portrait of the judge as passive mouthpiece of an ideal law, legal realism expected judicial pronouncements to vary significantly from one judge to the next, depending on his or her personality and background, even when presented by the same facts and law. Llewellyn had established himself as one of the progenitors of this philosophy with the 1930 publication of *The Bramble Bush: On Our Law and Its Study*, in which he announced that "divergencies in training, ability, prejudice, and knowledge still occur, and lead to differences in the [judicial] results upon like facts." Realism brings legal practice down to this realm and renders it susceptible to sociological (and anthropological) scrutiny.

By no means were Llewellyn and Hoebel the first to record disputes. Their originality comes from the methodological scrutiny to which the accounts were submitted. Schapera, for example, had included reports of disputes in his *Handbook*, but for him they functioned more as illustrations of legal norms he had arrived at by other means. In the hands of Llewellyn and Hoebel, however, they became the source material from which to extract those norms.

Despite the revolutionary innovation represented by their announced method, Hoebel and Llewellyn, like Malinowski before them, did not execute work at the level demanded by their own theory. While extolling the virtues of the case method, they did not themselves observe and record any actual cases. Instead, they relied completely on informants' recalled accounts, cross-checked when possible with other, similarly elicited memories. Some cases occurred years, even decades earlier (most from about 1820 to 1880), often when the informant, now aged, was but a child. Such source material cannot bear the weight of the theoretical burden the authors demand of it, to provide the means to discern the functional legal norms and ultimately to isolate a "Cheyenne way" of doing law that was distinctly their own. The writers' own practice would perhaps have been more apt to identify the legal *myths* prevalent within a population in which tales of prior events serve to explain or justify a current state of affairs including what could be expected in the way of law enforcement. As it was, it would be left to later fieldworkers such as Max Gluckman and Paul Bohannan to realize the true promise of the trouble-case method.

Suggestive Conclusions of *The Cheyenne Way*

John Conley and William O'Barr offer a bleak assessment of *The Cheyenne Way*. Conceding its stature in the (sub)disciplinary corpus, they admit that in their own classes they assign only the raw case histories—the first nineteen pages—"as an exercise in analysis, but . . . ignore the rest." Viewed more optimistically, granting that the book fails at many levels and even can be exasperatingly confusing at points, it still has much to offer that can be easily overlooked.

One particularly interesting line of argument put forward by Llewellyn and Hoebel is that, given the resource investment represented by the exercise of law, "it follows in the main that the fewer the demands that are made upon the law, the greater the good for the society. . . . [The] less call there is for law as law, and upon law as law (relative to the degree of complexity of a society), the more successful is that society in attaining a smooth social functioning." This opinion recalls Plato's belief that the ideal state shall need no law (see chapter 3). If the need for law is a function of the virtue of a society's citizens, moderately good states will need only some law, while bad states will require a lot to maintain even a modicum of order.

For us, the sociological implication appears to be that, because resort to legal solution represents at least a partial failure of other social mechanisms, not least being those intended to inculcate into the personality an aversion to disruption of social tranquility, excessive need for legal solutions to social problems can itself be a symptom of something gone awry, even if those legal solutions appear at the moment to be working well. Donald Black framed this observation with his generalization that "law varies inversely with other social control." Even in a healthy society, more kinds of norms of social regulation are required than law.

As an illustration, we might consider recent attempts to apply legal solutions to problems possibly more effectively addressed by other mechanisms of social control. Similar to local morality laws such as that in Hartford, Connecticut, which fines students for cursing, President Bush signed into law the Broadcast Decency Enforcement Act (Public Law 109-235, June 15, 2006). This legislation, enacted in response to Janet Jackson's "wardrobe malfunction" during the 2004 Super Bowl halftime show, increased tenfold the penalties the Federal Communications Commission could levy for violations for indecent language on television. These efforts to make decency a matter of law may indicate a breakdown of parallel regulatory institutions. According to Malinowski,

Not all rules can be enforced by the cumbersome external mechanism of court and police force. If you try to make this mechanism penetrate where it does not belong, you either make law ineffective or else when you try to make it effective you destroy the very institutions which you wish to build up. . . . Law is being used nowadays as a panacea. Politics are running riot. Every thing is to be settled by some grand council or committee of commissars. That way lies real savagery, such as is not to be found in primitive societies. Such artificial rules either do not work or work at such a cost to the fundamental institutions of mankind: family, religious community, school, and the communion of people for recreation, sport and pleasure, that all the substance of social life and culture is destroyed. From the practical point of view legislation and the use of law must be put in their proper place, or else civilisation will perish.

While there can apparently be too much law, so too can there be too little. Hoebel and Llewellyn appear to agree with Durkheim that no society can ever be crime free, and thus there will always be a need for a minimum amount of legal regulation. This inevitable minimum arises within their data because of traits that are virtues when directed outside the society—toward enemies and buffalo, for example—yet become irritants when directed inward. Because of the benefits of the external application, it would not be advantageous to suppress completely the qualities of impetuosity and impatience. The continued cultivation of these personality traits thereby incurs inescapable local costs in the form of legally sanctioned, antisocial behaviors.

As ethnography, *The Cheyenne Way* displays a sensitivity to context not seen in the works of Malinowski and Schapera. Particular attention is due to its repeated efforts to distinguish law from other closely related norms of social regulation, such as religion. The authors consider, for example, the forces working to affect the relative conservativeness of religion and law:

The importance of looking into the mechanics of the processes appears when one compares legal with religious institutions in the matter of unchanging continuance. . . . The peculiar additional force in religious institutions is a fear of slipping away from known efficacious procedures. . . . In legal institutions each of these elements is present, but with a further addition—the check, in most instances, of conscious interest-challenge to any departure. The resultant conserving mechanism in legal institutions is therefore in itself more powerful than that in the religious. Yet the latter tend to persist without change over longer periods than do the legal. Obviously, there should be in legal institutions some counterfactor or factors at work to force remodeling.

More important than any specific solution is the fact that the authors are asking these kinds of questions. The functional definition of law with which they are working requires a more nuanced elaboration of the criteria by which law can be separated from nonlaw social data since the observer can no longer blithely rely on external criteria or substantive content. Just as their method exceeds their execution, here too their theory outstrips their presentation. But the novelty of the conception of the phenomena they took as their subject should not be thereby diminished.

Comparative Overview of *The Law of Primitive Man*

Hoebel's contributions to legal anthropology did not end with *The Cheyenne Way*. As Hoebel summarized his research program ("The Study of Primitive Law," in *Some Uses of Anthropology* [1956]), his early work with Llewellyn proceeded according to four premises:

- "Law is a cultural phenomenon."
- "Law is behavior."
- "Social behavior is patterned."
- "Culture consists of a highly integrated, but arbitrarily selected and limited set of behaviors that eliminate a majority of the specific behaviors human beings are capable of."

This set of propositions proved useful, but in the end he found them inadequate to the task of fully accounting for patterns of legal behaviors.

Ruth Benedict had earlier published her argument for the configurational structure of society in *Patterns of Culture* (1934). In this classic work—one that forever put the word "culture" into the vocabulary of the general public—Benedict had represented cultures as elaborating on broad themes, in her analysis the Apollonian and Dionysian. The key to unraveling the significance of specific cultural details would then be to isolate their relationship to the underlying theme given tangible expression through that society's lifeways. "The master proposition that people select norms in accordance with basic cultural postulates is inferentially derived and, for the most part, indirectly substantiated. Whether 'true' or not, it is highly useful."

Similarly for Hoebel, "cultural themes, postulates for law, and social ideals fused in my own thinking to be recast as basic cultural postulates, basic cultural postulates of jural significance, and jural postulates."

This undertaking formed the thesis of Hoebel's *The Law of Primitive Man: A Study in Comparative Legal Dynamics* (1954). When discussing the Comanche way of life, for example, he formulates the society's "postulates" and "corollaries," such as the following:

Postulate I: The individual is supreme in all things.

Postulate II: The self of the male is realized in striving for accumulated war honors, horses, and women.

Postulate III: Women are sexually and economically desirable but are inferior and subordinate to men.

Corollary I: The sex rights of a husband to his wife are limited to himself and his brothers.

From one view, Hoebel here attempts to push the inductive method of the casebook one step further. Having inferred from cases the legal norms of the group, he would then use that result to inductively arrive at yet more fundamental principles, the values that dictate social life.

These doubly inferred rules—evocative of law's "double institutionalization" that will be proposed by Bohannan in chapter 9—are, in their turn, applied by Hoebel to identify broad "trends in the law." This evolutionary theorizing concludes that

> the trend of the law as it has been thus far explored is one of increasing growth and complexity. It is also one in which the tendency is to shift the privilege-rights of prosecution and imposition of legal sanctions from the individual and his kinship group over to clearly defined public officials representing the society as such.

The problem for Hoebel, as for all cultural evolutionary thinkers, is to justify the leap from the identification of types (which many critics would suggest presents problems enough) to arranging them along a sequential timeline, evocative of a quaint throwback to the days of Morgan's search for lines of unilineal cultural evolution. Despite the method and the speculative conclusions, the project itself does raise into sharp relief the kinds of questions asked by these early legal anthropologists: What (if any) are the universals of law, and how can they be identified? How do the rules of law relate to the other social institutions?

Summary and Conclusions

Unquestionably the whole of *The Cheyenne Way*'s enduring influence is contained in the phrase "trouble-case method." When announced, this borrowing from American legal education constituted a qualitative advance within legal anthropology. The unmixed blessing of the gift will be considered in chapter 14; any negative fallout, however, should not detract from the boldness of the innovation and the exemplary willingness of the authors to move legal anthropology into new directions.

Lacking formal training in law, Hoebel early allied himself with a professor at the Columbia Law School. The resulting collaboration yielded one of the canonical works in the field of legal anthropology. In his later reflections, Hoebel urges anyone similarly interested in the ethnographic study of law to take advantage of opportunities available for assistance to be found among law school faculties.

Hoebel and Llewellyn serve as a prototype for the cooperative studies that are not uncommon in subjects lying in the overlap between two disciplines. As lamentations grow about the unmanageable quantity of information generated by even one field, such interdisciplinary teams may be the most sensible solution to research programs joining multiple areas. This team approach will be echoed in another anthropologist–lawyer combination discussed in chapter 12, John Conley and William O'Barr.

BOX 7.2
Casebooks and Hornbooks

Hoebel plainly admits that "the trouble-case method . . . is derived directly from American law school and judicial practice." Given that intellectual heritage, we can note that this outcome was not predetermined. Legal education had at least one other format than the casebook that could have been turned to productive use. Given the enormous impact the model of the law school casebook has exerted over legal anthropology, a brief review of the format is warranted.

The era of the **casebook** commenced in 1870 when the dean of the Harvard Law School, Christopher Columbus Langdell, published the first half of the original *A Selection of Cases on the Law of Contracts with References and Citations, Prepared for Use as a Text-Book in Harvard Law School.* "Langdell's case method studied groups of judicial opinions on each issue to ascertain by means of a 'scientific' induction or logic a basic principle or rule that should govern the issue" (Kissam 2003). The outcomes of cases are used to infer the underlying rule of law that would bring them together as representative of a single legal norm.

The casebook format and method quickly spread throughout legal education. According to Matthew Bodie, 171 casebooks had been published by 1908, and between 1915 and 1941 "nearly one-hundred casebooks were published *each year*" (emphasis added). Although within the academy the editors of casebooks rarely earn significant money or prestige and professors grumble about the work required to guide students through the selections, few law school courses are so bold as to not require their purchase.

This pedagogical method has its reverse form in the **hornbook**. Here, the legal rules are synthesized and given to students—either as restatements of general principles or as codes—who are then challenged to apply them to specific fact patterns and to arrive at the "correct" outcome. Whereas the casebook method is inductive, the hornbook follows a deductive procedure.

While application of the casebook method to studies in legal anthropology was not inevitable, there were many factors that strongly pushed in that direction. Among these are the following:

- Its reliance on the inductive method, which had been so productively employed by Malinowski in *Crime and Custom*
- The familiarity of the lead author of *The Cheyenne Way*, Karl Llewellyn, with this technique to extract legal principles due to his teaching experience at the Columbia Law School
- The casebook's philosophical convergence with legal realism in that it highlights the behavioral aspect of law by concentrating on cases rather than rules

Was the hornbook then a viable alternative model? Although in retrospect it can be difficult to see how one can *begin* with the legal norms when doing ethnographic fieldwork, use of the hornbook might have been a logical possibility had the questions been differently framed. The casebook appears as the obvious choice when asking, "Do 'primitive' societies have law?" In response, the anthropologist collects instances of disputes and the means used to settle then and demonstrates that the procedures and rules applied are sufficiently consistent to fall within the broad category of the "law."

Asking a different question, however, could lead to a different method. If it had been assumed that "primitive" societies possessed legal norms (if not necessarily legal institutions), the research problem would have been to find examples of actions that fit into predetermined law-related categories.

To some extent it is this latter question, not whether traditional societies have law, that has sparked the more enduring debates. Are

(Continued)

BOX 7.2

Casebooks and Hornbooks (Continued)

there any legal concepts, principles, or categories that can be presumed to be present cross-culturally? Even if such legal universals exist, how do they relate to the Western legal vocabulary most likely to be employed when writing about law?

These problems will be addressed in later chapters devoted to the comparative anthropology of law. But while the casebook may seem to have been a felicitous choice, it is not too soon for the reader to realize its mixed blessings. The effect of the casebook on the legal education has been regularly criticized in scathing terms: "[Just] imagine a college physics course where only a few isolated experiments are studied, where the relationship of one to the other is not set out, where the theoretical underpinnings are not stated, and where virtually all of the writings of scholars are ignored. The result is absurd" (Watson 2005). If the casebook has not been generally recognized as doing an adequate job of isolating the legal norms of its home culture, how effective, we must ask, can we expect it to be as a tool to find them in less familiar contexts?

Suggestions for Further Reading

Llewellyn and Hoebel: N. E. H. Hull, *Roscoe Pound and Karl Llewellyn: Searching for an American Jurisprudence* (1997); Bronislaw Malinowski, "A New Instrument for the Interpretation of Law—Especially Primitive," *Yale Law Journal* 71 (1942): 1237–54; Leopold Pospisil, "E. Adamson Hoebel and the Anthropology of Law," *Law and Society Review* 7 (1973): 537–60; William Twining, *Karl Llewellyn and the Realist Movement* (1973).

Legal Realism: Benjamin N. Cardozo, *The Nature of the Judicial Process* (1921); Laura Kalman, *Legal Realism at Yale: 1927–1960* (1986); Julius Paul, *The Legal Realism of Jerome N. Frank: A Study of Fact-Skepticism and the Judicial Process* (1959); John Henry Schlegel, *American Legal Realism and Empirical Social Science* (1995).

Case Method: William P. LaPiana, *Logic and Experience: The Origin of Modern American Legal Education* (1994); Steve Sheppard, "Casebooks, Commentaries, and Curmudgeons: An Introductory History of Law in the Lecture Hall," *Iowa Law Review* 82 (1997): 547–644.

References

Donald Black, *Sociological Justice* (1989), at 78; Matthew T. Bodie, "The Future of the Casebook: An Argument for an Open-Source Approach," Hofstra University Legal Studies Research Paper No. 05-02 (March 2005), available at http://ssrn.com/abstract=691985; John M. Conley and William M. O'Barr, "A Classic in Spite of Itself: *The Cheyenne Way* and the Case Method in Legal Anthropology," *Law and Social Inquiry* 29 (2004): 179–217; Philip C. Kissam, *The Disciplines of Law Schools: The Making of Modern Lawyers* (2003); Bronislaw Malinowski, introduction to H. Ian Hogbin, *Law and Order in Polynesia* (1934), at lxix, lxxi; Alan Watson, *The Shame of American Legal Education* (2005).

CHAPTER 8

Gluckman and Identification of Legal Universals

MALINOWSKI HAD opened the door to the view that law could be a categorical cultural universal, one grounded in a psychological experience of a felt obligation arising from the binding mutual reciprocity of rights and duties. That conclusion, however, does not require that any uniformities exist across the legal systems themselves. That question would be the next to be asked.

Legal realists like Hoebel had persuasively argued that the best place to find law was through the "trouble case." Max Gluckman would run with this suggestion and find that "primitive" legal systems contained much that would be familiar to the student of Western law. Where once the former had not been recognized, now the claim was that they not only existed but were different from our own only in degree. The basis of Gluckman's surprising assertion would be his discovery of the "reasonable man" concept within the judicial process of the Barotse, a people within present-day Zambia. Explained more fully in this chapter, the reasonable man provides a legal standard against which a defendant's culpability could be evaluated. If he had behaved as a "reasonable" person would have under like circumstances, he might owe compensation but not a punitive penalty.

The claim that the reasonable man may be universal was controversial for many reasons. Recall first Maine's argument in chapter 3 that law emerged out of the historical influences of its own sociocultural past. Given that developmental path, it would be unexpected for independent legal systems to converge on anything as specific as the objective standard of the reasonable man. Gluckman's announcement, therefore, set off a heated debate concerning the proper method to analyze the field data collected by study of trouble cases. The outcome of that discussion will prove relevant to contemporary topics such as those involving human rights (chapter 16) and intellectual property (chapter 17). If the reasonable man is indeed a universal, we could imagine these other ideas to be present as well, reducing the global demand for their acceptance to a mere procedural or political obstacle rather than one of cross-cultural substantive incompatibility of ideas.

BOX 8.1

Gluckman Highlights

Born: 1911, Johannesburg, South Africa
Died: 1975, Jerusalem, Israel
Relevant Fieldwork: Barotse (present-day Zambia), 1940–1947
Teaching Appointments: Rhodes-Livingstone Institute, 1941–1947; Oxford, 1947–1949; Manchester University, 1949–1971
Significant Publications: *The Judicial Process among the Barotse of Northern Rhodesia* (1955); *Custom and Conflict in Africa* (1959); *Order and Rebellion in Tribal Africa* (1963); *The Ideas in Barotse Jurisprudence* (1965)
Law-Related Conclusions: Concluded that law among the Barotse resembled that of Western societies in the way its judges reached decisions, most notably through use of constructs such as the "reasonable man"

Perfection of the Case Method

Max Gluckman's *The Judicial Process among the Barotse of Northern Rhodesia* (1955) represents the first mature application of the trouble-case method devised by Llewellyn and Hoebel. His work constitutes the next step among the classic ethnographers, who had been much concerned to prove that all human societies possessed law, in the form at least of legal norms if not institutions. Gluckman was able to take as a given the possession of law by societies; he then asked whether this law was qualitatively different from our own.

In the foreword to *The Judicial Process*, A. L. Goodhart marvels that, "for the first time, we have a case book of early law," fulfilling the promise of the method described in *The Cheyenne Way*. The raw data for Gluckman's analysis came from cases argued before the *kutas*, or councils/courts:

> The litigants, supported by their witnesses and kinsmen, sit before the judges against the posts which hold up the roof. The plaintiff, without interruption, states his case with full and seemingly irrelevant detail. The defendant replies similarly. Their witnesses, who have heard their statements,

then speak. There are no lawyers to represent the parties. The *kuta*, assisted by anyone present, proceeds to cross-examine and to pit the parties and witnesses against one another. When all the evidence has been heard, the lowest induna on the right gives the first judgment. He is then followed by councilors on the three mats (indunas, princes, and stewards) in ascending order of seniority across from one mat to the other, until the senior councilor-of-the-right gives the final judgment. This is then referred to the ruler of the capital, who confirms, rejects, or alters it, or refers it back to the *kuta* for further investigation and discussion. It is this final judgment by the last induna to speak which, subject to the ruler's approval, is binding.

Gluckman offers a vivid overview of how he collected his information while attending the *kutas*:

The main part of my analysis is based on detailed anthropological enquiries over a period of thirty months between 1940 and 1947, and especially on cases I heard being settled in various *kutas*, in which I sat for several months. I do not mean here records of the bare bones of judgments: it will soon be apparent that these do not by any means reflect either the judicial process or the substantive law. The record of a case involves the pleas of the parties, the evidence of witnesses, and cross-examination, as well as the judges' decisions. It is of course impossible for me to reproduce any verbatim record of a whole case. The cases proceeded at high speed in Lozi, which I understood very well but not perfectly. I took down notes in a longhand mixture of Lozi and English. During the hearings I got lost over some details. It was particularly difficult for me to follow the references by parties and witnesses to others by various kinship terms. Where I got confused I asked the head of the *kuta*, next to whom I was invariably seated, to clear things up for me.

There is nothing complicated or mysterious about this method. The anthropologist witnesses events firsthand and records his experiences with copious notes in the native language. The work can be tedious, arduous, and frustrating, yet as the pages accumulate, hidden patterns eventually emerge (at least, that is the hope).

The improved data gleaned by this meticulous detailing of personally witnessed events go beyond being merely more or better than that acquired through eliciting informants' memories or consulting case abstracts. The information is qualitatively superior, as Gluckman was able to demonstrate. He compared his own version of a case (Case 1: The Case of the Biassed Father) with a summary by "an intelligent, trained Lozi" such as would have provided a recollected account under the earlier informant elicitation technique:

This summary was written some time after the case had been heard, and Mr. Sianga has not remembered correctly all the facts or which judges said what. I cite his summary, firstly, because it brings out that for a Lozi the case, as he remembered it, was not a garden-dispute, but a general quarrel involving a father and his "children." Secondly, this summary by a Lozi of a case I recorded fully evidences that the full implications of the judicial process cannot be extracted from texts: a Lozi does not consider that these implications need stating and he concentrates on the legal settlement itself. This shows that the Lozi have a distinctive body of legal rules, but makes clear my difficulty in using similar texts, on points on which I did not hear cases, for an understanding of how these rules are applied.

Reliance on such summaries would not only obstruct the accurate understanding of the events but even mislead. Legal anthropology therefore entered a truly new era with Gluckman's text and the methodology on which it is based. No work of significance on living peoples would again resort primarily to secondhand sources for the cases studied.

Further improvements are, however, always possible. Inquiries not fully pursued by Gluckman that contribute to the complete analysis of the social relationships at the heart of the trouble-case method include the contextualization of the court cases within society as a whole. People often use the law to complain of one matter, when the more enduring conflict is one embedded in the prior history between the parties. Why this dispute, now, when similar events provoked no such reaction? What else is going on? Although Gluckman does devote some attention to such questions, they move closer to center stage when taken up by the postclassic legal anthropologists and their process orientation (see box 8.2 and chapter 11).

The Reasonable Man

James March's review of *The Judicial Process* summarizes the five major questions Gluckman addressed:

- To what extent are the features of the judicial process and legal reasoning invariant throughout the cultures of the world?
- What is the role of certainty and uncertainty in the judicial process?
- Is there room in a modern theory of judicial determination for such concepts as "justice" and "the Law"?
- Granting that the norms of society do enter into judicial decision making, specifically how do they enter?
- What are the relevant questions that research into the judicial process ought to answer?

It was his answer to the fourth question, on the manner in which norms influence judicial decision making, that provoked the heartiest reaction. One tool, according to Gluckman, was use of the standard of the "reasonable man" to determine fault or guilt.

The gist of this tool of legal analysis is that the defendant's state of mind and personal beliefs are not relevant when judging his guilt. Instead, it becomes the idealized *observer's* state of mind and personal beliefs that determine the outcome, with the mere subjective opinions of the actor herself deemed inconsequential. What would the generic society member have done, known, and felt under like circumstances as those that confronted the defendant? The further the individual has deviated from this stereotyped expectation, the greater the perceived fault: she acted unreasonably.

Gluckman enshrines the reasonableness concept at the very root of his Lozi jurisprudence. Noting that the Lozi themselves understand law (*mulao*) to be "the things which ought to be done," Gluckman defines the category as "a set of rules accepted by all normal members of the society as defining right and reasonable ways in which persons ought to behave in relation to each other and things, including ways of obtaining protections for one's rights." The reasonable man standard is imported into this definition through inclusion of the "normal" qualifier.

The *kuta* provides the stage whereby persons deemed by their neighbors as deviating from the way things ought to be done have an opportunity to defend themselves. "The essence of the judicial process is to state these norms to the world and to assess against them the behavior of the parties in a specific series of situations." It is in this light that Gluckman's use of the word "reasonable" becomes significant.

Having the benefit of formal legal education, Gluckman was versed in the categories of thought in Western jurisprudence. He was not afraid to use them to analyze the legal system of a traditional jurisdiction. Gluckman begins by asserting that "the reasonable man is recognized as the central figure in all developed systems of law, but his presence in simpler legal systems has not been noticed."

The standard of the reasonable man has never been unproblematic even within those "developed systems of law." Alison Dundes Renteln insists that the "'objective reasonable person' standard is culturally biased because it is simply the persona of the dominant legal culture, namely the Anglo-American." The test is therefore not "objective" at all but merely the unreflective presumptions of the cultural majority. The legal analysis differs little if at all from a mere culture-conformity test: did the defendant behave in a way that an idealized, stereotypical *American* would behave under like circumstances?

Women particularly have argued that the "reasonable man" was precisely that, a *man*, and therefore prejudiced the claims of females about what would be reasonable from their perspective. Although touted as a generic standard, the "reasonable man" is intrinsically sexist, and not by accident. Reason has historically been a cognitive ability withheld from the list of feminine attributes, earning women a significant amount of paternalistic protection from the law "for their own good."

Beyond such substantive critiques, the concept can also be problematic because of its vagueness. Raphael Powell counts at least six different meanings that can attach to the word "reasonable." Two of these variants can be found already in the few excerpts from Gluckman's text already given: "reasonable" is used to describe both *ways* and *man*. One single definition, therefore, would not suffice to clarify what he means by the term since it is claimed to be a property of both human beings and actions. This one observation hints at the quagmire into which Gluckman attempts to lure his reader.

As the Lozi presumably unpack the concept,

> unreasonable actions include deviations both from custom and from commonsense behaviour. The court works with certain stabilized norms to check the evidence: these norms are present both in the physical and biological world (e.g., cosmological, ecological, and physiological time, and topographical space), in the usual reactions of persons (e.g., a father would not accept marriage-payment from a daughter's abductor), and in the instituted customs and usages of the different social positions which one or more parties and witnesses occupy.

Among the Lozi, the reasonable man would be distinguished from the "upright" man. The upright man is one who behaves according to the ideal; the standard for reasonableness falls something short of such perfection. He need not be the best but only observe certain baseline levels of sociability. Law does not enforce the ideal standard of uprightness but only the minimal criteria of "reasonableness."

In some sense, Gluckman means the term to gloss the expected (ordinary, customary, average, stereotypical) ways of acting, given a person's role and status, but also the rational, sane, and reasoned. The conceptual difficulty is that very often the usual way of doing things is not the reasonable, putting the two prongs of the term in direct conflict. Admitting the confusion into which that the standard throws Anglo-American common law judges, one must seriously question the helpfulness of raising it to the level of a universal legal principle. As we saw for "customary law," we hear a similar call that the word "reasonable . . . ought never to be used again" (Diamond 1956).

Gluckman should, of course, be recognized as having isolated a meaningful principle of judicial reasoning. By wedding it to the label of the "reasonable man," however, he was forced to expend more energy defending the term rather than the ethnographic insight it encoded. That situation would, in the end, describe the gist of the Gluckman–Bohannan exchange (see chapter 13).

Disciplinary Reverberations

The claim that the Barotse recognize and employ the standard of the reasonable man when deciding cases is the keystone to Gluckman's argument that the law of these "primitive" people is nigh indistinguishable from our own:

> In general terms, their courts aim at the same ends as courts in highly developed societies: the regulation of established and the creation of new relationships, the protection and maintenance of certain norms of behaviour, the readjustment of disturbed social relationships, and the punishing of offenders against certain rules. Their jurisprudence shares with other legal systems many basic doctrines: right and duty and injury; the concept of the reasonable man; the distinctions between statute and custom and between statute and equity or justice [see box 10.2]; responsibility, negligence, and guilt; ownership and trespass; etc.

As such, "the Lozi judicial process corresponds with, more than it differs from, the judicial process in Western society."

As soon as these words are spoken, however, the fault lines developing within the anthropology of law should break into our attention. Gluckman may well represent the last of the legal anthropologists—excepting Leopold Pospisil—dedicated to the identification of cross-cultural universals about law. Henceforth, the trend would focus on elaboration of culturally specific legal institutions, with only the most timid generalizations. The tipping point would be the clash of titans between Gluckman and Bohannan.

Later theorizing has suggested that Gluckman's conclusion, however desirable from a liberal viewpoint, was probably overstated given his data. At best, his result is supportable only if the premise on which it was based—that Gluckman was studying a traditional Lozi legal system—is valid. The likelihood of that, however, is small. Colonial administration had already "contaminated" the Lozi legal system by creating the system of customary law that the Lozi inhabited. Far from being a pristine, precontact legal system, the Lozi system may have looked like European law because European law had left its mark on the Lozi system. Gluckman was not able to eliminate this possibility, and therefore his conclusions should be couched in more qualified tones.

Looking Ahead: The Furor over Language

Reaction to Gluckman's ethnography focused less on the details of his theory than the manner in which he expressed it. The negative response at this level is understandable: to read *The Judicial Process* barely differs from studying a casebook in civil procedure during the first year of law school. The pages are strewn with technical vocabulary and concepts from Roman and English law. In addition to the already discussed "reasonable man," terminology and concepts alien to the Lozi include movable versus immovable property, chattel, jus naturale, jus gentium, res judicata, corpus juris, jura in rem, stare decisis, and Latin legal maxims like *ex turpi causa non oritur actio* ("no action arises from an immoral agreement") and *in pari delicto potior est conditio defendentis* ("in equal guilt the position of the defendant is stronger").

Liberal reliance on Western legal concepts begged the question of the extent to which Gluckman's own categories had influenced what he found among the Lozi. Had they appeared so amazingly Western-like because he fit the data into preexisting, Western categories, essentially determining the outcome? This would be the question at the core of the Gluckman-Bohannan debate. Chapter 13 reviews this episode in the history of legal anthropology, and thus elaboration of the issues involved will be deferred to that discussion.

One point, however, bears raising. In earlier chapters, it has been suggested that anthropologists implicitly use their own cultural background as the standard of comparison when they enter the field. Gluckman's text offers itself as a vivid example of this phenomenon on at least two levels. First, his explicit objective was to achieve just such a favorable comparison between the legal system of the "undeveloped" Lozi and his own English common law. Second, while it may be easier to hide the cultural disruption that occurs when describing any society in a language not its own when using only "ordinary" words, Gluckman's text shocks us back into awareness of the problem by its extensive (and some would say excessive) employment of technical legal vocabulary. But this is a difference of degree, not of kind.

While Gluckman has been accused of exacerbating the difficulties of ethnographic description by cloaking the data in foreign words, few could claim that his work was qualitatively more problematic than the offerings of ordinary, less controversial writings. On the contrary, although his methodological transparency exposed Gluckman to extensive and often withering criticism, his openness about his thoughts and his attempts to reconcile his background with his field data stand as models for future ethnographers.

Summary and Conclusions

The goal of the Lozi court is "to be conciliating; it strives to effect a compromise acceptable to, and accepted by, all the parties." Laura Nader and Harry Todd offer a schematized summary of Gluckman's model of how judges handled the disputes that were brought before them (see table 8.1).

As a statement about the function of law within society, this result is significant. To the extent the law is what the courts say it is (i.e., legal realism),

TABLE 8.1 Nader and Todd's (1978) Summary of Gluckman's Model Relating Disputants' Relationship to Outcome

Disputants in multiplex or continuing relationships	will rely on	Negotiation or mediation in settlement attempts	which will lead to	Compromise outcomes
—and—				
Disputants in simplex relationships	will rely on	Adjudication or arbitration in settlement attempts	which will lead to	Win-or-lose decisions

among the Lozi law is primarily a work of social cohesion. As modeled in Nader and Todd's summary, the form of the outcome depended on whether the litigants shared a relationship that society wished to preserve (as between family members or regular trading partners) or whether they were relative strangers. Only in the former circumstance was a mutually satisfying compromise the goal of the court. This divergence in goals matters to Gluckman, especially in contexts like the Lozi, where "four in five cases in Lozi courts are matrimonial disputes." The intention of the court is not only to resolve disputes but also to resolve them in such a way that even the loser is inclined to accept the unfavorable outcome.

Thus is peace within the community preserved, and thus are the ties of the group maintained and even strengthened. The patterned variability of this rule demonstrates the purposefulness of the goal: "Matters of property-rights, contract or injury in permanent multiplex relationships require reconciliation; the same matters between strangers do not." All of Gluckman's analysis goes to demonstrate how this end is attained.

BOX 8.2

Case Studies and Extended Case Studies

Max Gluckman intended *The Judicial Process* to be the first of three volumes documenting law among the Barotse people. The second, *The Ideas in Barotse Jurisprudence*, followed ten years later. The envisioned third volume, *The Role of Courts in Barotse Life*, however, never materialized. The explanation for this lacuna in Gluckman's corpus lies in further developments in the case method.

Gluckman described the case method as it had been developed in his generation of researchers:

> [Faced] with a great variety of tribal systems, [we] illustrated an analysis of the interrelation of the parts of the social system, and how it functioned as a whole, with examples culled from the experience of different persons and groups. . . . Examples to illustrate various social principles were not connected with one another.

Granting the success of the case method at uncovering the principles governing the legal institution, strictly applied it could not fully articulate it with the other components of the social structure. At best, the rich details of the cases Gluckman recorded only suggested the information needed to achieve this wider view, information he realized he did not have and was ultimately never able to acquire. In contrast to this earlier, limited case study approach,

> some younger anthropologists have ceased to use occurrences and actions thus to illustrate general principles of social organization, and instead have begun to analyse occurrences and actions themselves so as to extract dynamic social processes set in a social-cultural framework.

As Gluckman explains, this broader method, the **extended case method**, examined not only the case itself but also how the case found its way into the court, mapping out the experiences of the parties both before and after the court decision ("Limitations of the Case-Method in the Study of Tribal Law," *Law and Society Review* 7 [1973]: 611–42). J. van Velsen explained that the extended case method aspired toward "a synchronic analysis of general structural principles that is closely interwoven with a diachronic analysis of the operation of these principles by specific actors in specified situations."

"Case" then took on two meanings. Although originally referring to the legal event in a court or its cross-cultural equivalent (i.e., a dispute resolution process before a third party), it now meant something akin to a "story," with a beginning, a middle, and an end, of which the official legal proceeding would be but one element.

Taking this different unit of analysis, the extended case method facilitated the application of the case method to contexts that lacked

(Continued)

BOX 8.2

Case Studies and Extended Case Studies (Continued)

formal legal apparatus. Elizabeth Colson was thereby able to use the extended case method to show how the Plateau Tonga of northern Rhodesia, a group lacking "obvious political institutions concerned in the maintenance of order," were still able to preserve cohesion:

> To understand how social control operates among the Tonga, it is first necessary to review the basic elements of their organization; we can then trace the interplay of these elements in an actual incident, and see how different systems of relationship act as checks on any general mobilization of one group against another, while at the same time influence is brought to bear upon the contestants to bring about a peaceful settlement of the dispute.

Applying this method, she uncovers that

> Tonga society, despite its lack of political organization and political unity, is a well-integrated entity, knit together by the spread of kinship ties from locality to locality, and the intertwining of kinship ties within any one locality. It obtains its integration and its power to control its members and the different groups in which they are aligned, by the integration of each individual into a number of different systems of relationships which overlap.

The extended case method would later prove to be not a mere elaboration on or extension of the traditional case method but the leading edge of a paradigm shift slowly emerging within legal anthropology.

Suggestions for Further Reading

Reasonable Man Standard: A. L. Epstein, "The Reasonable Man Revisited: Some Problems in the Anthropology of Law," *Law and Society Review* 7 (1973): 643–66; S. F. Nadel, "Reason and Unreason in African Law," *Africa* 26 (1956): 160–73; Michael Saltman, *The Demise of the "Reasonable Man": A Cross-Cultural Study of a Legal Concept* (1991).

References

Elizabeth Colson, "Social Control and Vengeance in Plateau Tonga Society," *Africa* 23 (1953): 199–212, at 200; Arthur S. Diamond, "Review of *The Judicial Process among the Barotse*," *International and Comparative Law Quarterly* 5 (1956): 624–28; James G. March, "Sociological Jurisprudence Revisited: A Review (More or Less) of Max Gluckman," *Stanford Law Review* 8 (1955–1956): 499–534; Laura Nader and Harry F. Todd Jr., *The Disputing Process—Law in Ten Societies* (1978), at 13; Raphael Powell, "The Unreasonableness of the Reasonable Man," *Current Legal Problems* 10 (1957): 104–26; Alison Dundes Renteln, *The Cultural Defense* (2004), at 36; J. van Velsen, "The Extended-Case Method and Situational Analysis," in *The Craft of Social Anthropology* (1967), 129–49.

CHAPTER 9

Bohannan and Relativism

DEPENDING ON the context, "relativism" can be an insult or an aspiration. An important dimension of that context is whether the relativism involved is cultural or moral. Related by distinct concepts, both have played influential roles within legal anthropology.

The central dilemma has been whether there exist generic categories for the analysis of legal systems. Granting Malinowski's argument that law itself is a cultural universal, was it necessary to go as far as Gluckman to claim that the world's many examples of law can be studied through one lens? And a lens that happened to coincide with the categories of Anglo-Roman law? Or will our understanding of legal phenomena be advanced if we approach each cultural occurrence as self-contained and sui generis?

Paul Bohannan urged the latter approach, and for most purposes his perspective has become the disciplinary standard. That debate, however, has not exhausted the problem of relativism for anthropology. If indigenous legal systems should be understood from the "inside" as it were, are we still able to render an ethical judgment concerning those systems?

Such questions become particularly pointed in today's milieu in which each society seems concerned to judge the details of others as being in compliance with what universal standards of "civilized" conduct have consensually emerged: Is female circumcision a violation of "human rights" (chapter 16)? What sets someone apart as a "terrorist" (chapter 19)? Solutions to the first kind of relativism, the cultural and legal, will help shape society's assumptions about the second, moral relativism.

Folk and Analytic Systems

Employing a methodology similar to Max Gluckman's, Paul Bohannan settled any remaining questions about a core technique to study local legal systems and even the manner in which the information could be effectively

BOX 9.1
Bohannan Highlights

Born: 1920, Lincoln, Nebraska
Died: 2007, Visalia, California
Relevant Fieldwork: Tiv (Northern Nigeria), 1949–1953
Teaching Appointments: Oxford, 1951–1956; Princeton University, 1956–1959; Northwestern University, 1959–1975; University of California at Santa Barbara, 1975–1982; University of Southern California, 1982–1987
Significant Publications: *Justice and Judgment among the Tiv* (1957); edited volumes: *Law and Warfare: Studies in the Anthropology of Conflict* (1967); *Law, Biology and Culture: The Evolution of Law* (with Margaret Gruter, 1983)
Law-Related Conclusions: Argued for the uniqueness of the folk culture, eschewing unnecessary transformation of local legal concepts into Western legal categories as well as broad comparative projects

presented. Bohannan's ethnographic text aims to deal "with that aspect of 'repairing *tar*' [a broad term glossing the territory or homeland of the Tiv of Nigeria] which centers around arbitration and government. It is concerned, that is, with jural institutions embraced in the Tiv concept of *jir* meaning 'court, case, moot.'"

As compared to Gluckman's attention to the decision-making process of judges in Lozi courts, Bohannan's theory attends to the legal institution itself and how it articulates with other aspects of the social structure. At the level of methodology, a cursory glance might suggest that he has followed the same trouble-case model proposed by Llewellyn and Hoebel and realized by Gluckman; that is, he has witnessed several legal proceedings, recorded them in much detail, and then analyzed them with an eye to solve the immediate problem he has posed.

To this basic characterization, however, Bohannan has added his own innovations that devote special attention to the "translation problem" and its ramifications. The translation problem refers to the previously mentioned difficulty to accurately convey indigenous meanings in a nonlocal language, typically English. Any effort to do justice to the field data must be counterbalanced by a concern to place the new information "in relation to a body of knowledge already in existence," which he terms the "theoretical or comparative problem."

Having identified two challenges to the successful completion of any research project, Bohannan sensibly intends to construct his report in layers, one to correspond with each of the two problems. The **folk system** is the report of local interpretations of social events, while the **analytical system** construes the data through the tools of the scientific methods developed by "the anthropologist *qua* anthropologist to explain the material which he has gathered *qua* ethnographer."

The danger according to Bohannan arises when anthropologists intermingle the two systems. Confusion results when the ethnographer does not report the folk system in its true local perspective but frames it to anticipate the analytical perspective that the anthropologist intends to employ later to explain the data. Description then becomes part of the explanation rather than a distinct and independent intellectual undertaking. For example, if the intention is to argue that the criminal and civil dichotomy exists indigenously, it can be problematic if the description of the local system includes terms found in the definitions of those categories. Not coincidentally, moreover, it will be the fieldworker's own legal local system that has been elevated to the status of a purportedly objective analytic system, giving it "wider application than its merit and usefulness" would otherwise allow.

It should not be difficult to guess the intended target of Bohannan's comments. From one view, *Justice and Judgment* represents an extended critique of Gluckman's *The Judicial Process*. Explicit references to Gluckman are few, however, such as when Bohannan comments that "Tiv have 'laws' but do not have 'law.' To speak of a *corpus juris* among Tiv, as Professor Gluckman speaks of it among Lozi, would imply reference to an analytical system, not a folk system." The bulk of Bohannan's criticism comes in the way of a counterexample, a demonstration of how legal ethnography should be conducted and reported, one that respects local realities in a way that Gluckman apparently failed to do.

As a side note, if matters are truly as bad as Bohannan depicts, we may see in his concerns the best argument why legal anthropologists should *not* have prior legal training. If anthropologists are already prone to apply their own technical legal concepts to describe what they witness in the field, then perhaps the fewer of those concepts they possess, the better. On the other hand, we should also consider that John Comaroff and Simon Roberts judged harshly earlier work that "relied heavily on naive accounts of Anglo-American arrangements, which postulated an unproblematic relationship between rule and decision in settlement processes." Too little technical legal knowledge can apparently inflict as much damage to the project as too much. Legal anthropologists must, it seems, walk a fine line.

The *Jir*

Bohannan identifies two folk systems active in Tivland: that of the British administrators and that of the Tiv themselves. These folk systems interact when the Europeans take up what they assume to be the traditional Tiv legal system, reinterpret it to meet their own needs, and then impose it back on the Tiv people (creating what chapter 6 explained as "customary law"). That perceptions of the same legal machinery can be at cross-purposes becomes apparent when "administrative officers and other Europeans living in Tiv-land refer to those bodies officially termed 'Grade-D courts' as 'native courts,' while the Tiv refer to them as 'government courts.'"

Many fieldworkers might find labeling these institutions as "courts" an unproblematic gloss. But the conceptual boundaries of what the Tiv call *jir* are not coterminous with what the European administrators call the "native courts." *Jirs* also include the "moots," or the "*jirs* at home." These are dispute-resolving events that lack the colonial authority of the "native courts." Moots "are concerned primarily with disputes *within* a social group . . . [while courts] fundamentally are concerned with disputes *between* social groups or between individuals." Both, however, are covered by the one word, *jir*.

> In order to retain the essential ambiguity of the Tiv concept, I am retaining the Tiv word *jir*. I realize that this throws a burden on the reader, in that he must call up a new and, at first, unnatural meaning and image. But only the effort of calling it up will eventually lead to its clarification as a concept rather than a welter of parts fitting into familiar pigeon-holes. I cannot translate *jir* by one English word; to translate it with several is to dissipate its force and truth.

Indeed, by the end of the book and the eighty-three trouble cases it reports, the reader has had inflicted on her a plethora of Tiv vocabulary terms that Bohannan deems it inadvisable to translate. "Good ethnography is hard to read," Bohannan has told us ("Ethnography and Comparison in Legal Anthropology," in *Law in Culture and Society* [1969]).

The purpose of the *jir*, according to Bohannan, "involves pointing out a mode of action that will be satisfactory, or least unsatisfactory, to both parties; action to which both will agree, and which will resolve the dispute. . . . The purpose of most *jir* is, thus, to determine a *modus vivendi*; not to apply laws, but to decide what is right in a particular case. They usually do so without overt reference to rules or 'laws.'"

The word that Bohannan has said means "right" is *mimi*, which "means both the morally good thing and the socially correct thing." In this light, the goal of the *jir* can be related to the enforcement of the "fair" as it is understood in that culture. This conclusion earns further support from the fact that judges are described as expecting litigants to speak not *vough* (what is "factually correct") but only what is *mimi*. "[No] Tiv would blame a witness for telling what we should consider to be untruths, if by so doing the criterion of *mimi* were maintained, and the judgment could still be wholeheartedly concurred in by both principals." The distinction between the "socially correct" and the "factually correct" problematizes the view of adjudication as a search for the "truth" that many people hold (see box 9.2). Different societies have adopted divergent positions on this issue.

The legal process among the Tiv is one meant to resolve tears in the social fabric and not necessarily to uncover the truth of the matter. This conclusion can be ratified by the observation that Tiv apply a different set of rules to settle disputes among themselves than they do when a foreigner is involved (as we also saw among Gluckman's Lozi). Where the two interests of restoration and truth are opposed, it will be the former that is given the higher priority: "'Truth' in Tivland is an elusive matter because smooth social relationships are deemed of higher cultural value than mere precision of fact."

For these reasons, concurrence in the outcome of the dispute must come not only from the litigants but also from the community as a whole. The "correct" outcome of a case is not one that correctly applies the "law" but one that everyone agrees is desirable. This preference for consensus can be contrasted with that seen in the previous chapter: Lozi judges, while trying to find the outcome that satisfied both law and justice, in the end, if that proved unobtainable, ruled according to law. The Tiv, it would seem, would rule according to justice, which to them refers to what the community perceives as the appropriate resolution in that specific altercation (the contrast between law and justice is further discussed in box 10.2).

Legal Institutions

The last sentence of *Justice and Judgment* is a quotation from William Seagle: "Developed systems of law at least deal with nothing less than the whole of life, and the law is the one art which, unfortunately, has no subject matter of its own." Bohannan took this opinion to heart and made it the foundation for his theory about the rise of legal institutions.

In his often-reprinted article "The Differing Realms of the Law" (*American Anthropologist* 67, no. 6, pt. 2 [1965]: 33–42) Bohannan set out his own solution to the enduring problem of differentiating law "from norm and from custom." For Bohannan, "norm" refers to "a rule, more or less overt, which expresses 'ought' aspects of relationships between human beings. Custom is a body of such norms—including regular deviations and compromises with norms—that is actually followed in practice much of the time" and that governs "the ways in which people must behave if social institutions are to perform their tasks and society is to endure." Customs, in other words, are norms that have been **institutionalized** to perform the required tasks of a specific social domain.

Society cannot long endure with a number of independently operating institutions. There must exist some higher mechanism that can "interfere in the malfunctioning (and, perhaps, the functioning as well) of the . . . institutions in order to disengage the trouble-case." This responsibility falls to the legal institution.

The legal institution is comprised of laws that are distinguished from mere customs by being "both greater and more precise." Although custom can display many of the "stigmata" associated with law through the force of reciprocity identified by Malinowski, what further separates these two levels is that "whereas custom continues to inhere in, and only in, these institutions which it governs (and which in turn govern it), law is specifically recreated, by agents of society, in a narrower and recognizable context." Laws are, if Bohannan is to be credited, customs that have been removed from their specific context through a process of **reinstitutionalization**, demarking "a transition from the purely social to the legal when certain customs are selected by legal institutions to provide the criteria according to which disputes which threaten the efficient functioning of other social institutions can be settled" (Rouland 1994).

Figure 9.1 presents the tiered relationship described by Bohannan relating norms, customs, and laws. From a cultural repertoire of norms—general prescriptions for appropriate behavior but lacking either specificity or authority—a subset comes to serve as the customary rules for discrete institutions. While functioning in a lawlike manner within their specific domains, customs are unable to settle conflicts that arise between customary social institutions. Hence, a small portion of these institutionalized customs rises to serve as regulatory rules for all institutions by elevation into the legal institution.

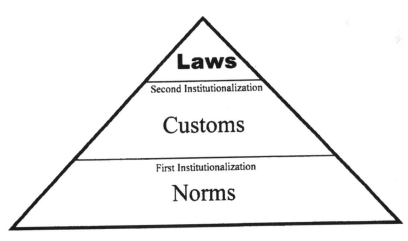

FIGURE 9.1

Schematic Representation of Bohannan's Model of Double Institutionalization

Through this process of **double institutionalization**, select norms become laws, now charged to regulate activity among all the social institutions and not merely their own. Unlike customs, which govern specific domains, laws—echoing Seagle—have no unique domain, instead governing all others. According to Bohannan, law is not one type of norm of social regulation but is the "master" norm hierarchically superior to all others whose only work is to regulate the customary institutions. If law is a social necessity, it is only because of the imperfect ability of customs to govern their domains and not because law has an irreducible domain of its own (such as inculcation of normative standards). The form and content of an indigenous legal system will vary less because of the demands of law itself (although Bohannan does identify some of these: the legal institution must contain both rules of procedure and rules of substance) than because of the customary institutions whose malfunctions it is intended to resolve.

Perhaps the greatest strength of Bohannan's theory of double institutionalization is that it captures the often lawlike aspect of custom. By regulating their own institutions, customs function locally very much as do the more globally active laws. That appearance can lead the casual observer to confuse law and custom, as indeed many, including anthropologists, have done.

The weaknesses of Bohannan's pyramidal scheme arguably outweigh any benefits it confers. Stanley Diamond challenges whether double institutionalization uniquely characterizes legal rules. We can also observe that if custom and law have the relationship Bohannan describes, then the term "customary law" becomes meaningless, belying its common use. More seriously, as Rouland observes, the theory of double institutionalization treats as the *sole* function of law dispute resolution, the stepping in and resolving the "malfunctioning" of institutions. American legal anthropology does work under just that equation (see chapter 14). Those who assign law additional tasks beyond these—a point of some ambiguity among many contemporary legal anthropologists—will find unsatisfactory a theory that does not merely highlight this responsibility but elevates it definitionally into the only legitimate work that law performs.

Summary and Conclusions

Bohannan deemed as "the cardinal error of ethnographic and social analysis the grossly ethnocentric practice of raising folk systems like 'the law,' designed for social action in one's own society, to the status of an analytical system, and then trying to organize the raw social data from other societies into its categories." Notably for those who turn to sanction as the definitional sine qua non of law, Bohannan considers sanction as another instance of the Western local concept that has been illegitimately elevated to the status of the analytic.

Instead of sanction, "explanation in terms of a series of social actions which show the interpenetration of institutions . . . seems more comprehensive and economical." He also identifies the civil/criminal divide in law as a distinction rooted in the Western folk system with little general utility.

Stated in this manner, one would be hard pressed to disagree. To see the deeper problem, one must look again at what Bohannan identified as the two problems of ethnography: the translation problem and the comparative problem. The consensus has been that Bohannan's meticulous attention to solving the first has raised obstacles to fulfilling the second. A rigid refusal to translate terms, insisting on using only the specific vocabulary of the indigenous people, makes the resulting data increasingly incomparable with any other.

This point can be better appreciated in the abstract. If X and Y are to be compared, it is because they are both instances of A, in which case X and Y can be translated to A (with appropriate caveats). Some contexts might require preserving the distinction between apples and oranges, for example, but in others it is enough to know that they are both instances of "fruit." Refusal to relate X to the common category A, however, precludes any comparison of X with Y. Unless the problem Bohannan describes can be surmounted or some principled middle ground found, ethnography faithful to the folk system will produce deep local detail but little that can contribute to a comparative anthropology of law.

How one handles the problem of legal relativism—whether through a heavy emphasis on local specificity such as that argued by Bohannan, or some other view—impacts the subsequent posture toward moral relativism. To the extent that human groups are viewed as being incommensurable, then arguably to that same extent our responsibilities to treat them equally are also diminished since evaluations of equality are as much a comparative judgment as are those of difference, and it is just that kind of comparison that is argued to be problematic. These kinds of conundrum will become critical at both ends of the spectrum when we wish to speak of a unitary group entitled to "human rights" and engage in the discourse of dehumanization for labeling a "terrorist."

BOX 9.2

Inquisitorial and Adversarial Legal Systems

Bohannan's description of the Tiv legal system juxtaposes the search for the truth of the matter and the search for the communally supported resolution.

(Continued)

BOX 9.2
Inquisitorial and Adversarial Legal Systems
(Continued)

The relationship of truth to law—especially criminal law—follows from the task of law to assign responsibility. Some systems recognize a theory of **strict liability**, either entirely or for certain infractions. Under strict liability, responsibility is presumed to lay with one party or another because of some fact, such as their role in the incident; it is not necessary to prove that they were negligent or otherwise behaved in a criminal manner.

A related concept is **collective responsibility**, which holds the group liable for the actions of any of its members. If a member kills someone belonging to a different group, for example, revenge can be exacted on any relative of the murderer simply because of their relationship. It is not always necessary to identify and punish the one who actually committed the crime. Feuds often operate under justifications of collective responsibility.

In situations where responsibility must be assigned to a specific individual before punishment can be exacted, however, truth—always a background concern—rises to dominate the legal process. Legal systems can sometimes be usefully distinguished according to where the locus of truth is presumed to be and the means to discern it.

In the Western tradition, the great divide is between **inquisitorial** and **adversarial** legal systems. Broadly speaking, these two legal traditions constitute a continuum of approaches, characterized by the Netherlands as extremely inquisitorial and the English/American systems as extremely adversarial.

The prototypical adversarial system of law envisions a contest of formal equals before an impartial judge and a verdict-rendering jury. To preserve the formal (which is different from actual) equality, adversarial systems are much concerned about the fairness of the process. It is only a slight exaggeration to claim that procedure becomes more important than outcome: later exculpatory evidence will not necessarily exonerate a person who has been found guilty by a procedurally unflawed trial.

Each side advances the facts in a manner most favorable to its own position. Although neither side can deliberately lie or mislead the court, neither must they fully divulge all the facts. The objective is to persuade the jury to its point of view, not to uncover the truth. From the jury's perspective, the truth emerges in the contested space between the two competing accounts (if anywhere at all).

Inquisitorial systems, by contrast, seek to uncover the true facts of the matter. The court, far from being impartial, plays an active role in evaluating the evidence and questioning witnesses. Perhaps the most significant difference between the two systems is that whereas in adversarial process the procedure is sacrosanct, in inquisitorial proceedings "whenever technicalities of fair play threaten to get in the way of finding the truth, they are put aside" (van Koppen and Penrod 2003). Rights such as those against illegal searches consequently loom larger in adversarial than in inquisitorial jurisdictions. Of particular interest are claims that "inquisitorial and adversarial procedures are *not* alternative ways to serve the same process [of assigning criminal liability]. They represent basically different views of what the purpose of law is, and even of what is the purpose of the state" (Crombag 2003).

Related to the adversarial/inquisitorial distinction is another that closely matches the same sorting, that between **common law** and **civil law**. Common law states tend to be adversarial, with civil law countries preferring inquisitorial processes. Common law refers to the body of rules and principles deriving authority from customs and from decisions by judges. Civil law adheres to enactments of legislators and is characterized by possession of formal codes. The task of judges in civil law jurisdictions is to apply the code, while common law judges must also consider judicial precedent. Contemporary American worries about "activist judges" frequently include a misunderstanding of the traditional expansive role of judges in common law jurisdictions.

Most of the nations of the world are technically civil law jurisdictions. Common law is applied only by states that were former members of the British Empire. In the United States, all states are common law jurisdictions except for French-settled Louisiana. In practice, however, most jurisdictions are mixed.

While these comparisons are of interest in their own right, they are also a basis of contrast between the backgrounds of fieldworking legal anthropologists. To the extent that an anthropologist's view of law is shaped by the legal traditions of her own society, those from common law/adversarial backgrounds will bring to the field different expectations of what law looks like and what functions it should perform than those from civil law/inquisitorial systems.

Suggestions for Further Reading

Translation Problems: Gísli Pálsson, ed., *Beyond Boundaries: Understanding, Translation, and Anthropological Discourse* (1993); Paula G. Rubel and Abraham Rosman, eds., *Translating Cultures: Perspectives on Translation and Anthropology* (2003).

Inquisitorial/Adversarial Legal Systems: Matthew T. King, "Security, Scale, Form, and Function: The Search for Truth and the Exclusion of Evidence in Adversarial and Inquisitorial Justice Systems," *International Legal Perspectives* 12 (2002): 185–236.

References

John L. Comaroff and Simon Roberts, *Rules and Processes: The Cultural Logic of Dispute in an African Context* (1981), at 8; Hans F. M. Crombag, "Adversarial or Inquisitorial: Do We Have a Choice?" in *Adversarial versus Inquisitorial Justice* (2003), 21–25, at 22; Stanley Diamond, "The Rule of Law versus the Order of Custom," *Social Research* 38 (1971): 42–72; Norbert Rouland, *Legal Anthropology* (1994), at 123; William Seagle, *History of Law* (1946); Peter J. van Koppen and Steven D. Penrod, eds., *Adversarial versus Inquisitorial Justice* (2003), 1–19, at 3.

CHAPTER 10

Pospisil and Differentiating the Institutions of Social Regulation

F EW WORKS OF legal anthropology have had as much crossover appeal as Leopold Pospisil's *Anthropology of Law* (1971), read equally by lawyers, anthropologists, and an interested public. No small part of his broad popularity should be attributed to the coherence of his theoretical vision. Rather than deep but narrow study of a limited topic or even wide-ranging erudition on disconnected subjects, he developed a thoughtful portrait of legal institutions where each new insight served as the starting point for the next exploration.

Perhaps more than any previous worker, Pospisil directly confronted one of the more intractable problems within legal anthropology: what is "law," and how is it different from other forms of social regulation like custom and religion? The original search for a workable definition had remained unsettled, a condition Pospisil hoped to remedy. Malinowski had made an unsuccessful effort to distinguish law from custom, and Bohannan had characterized law as the master normative order due to its double institutionalization. That process may clarify law's relationship to custom but leaves unclear how law then relates to parallel institutions like religion. Pospisil would work simultaneously with a wider range of regulatory phenomena and identify in precise terms how each differs from all the others. For those looking for a comprehensive theory of social order, Pospisil's models are both insightful in their conclusions and provocative in the methods he employed.

Methodological Notes

His popular *Anthropology of Law* expanded on themes present from the beginning in Pospisil's ethnographic works. Many of the enduring hypotheses had been voiced in *Kapauku Papuans and Their Law* (1958), a book that

---

BOX 10.1
Pospisil Highlights

Born: 1923, Olomouc, Czechoslovakia
Died: N/A
Relevant Fieldwork: Kapauku Papuans (Netherlands New Guinea),
    1954–1955+
Teaching Appointments: Yale University, 1956–1993; Peabody
    Museum, 1956–1993; Yale/Peabody Emeritus, 1993 to present
Significant Publications: *Kapauku Papuans and Their Law* (1958);
    Anthropology of Law (1971); *Ethnology of Law* (1972)
Law-Related Conclusions: Proposed four attributes of law: authority,
    intention of universal application, obligatio, and sanction; articu-
    lated the phenomenon of "legal levels"

---

he, like Schapera among the Tswana, was surprised to learn was used by Dutch colonial administrators as the basis for their rulings on customary Kapauku law.

Pospisil offered his own spin to the now established trouble-case method. His predecessors had accumulated a body of cases from which they inductively derived general rules of substantive and procedural law. Pospisil used the case method not to distill the Kapauku rules of law but to test theories about the features of law generally. As he comments, the fieldwork he conducted was designed "to demonstrate with the help of the Papuan data the effectiveness of a theory of law formulated on the basis of a comparative study of thirty-two cultures and a survey of an additional sixty-three."

We see here anthropology as it is unfortunately rarely conducted. Pospisil used existing data—the currently disdained "library research"—to devise a theory that he then tested against extensive fieldwork designed for that purpose. His goal was to arrive at cross-culturally useful generalizations where the data supported them. This is anthropology practiced as a science, a method that is far from a disciplinary ideal. In an era much influenced by text-based interpretive models, it is no surprise that Pospisil has been specifically criticized on this point. For example, Mark Goodale opines that Pospisil's work improved only after he retreated from such "scientism."

Of the 176 cases of dispute recounted in *Kapauku Papuans and Their Law*, most were reported from informants rather than witnessed and recorded, as Gluckman and Bohannan had done. While the lack of personal observation of the disputes would count as a shortcoming in a pure ethnography, Pospisil's theory-oriented goals provide the standard against which he should be judged.

Given that methods should always be tailored to the project goals and that for Pospisil the goal was less to create a free-standing description of a social institution than to study the merits of an initial theory, the indirect nature of his legal data poses no obstacle to achieving that aim.

Attributes of Law

The overarching challenge for Pospisil was to clarify the category of law in such a way as to usefully distinguish it from other norms of social regulation:

> [Law] has not been defined in a way that is satisfactory to most ethnographers. . . . Even if an ethnographer were to select one of the existing theories of law, the differentiation of law from other social phenomena is usually so unprecise and vague as to militate against the use of the concept as a tool for analysis. Many theories provide no objective criteria to guide the ethnographer, and as a result he completely omits the category of law from his monograph.

Particularly problematic—as should be familiar by now to the reader—was the relationship of law to custom. Some theories argued that laws emerged out of custom, while others assumed the opposite.

The trouble cases Pospisil collected allowed him to examine the viability of his own theory of law:

> Four attributes of law which the writer has abstracted from the legal cases of the thirty-two cultures studied will be presented. These attributes not only represent analytical constituents of the legal phenomena; they may also be used as criteria which help to differentiate law from other social phenomena, as for example from political decisions or purely religious taboos and observances.

Pospisil by his own admission stands squarely in the ranks of the legal realists ("Corrections of a Reappraisal of Leopold Pospisil," *Journal of Legal Pluralism* 46 [2001]: 115–20). As with them, for him law is comprised of the decisions of authorities rather than mere codes or litigant behaviors. This is essentially the same trilogy analyzed by Llewellyn and Hoebel (see chapter 7) when they reviewed the different approaches to study law, concluding that their own dispute-centered approach was the superior method:

> [If] law is conceived as "rules or modes of conduct made obligatory by some sanction which is imposed and enforced for their violation by a controlling authority," then the analysis of such legal phenomena reveals a common pattern of attributes rather than one sweeping characteristic of

法 law. These attributes if considered in turn as criteria of law separate it
η objectively from all other social phenomena.

The four identified attributes (see table 10.1) are the following:

- **Authority**: Functionally defined as "one or more individuals who initiate actions . . . and whose decisions are followed by the majority of the
group's members."
- **Intention of universal application**: "Not only does the decision solve
a specific case, but it also formulates an ideal—a solution intended to
be utilized in all similar situations in the future." Behaviors that are
repeated but without imposition by an authority are only custom; a ruling intended to apply to the given situation only, with no universal application, is an exercise in politics, not law.
- **Obligatio**: Recalling the central role that Malinowski assigned to reciprocity, obligatio is "that part of the decision of an authority which
determines the rights of one party and the duties of another." This is a
new relationship created by the decision, not a reliance on anything preexisting, such as the previous rights and duties, the breach of which pre-
cipitated the dispute to be resolved by the authority's decision.

  All parties must be living to qualify as having a legal interest in this
sense. Because nonreal entities possess no rights and are incapable of
obligations, duties to the dead and other supernaturals fall outside of
law and are the province of religion alone. Religious law, however, arises
when the interests of the supernaturals are represented by living beings,
such as priests.
- **Sanction**: "Effective social control is the important qualification of a
legal sanction." So long as this goal is achieved, the form of the sanction matters little. Thus, according to Pospisil, psychological sanctions—
and not just the physical sanctions required by Hoebel—can satisfy the
criterion and count as legal sanctions. Loss of reputation, for example,
can perform this function as well as the whip.

Equipped with these criteria, Pospisil is able to disqualify forty-four of his
original 176 cases from the category of the legal because of their lack of one
or more of the attributes. These excluded examples presumably belong
within one of the other categories of norms of social regulation.

Perhaps the primary criticism of Pospisil's method is that, although working with an initial hypothesis concerning the attributes of law that he had
generated from his library research of many other cultures' legal systems, the
data are not such as could lead to a rejection of that hypothesis. Where the
reader might have expected a challenge to the hypothesis that could result in
its falsification, instead we get results that could only support the a priori

position. The sole question seems to be what form the validation would ulti-mately assume. If the outcome could have been otherwise, Pospisil does not make clear what that falsifying result would have looked like.

This may be less a fault of Pospisil than the limitations on conducting scientific theory testing in the field. At a time when few were performing work so closely adhering to the scientific method, however, Pospisil should be credited for what he achieved rather than criticized for shortfalls in the execution.

Aside from any methodological criticisms, some of the attributes raise problems in the identification of "law" because they result in counterintu-itive outcomes. For example, a strict requirement for an intention of uni-versal application would mean that trial-level court rulings in the U.S. system are technically nonlegal. Such rulings explicitly lack binding prece-dent and impose an obligation on no one other than the parties to the spe-cific suit. Only appellate-level opinions can acquire precedential value. It seems that any standard that forces trial-level rulings outside the field of law leaves something to be desired. In this same vein are implications of his dis-cussion about sanction (especially in the later *Anthropology of Law*) that would deny the status of "law" to international law.

An important element of Pospisil's scheme is the reasonable expansion of the concept of sanction to include psychological constraints in addition to the physical punishments to which earlier workers like Hoebel had lim-ited themselves. The result is that we now see sanction as an attribute of all the forms of social regulation and not a special property of the legal system.

Legal Levels

With law defined by the four attributes, several implications follow almost immediately. Stimulated by the references of Llewellyn and Hoebel to "sub-law-stuff," Pospisil understood there to be no requirement limiting law "to the society as a whole. Every functioning subgroup of the society has its own legal system which is necessarily different in some respects from those of the other subgroups." So long as the four attributes are present, law exists:

> We dare to say that it is inconsistent to make a qualitative distinction
> between the law of the state and the "criminal gang's ethics." Both of
> these phenomena contain all four legal attributes and thus belong to the
> same category; both should be classified as laws. It is unfortunate that in
> the West the concept of law has acquired a moralistic connotation.

As an aside, we can observe that the lamented "moralistic connotation" the West assigns to law is in large measure, of course, the history of the relation-ship between law and theology and natural law particularly (see chapter 3).

Pospisil's theory of legal levels is an early precursor to the theory of legal pluralism, which is taken up in chapter 15. For present purposes, we should note two observations. First, the existence of the legal levels follows inevitably from the definition of law that Pospisil has constructed and defended. Given that definition, the levels are undeniable. This elegantly reasoned model should be contrasted with those who adopt the contradictory stance of accepting legal pluralism on the one hand while refusing to define law on the other. This feat requires control of the concept of law sufficient to identify multiple interrelated instances of its occurrence while denying that the concept can be controlled at all. Pospisil's theory of law stands as a coherent intellectual accomplishment that has been undervalued by today's legal anthropologists.

Second, Pospisil, in *Kapauku Papuans and Their Law*, does not develop the full implications of the existence of these legal levels. There are questions to be asked pertaining to the relationships of the structures themselves—how does a legal system articulate horizontally and vertically with the other legal systems in the society? He does offer some suggestive ideas where such investigations might lead in his brief description of legal relativity: given that law exists at different levels and that there are different types of social norms, Pospisil considers whether "the same law which is customary on the level of a more inclusive group at the same time might be authoritarian when considered as the law of subgroups that have not yet internalized it." Very quickly, the networks of legal systems, given the numbers of systems and the ways they might react to the legal norms of one another, can become quite dense and may well blossom out of the control of the solitary social scientist.

Further questions to be asked of the phenomena of legal levels speak to the techniques used by persons to navigate between and negotiate among the legal systems in which they are simultaneously participating. How do people decide which legal norms should prevail in a context in which multiple systems apply? At this point, one begins sensing the problems of process that would become the new paradigm (see chapter 11).

Legal Dynamics

Perhaps the most complicated section of Pospisil's discussion occurs when he turns to the question of how law relates to politics and customs. In the broad sense, much of the distinction follows directly from the qualities of the attributes: political decisions are those lacking an intention of universal application, while custom lacks authority. Such lines are not static, however, as customs can evolve into laws and vice versa at the same time that political decisions are reinterpreted into laws.

Pospisil attempted to graphically capture the dynamism of a society's legal system (see figure 10.1). Using the attributes to organize the norms of social

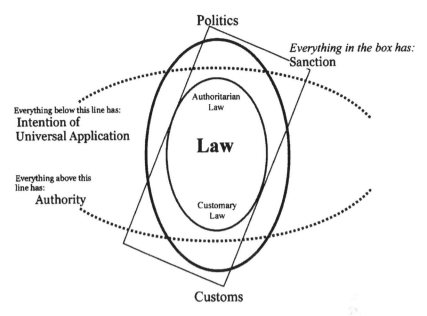

FIGURE 10.1

Relationship of Pospisil's Attributes of Law

regulation, Pospisil shows the relative positions of politics, law, and custom. Law sits at the center of the graph, where all attributes converge, while politics dwells in a zone beyond the intention of universal application. Custom, on the other hand, falls to the bottom of the graph, outside the area of authority.

The closer a law drifts to one pole or the other, the more it takes on the characteristics of that nonlegal norm. Thus, customary law as Pospisil uses the term refers to "a law that is internalized by a social group. We call a law internalized when the majority of the members of the group consider it to be binding, as when it stands for the only proper behavior in a given situation. . . . Conformity to such a law is not much effected by external pressure—it is produced by a different, internal mechanism which we may call conscience in some cultures and fear of shame in others." Authoritarian law, on the other hand, "is not internalized by a majority of the members of the group."

Individual laws may float between one type and the other. As an originally authoritarian rule becomes internalized over time, it can become law, then customary law. By the same token, laws that are no longer officially enforced will fall into mere custom.

While instructive in the three-way contrast Pospisil intended it to capture, the graph is incomplete. The absence of religion is particularly noticeable, as is the attribute of the obligatio previously identified as serving to distinguish law from it. Even supposing that a separate graph could be constructed that would capture those omitted relationships, it strikes the reader as inelegant that all attributes and all norms cannot be presented within one dynamic system.[1]

Summary and Conclusions

All the foregoing themes from his 1958 ethnography are developed further in his later *Anthropology of Law: A Comparative Theory* (1971). In this latter monograph, he seconds Gluckman's conclusion about the respective differences of legal systems: "The explicit conclusion of my comparative studies is that there is no basic qualitative difference between tribal (primitive) and civilized law."

Employing a method more scientific than the merely inductive, he isolated four attributes essential to the identification of law cross-culturally. This result in turn generated additional insights that challenge legal anthropologists to this day. Perhaps the most enduring of his contributions would be the description of legal levels, laying the groundwork for later work in the problem of legal pluralism.

BOX 10.2
Law and Justice

Pospisil tells how the Papuan Kapauku "distinguish between what they consider 'legally just,' expressed by the verbal suffix *-ja* . . . and either what they call good or what they are ashamed of. To the latter we may assign the name morality."

He touches here on a tension that also runs through Western jurisprudence: what is the relationship of law to justice?

Strict adherence to the law fosters consistency and uniform application of authority, which can offer a measure of security to people outside the dominant power structures. Adhering to any rule blindly can, however, render unintended and undesirable outcomes that should be tempered with mercy, or **equity**, a concept Pospisil explicitly invokes: "There is another type of justice which the Kapauku call '*uta-uta*, half-half.' The meaning of the phrase comes very close to what we call equity."

As Pospisil reviews in *Anthropology of Law*, within the English common law tradition there were in fact separate courts of law and

---

1. This critique refers only to Professor Pospisil's published works. In correspondence he has graciously shared an unpublished revision of this figure that does attempt to incorporate the attribute of obligatio and the institution of religion on the left-hand of the drawing.

courts of equity. When law did not recognize a remedy yet manifest injustice would result from allowing the circumstances to continue, the plaintiff could seek relief from a court of equity. The remedies available were often limited but included actions such as injunctions that would minimize any injury. Eventually, the courts of law and equity merged into a single system, although conceptually they remain distinct.

As suggested by Pospisil's data, however, the distinction between law and equity is not limited to Western cultures. In the course of his analysis, Gluckman notes of the Lozi legal system that "the highest duty is to law and justice; and justice must give way to law," yet nonetheless "the judges are reluctant to support the person who is right in law [*mulao*], but wrong in justice [*tukelo*]." This position can be contrasted with the Canela of Brazil, for whom justice also yields to a higher value. Unlike the Lozi, however, that value is not law but peace (Crocker and Crocker 2004). The Mexican Talea studied by Laura Nader (1990) report a similar preference, saying that "a bad compromise is better than a good fight."

Among the Barotse, the desire to reconcile the two goals leads to changes within the legal system itself, as a sympathetic judge "may combine different principles of law so as to create, in effect, new law, and he does so in order to satisfy the requirements of justice." The flexibility and ambiguity of legal principles that would allow such novel yet desirable outcomes are thus, for Gluckman, essential attributes of a working system of law. The precision that some might admire as the height of the legislator's craft can in practice be counterproductive in a society that aims at not merely the rule of law but also the dispensation of justice.

The concept of justice may relate to law in still another way. According to Laura Nader (2002), "The movement in the law came from the experience of total injustice rather than from the demand for total justice." Contrary to the ordinary idea, justice and injustice may be sufficiently distinct that they fall within the scope of different norms of social regulation. Accordingly, while the center of balance in the *legal* system may be the minimization of *in*justice, justice as a positive quality falls within the moral systems devoted to the articulation of cultural ideals such as religion. By this interpretation, fairness is related not to the maximization of justice but to the avoidance of injustice. This understanding of the proper realms for the two systems gains further support as Nader expands on her thinking: "Justice is contemplative. Injustice is dynamic," and it is injustice, and not justice, that is "the life of the law."

Suggestions for Further Reading

For additional background information about Pospisil, see Rebecca R. French, "Leopold J. Pospisil and the Anthropology of Law," *PoLAR* 16 (1993): 1–8; Csaba Varga, *Anthropological Jurisprudence? Leopold Pospisil and the Comparative Study of Legal Cultures* (1986).

Justice/Equity: Wesley Newcomb Hohfeld, *The Relations between Equity and Law* (1913); Louis P. Pojman, *Justice* (2006); D. D. Raphael, *Concepts of Justice* (2001).

References

William H. Crocker and Jean G. Crocker, *The Canela: Kinship, Ritual, and Sex in an Amazonian Tribe* (2nd ed., 2004); Max Gluckman, *The Judicial Process among the Barotse of Northern Rhodesia* (1955); Mark Goodale, "Leopold Pospisil: A Critical Reappraisal," *Journal of Legal Pluralism* 40 (1998): 123–49, at 143; Laura Nader, *Harmony Ideology: Justice and Control in a Zapotec Mountain Village* (1990), at 1; Laura Nader, *The Life of the Law: Anthropological Projects* (2002), at 183.

Postclassic
Ethnography

C HAPTER 10'S ACCOUNT of the scholarship of Leopold Pospisil
brings to a close our review of the "classic" legal ethnographers. As
a group, they tended to be functionalists of one variety or another,
looking at law from the perspective of rule-governed institutions. Beginning
in the 1960s, that orientation would begin to change. The questions asked,
the theories explored, and the philosophies espoused would take legal
anthropology in new directions. The remaining chapters in this part look at
only two examples from a much longer list of preeminent modern legal
anthropologists, chosen not only for their own accomplishments but also
for the disciplinary trends they represent.

CHAPTER 11

Nader and Processualism

THE NAME OF Laura Nader is all but synonymous with contemporary legal anthropology. Commencing her researches almost half a century ago, she has guided the discipline to a degree unmatched by any other single practitioner. Invariably, the student finds himself consulting either one of her own groundbreaking publications or those of her many protégés. Her unrelenting attention to cultivate the next generation of legal anthropologists may challenge Nader's own theoretical contributions as her most enduring legacy.

Born in 1930, Nader has spent her professional career as faculty member at the University of California, Berkeley. She entered the field in 1957 to study the Zapotec of Oaxaca, Mexico, and became one of the first legal anthropologists to incorporate filmmaking into her work ("To Make the Balance" [1966]). Her own ethnographic monograph, *Harmony Ideology: Justice and Control in a Zapotec Mountain Village* (1990), was perhaps delayed because of her immersion in innovative group projects that culminated in groundbreaking edited volumes.

Because of the breadth of her scholarship, Nader is discussed in two contexts. This chapter considers her specific ethnographic achievements and the idea of **harmony ideology** she employs to explain the strategic use of legal institutions by her Zapotec informants. First, however, it places her in the context of the new anthropologists who succeeded the classic legal ethnographers, effecting a paradigm shift in the discipline from a rules to a process perspective. Chapter 14 considers her long-term study of dispute resolution, paying particular attention to her views on the role of alternative dispute resolution techniques within the American legal system.

From Cases and Rules to Disputes and Processes

The expansion of the case method into the expanded case method (described in chapter 8) seems almost a natural progression from an anthropologist's perspective. The initial focus on the institutionally bounded proceedings made sense at the time given the recognized alternatives: formal code compilations, which, if they existed at all in a given locale, limited themselves to normative ideals, and behaviors, which reduced the norm to the mean of the behavioral aggregate (recall this discussion by Llewellyn and Hoebel). Concentrating on the case and its resolution allowed for the isolation of a cross-culturally meaningful unit of analysis as well as a technique to identify the legal norms through their invocation when resolving real conflicts. The disciplinary curiosity of anthropology would inevitably push those boundaries outward to reflect its broader sociocultural interests.

To fully analyze the resolution of the case, especially as to whether it was effective at healing the underlying social breach, the fieldworker needed to become deeply familiar with the dispute itself and not simply the face it showed during the short phase it manifested as a legal case. Often the precipitating argument was but the latest in a long-running series of clashes. To look only at this most recent outbreak missed the subterranean psychological and emotional dynamics that already bound the parties in a history of demands and expectations and thus was to misunderstand the reasons why the institutional solution was or was not acceptable to the complainants. Even within a judge-oriented methodology, to remain ignorant of such details may be to misinterpret why the case resolver ruled as he did from the options available to him. Pursuing the necessarily wide-ranging background of the conflict involved the anthropologist in longitudinal analyses of disputes, of which institutional intervention in the form of a "case," if any occurred at all, would be only one event in a longer chain of interactions between parties.

We can see how the desire to realize the goals of the case method inevitably leads one to adopt the extended case method's wider focus and to the study of disputes. On the surface, the extended case method is exactly what the name suggests, a broadening of the case method, but still essentially the case method as it had been practiced. Although the transformation was significant, it was still a change in degree at the level of methodology. The consequences to theory, however, were startlingly of kind, ushering in not simply more or better ethnography but something qualitatively different. The ramifications constituted a shift in paradigm of what it means to study law in the field.

Case-centered research did not focus on rules in the sense of codes, but it remained essentially a rules-oriented theory nonetheless. It restricted attention to formal decision-making events and to the norms incorporated into those official resolutions. This view characterized law as the kind of stable, structured, if not always consciously articulable system favored by classic functionalists. The use of the extended case method, however, necessarily introduced a new dimension into the field of law that was not easily accommodated by functionalism: time. The methodologically incremental transition from case study to extended case study therefore almost immediately kicked off a new period of nonfunctionalist theory about law. Rules and law were no longer stable standards by which cases could be settled but instead tools to be selectively employed throughout the disputing life cycle. Thus, the new orientation turned toward **process**.

Laura Nader was one of the first to fully appreciate the new direction being taken by legal anthropology and to encourage the development of techniques to exploit the novel perspectives it introduced. "The shift from structure to process," she and coeditor Harry Todd observed, "brings with it a shift in the level of interest from institutions and social groups, to the individual and the choices which he or she is forced to make in disputing" (*The Disputing Process—Law in Ten Societies* [1978]). Instead of following the case as defined institutionally, the new process-oriented methodology followed the parties engaged in the dispute. By placing the individual at the center of analysis instead of the case and its resolution by third parties, questions that had gone unnoticed by earlier ethnographers become the primary issues for the next generation:

> It is no longer sufficient to generalize that in a face-to-face society disputes between two members of such a society will be resolved through some kind of compromise or reconciliation mechanism. The ties between and among litigants, and among litigants and remedy agents, may be rooted in a variety of principles: kinship, residence, patron-client, friendship, competition. It is this variety that must inform a dynamic understanding of the social relational dimensions of disputing.

In addition to a fuller description of the ties of the disputants, both between themselves and with other members of society that might be impacted by the outcome, new attention focused on how people chose from among the dispute resolution options available to them. A complex calculus emerged out of the perceived injury, the relative attributes of the parties, any prior history, and costs associated with each resolution option, to mention but a few considerations.

It is possible to appreciate this vital new perspective in legal anthropology without going so far as John Comaroff and Simon Roberts, who argue that a necessary entailment of the process orientation toward law is that legal anthropology should cease to exist as a discrete field of study. As they argue the point, processual legal anthropology has its roots in Malinowski's *Crime and Custom*. Unlike the rules orientation—exemplified by Schapera's *Handbook*—which views stability as the norm and conflict as pathological, process adopts the position that conflict is an endemic feature of social life. . . . An adequate account of a dispute therefore requires a description of its total social context. Once disputes are no longer seen as discrete and bounded pathological events, they may not be neatly excised from the ongoing flow of community life, even for heuristic purpose. . . . [Taken] to its final conclusion, the subdiscipline of legal anthropology would no longer enjoy analytical hegemony over *any* demarcated field of social action.

This claim recalls Bohannan's conclusion that law has no unique domain but instead serves to govern all other social institutions. Comaroff and Roberts take this belief about law to its logical extreme: if law has no object, then legal anthropology has no subject.

Any competent ethnographer, they appear to argue, would do what a processual legal anthropologist should set out to accomplish, no special training or intention required. The expanded case method has in their view grown to encompass all of anthropology, rendering "legal anthropology" equivalent to anthropology itself.

While theirs stands as an influential exercise in the processual method, it remains an open question how many have followed Comaroff and Roberts to quite these extreme disciplinary implications. I should add that even I am not unmoved by the argument. If, as the introduction claims (as well as chapter 4 of *Anthropology and Law*), law and society in some meaningful sense came into existence simultaneously, then at that level the two concepts are indeed coextensive. To study the one entails study of the other with no special effort required. Even, however, if this is how the reality is truly related, it is not how academic disciplines have been structured. At that level, at least, it remains counterproductive to call for the elimination of a distinct expertise in the anthropology of law.

The only way to avoid the rational force of this agenda, however, must be to argue that legal anthropology does indeed study something unique in the social milieu and that law in some sense is not completely reducible to the ordinary cultural analysis pursued by general ethnography. The burden is once again on legal anthropologists to articulate what it is that they study, what is their special "demarcated field of social action." There seems no avoiding the problem of definition, however out of vogue such philosophical inquiries have become.

Transition to Nader's processualism was not, however, without consequences. While offering a superior solution to the problem of the cross-culturally valid unit of analysis—disputing between parties is a cultural universal in a way that the legal case is not—it limited legal anthropology's theoretical options in other ways. The part had become the whole of law, with little or no elaboration of what that meant for a self-avowed anthropology of "law."

The combination of influences of the philosophy of legal realism and the methodology of the casebook demanded a practical dependence on case decisions that would lead scholars to conclude that law is *only* about dispute resolutions. This elevation of dispute resolution to the sine qua non of legal anthropology was driven home through Nader's characterization of her ethnographic ideal:

> (1) a stress on law as a process rather than a framework—on the settlement of a conflict and the mechanisms through which this is achieved, rather than on the definition of legal rules and the identification of particular agencies or parties formally backed by force and endowed with authority; (2) an interest in the social context of dispute resolution and in the influence of this context on the process; (3) (as implied in part by 2) an interest in the litigants and in their relationships to each other as well as to all other persons involved in settlement procedures; (4) an interest in multiple systems within one society and in the bases for and strategies involved in choosing one resolution mode over another; (5) the use of an extended case, or a sequence of related cases, to illustrate in detail the processes and strategies involved. (Nader and Yngvesson 1973)

While many have noted and commented on the (over)emphasis of American legal anthropology on dispute resolution (e.g., Snyder 1993), it should be noted that this outcome was not unambiguously required by the terms in which Nader had originally conceived the new paradigm. Like Malinowski, she recognized both the positive and negative functions of law:

> [It] is not always clear whether the social control functions of law are to "clean up social messes" [as argued by Llewellyn and Hoebel], or to maintain order [which was Malinowski's position], although how the law handles the breach is usually clearer than how in fact it serves to maintain order.

If it is indeed true that legal anthropology has acquired a singular mania for dispute settlement at the expense of understanding other aspects of the law, this is the outcome of contingent historical factors and not of a reasoned theory of law. Nader allows that law includes more than the dispute resolution studied by processualism, however much her own method leaves no room for these alternative functions.

A major consequence of the new processual research was that it did not support realism's equation between official acts, disputing, and law, which had originally defined these variables as coterminous concepts (see figure 11.1). Within the realist paradigm, any legal observation Z could be unproblematically related to any of the three since it is stipulated to contain both law (L) and dispute resolution (DR) events.

FIGURE 11.1
Realist Equation of Officials, Disputes, and Law

Fieldwork conducted within the processual model produced a more nuanced view that these variables interacted but remained severable in any analysis, not least because disputing encompassed the choices among alternatives by individual plaintiffs and was therefore not reducible to official actions. Dispute resolution can be achieved through law, but it can also be the result of nonlegal practices such as mediation and arbitration (both formal and informal). Likewise, while on the surface a good bit of law could appear to be concerned with the resolution of disputes, its field of operation is, as Nader recognized, much wider.

Figure 11.2 depicts the newly recognized relationships between the variables of acts, disputes, and law. The three variables that were equated in legal realism have diverged after the improved cross-cultural observation under the influence of legal processualism. The field's explicit methodology, however, limits its attention to the increasingly diminishing area where the three continue to be equivalent (i.e., the hatched area, or events Z). The relationship between events of the types X_{DR} and Y_L—once defined as synonymous—must now be clarified. In practice, however, expansion of the discussion beyond the small area of overlap relies primarily on rhetorical strategies, such as uncritical changes from one term to another, to expand conclusions about this core to the outer boundaries of the categories. For legal realism, such transitions were not a problem since it had defined the law, disputing, and official actions as equivalent; legal processualism had demonstrated the error of this view without taking the additional step of explaining how one moves from one field of action to the other.

Indicative of processualism's slippage between theory and method is that the casebook organization of disputing cases (extended and otherwise) remained the distinctive technique of legal anthropology even as it was receiving heavy criticism in its original context of legal education. What is

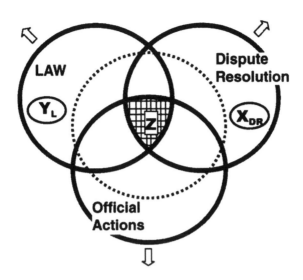

FIGURE 11.2

Diverging Processualist Relationships between Officials, Disputes, and Law

not self-evident, however, is that an analytical technique created to foster legal formalism and adapted to advance the thesis of legal realism serves well when applied to analysis of antirealist processual theses. That which should have been argued was instead only presumed.

In short, legal processualism both exacerbated some strands of legal realism, such as the emphasis on the negative, disputing aspect of legal processes while contradicting others, like the equivalency between law and official acts. Deviation from the inherited tradition, however, did not noticeably influence either the analytical or the discursive style of the discipline.

Harmony

Both the strengths and weaknesses of the new paradigm can be seen in Nader's legal ethnography, *Harmony Ideology*. Here she outlines her thesis that "harmony ideology in Talea [a village in the Rincón area in the Mexican state of Oaxaca] today is both a product of nearly 500 years of colonial encounter and a strategy for resisting the state's political and cultural hegemony." An ideology of harmony, maintained in the face of almost constant disputatious litigation, "promotes" local solidarity and preserves the community from intrusive oversight by the state government.

Nader's commitment to the processual orientation is captured by her motto that the *plaintiff* rather than the judge is the "life of the law." Nader carefully maps out the options available to potential litigants throughout the course of a dispute, shaping its course and outcome. Unlike almost all of the classic ethnographers, she inquires into the variables influencing a person's choice to resort to the courts:

> [A] few basic guidelines determine if citizens decide to mobilize to do something or to leave well enough alone. First, citizens see themselves as empowered. . . . Second, relations that are by nature potentially long-term, such as loan-debt relationships, usually become part of a well-thought-out long-term strategy for recouping the debt. . . . Third, group responsibility for decision-making is stressed in all decisions that might trigger or initiate relations with the state.

Uniquely encapsulating the folk attitude to the legal system is the maxim, "A bad agreement is better than a good fight." In terms that evoke Pospisil's Kapauku, Nader explains that "the duty of town officials in handling cases is to *hacer el balance*, to make things balance out." "Winning" is not the primary social objective for these legal proceedings:

> One constant that runs through case materials from the Talean court may, for present purposes, briefly be described as the value placed on harmony and on achieving balance or agreement between the principles in a case. . . . The *settlement* to a dispute may be designed to fine, jail, ridicule, or acquit the principals in a case, but the *outcome* desired is rectification.

In case after case, the court officials are shown as more concerned to reconcile the parties, to bring about an amicable settlement, than to "apply the law." Echoing the objectives of legal systems we have encountered in earlier ethnographies, the official "is expected to render a verbal and written agreement for each case—an agreement that town consensus would consider equitable." Peace is to be made not only between the disputants but with the entire town. The "Talean style of justice . . . is more concerned with wider questions of order and group interest." Much of *Harmony Ideology* is devoted to documenting how these resolutions are achieved.

The emerging insight is that the people do not espouse harmony because they fear confrontation. So long as the dispute can be contained within the confines of the town, there is no hesitancy to press their cases. The fear is that disputes will become unmanageable at the local level and thus the villagers will lose control over their lives when the state government intervenes to maintain the peace. Thus, among Nader's Talean society, escalation looms as the social evil to be avoided at any cost. She documents this concern from several angles, including the relatively low referral of cases to the district court in a distant city:

Taking a case to the district court is escalation, and Rinconeros do not escalate disputes both because escalation to an external system is linked to a loss of local autonomy and because village law is more elastic than the state system. The state system narrows disputes in a way that does not permit participants the possibility for creative harmony.

Frequent litigation in fact is an escalation-avoidance strategy intended to keep resentments and other antisocial emotions from building until they can no longer be locally negotiated.

Nader underscores that this is the positive face of harmony ideology. In colonial contexts, it was used by Christian missionaries "to suppress peoples by socializing them toward conformity. . . . Harmony ideology is most likely part of the hegemonic control system that entered Middle America by means of Spanish law and Catholic missionaries." Harmony law models, she expands elsewhere (*The Life of the Law: Anthropological Projects* [2002]), are "coercive when they mandate unity, consensus, cooperation, compliance, passivity, and docility—features often taken for granted as humankind's normal state and considered benign."

Talean Zapotec use of harmony turns this model on its ear. "[Both] in its cultural and in its social-organizational form [it] is counter-hegemonic. Harmony and controversy are different poles of the same system of control: the disputants bring controversy, and third parties apply the rhetoric and practices of harmony."

Bringing the themes of this chapter together, Nader explicitly equates the colonial sense of the harmony model with the structural-functionalist framework: "Such studies were often ahistorical, generally focused on artificially bounded communities, and tended to use the equilibrium or harmony model to describe social relations" ("The Crown, the Colonists, and the Course of Zapotec Village Law," in *History and Power in the Study of Law*, 320–44 [1989]). She apparently means that the rules-centered perspective incorporated by the classic ethnographers, in which judges used laws to resolve cases, kept the peace by quashing dissention.

The counterhegemonic spin put on harmony ideology by the Taleans would have escaped the notice of preprocessualist ethnographers. The inversion of the Christian antidissension morality that favored the colonial powers could appear only in that new light, which moved the focus from the case-settling officials and onto the dispute-strategizing plaintiffs.

Harmony Ideology is not without its problems. Peter Just warns against her denial of "autochthonous origins for harmony ideology in the absence of any account of what Zapotec dispute settlement was like before the Spanish conquest." As indicated at points, Nader's description of the function of courts in Talean society bears strong similarity to that described in other cultures unmarred by Christian missionizing, particularly Pospisil's Kapauku. While convergence of cultural forms is not impossible, that explanation should not be resorted to if another can account for both instances with a single stroke.

The text's discussion also points out some of the theoretical weaknesses within processual approaches. As the previous section discussed, legal processualism demonstrated the nonequivalence of law, official acts, and dispute resolution. The drawback of this insight, however, is that transitions from one discussion to any of the others now requires justification since the definitional equivalence of the terms that had been asserted by legal realism could no longer be sustained. Yet we find Nader making statements when describing her methodology that while she "make[s] central use of the *dispute case*," she uses these data "to reveal how social organization in general and how the social organization of *law* in particular relate to control, to relative power, and to autonomy over an extended period of colonization" (emphases added). The transition from data about disputing to conclusions about law is undiscussed, implying that the relationship between the two is unproblematic. Nothing in the text dispels that impression. Yet even if dispute resolution were always and necessarily a legal topic (and her own data disprove that simple equation), that reality would not eliminate the possibility of meaningful remainders, that is, the positive, non–dispute resolution dimensions of law that she herself recognizes. If law possesses such reminders, the transition she employs is a point to be argued and not assumed.

Summary and Conclusions

Any text that surveys the major landmarks of legal anthropology's history and theory could not fail to prominently highlight Laura Nader. Among the many notable contemporary practitioners in the discipline, she stands without peer for her continued productivity and influence over the next generation of workers.

From the vast range of her achievements, this chapter selected that portion that highlights her role in the transition of legal anthropology from the classic to the postclassic ethnographies, indicated by a methodological shift from the case to the extended case method and a theoretical sea change from a rules and cases focus to a dispute and process orientation. Although some chroniclers might characterize this change as a radical break with the past, the new paradigm is best understood as flowing organically from the received tradition: "Criticism of the structuralist tradition is a matter of amplification and difference in emphasis rather than a radical departure from this tradition in the way that the new fieldwork techniques and analytical methods of the structuralists differed fundamentally from those of the pre-structuralists" (van Velsen 1967). Working out the full implications of the earliest method compelled the transformation rather than the importation of an utterly novel perspective.

Nader's own work, not least *Harmony Ideology*, has demonstrated the productivity of this advance. Power would become a central issue for processual legal anthropologists, recognized as a factor influencing the use of legal forums. Always present in her thinking, considerations of power would become an especially important variable in her work on alternative dispute resolution (see chapter 14).

BOX 11.1

Rules and Processes (A Third Sense)

The distinction between rules and processes has previously been asserted in two distinct senses. In the first, broadest sense, rules in the form of codes, and processes as embodied in behaviors, represented two of the three approaches to the study of law identified by Hoebel and Llewellyn. These were rejected as unsuitable, and the trouble-case method was introduced.

The second sense, rules in the sense of the normative order presented by the judge-decreed resolution and processes in the sense of the life span of the dispute, has been introduced in this chapter. This is the most common connotation of the contrastive terms and represents a major historical divide in the development of legal anthropology's method and theory.

There remains a third sense in which the pair of "rules and processes" can be understood. The meaning of the terms can relate not to the source of data for analysis or the unit of analysis but to the locus of justice.

Legal systems can vary according to the standard by which parties can determine whether they have received a fair outcome. For some, justice is served when the *rules* have been evenly applied, guaranteeing a uniform outcome. These systems—here best represented by Schapera's *Handbook*—are concerned less about procedural process than about the substance of the rules. Unwarranted deviation from the stated norm provides grounds to claim that the hearing was biased and unfair.

For others, justice has been served when the *process* used to arrive at the result has been fair, even if the outcome is idiosyncratic. This is **procedural justice**, perhaps best known today from the works of political philosopher John Rawls.

(Continued)

BOX 11.1
Rules and Processes (A Third Sense) (Continued)

Studies of legal proceedings frequently contain observations such as this from New Guinea: "The councillor's court was not simply a vehicle for settling disputes; it was also an instrument people could use to ensure a public hearing of grievances" (Reay 1974). Sometimes this is all that people really want: to be taken seriously as a human being. Once their grievance has been seriously attended to, the actual outcome becomes secondary. Many of Nader's own cases appear to respond to this analysis.

In such settings *procedure* is often the primary determinant of fairness rather than substantive rules of law and their rigid enforcement. John Conley and William O'Barr refer to this as "law as therapy" and invoke it to explain why a small-claims court litigant who had won her case nonetheless felt cheated because she had not been allowed the opportunity to "tell her story."

Suggestions for Further Reading

Process: Jane F. Collier, "Legal Processes," *Annual Review of Anthropology* 4 (1975): 121–44; Sally Falk Moore, "The Ethnography of the Present and the Analysis of the Process," *Assessing Cultural Anthropology* (1994), 362–74; June Starr and Jane F. Collier, eds., *History and Power in the Study of Law: New Directions in Legal Anthropology* (1989).

Case Method: Max Gluckman, "Limitations of the Case-Method in the Study of Tribal Law," *Law and Society Review* 7 (1973): 611–42; J. F. Holleman, "Trouble-Cases and Trouble-less Cases in the Study of Customary Law and Legal Reform," *Anthropology of Law in the Netherlands*, ed. Keebet von Benda-Beckman and Fons Strijbosch (1986), 110–31; Marian Kempny, "History of the Manchester 'School' and the Extended-Case Method," *Social Analysis* 49 (2005): 144–65; Philip C. Parnell, "Hoebel's Crucible: Information and Misinformation in Case Studies in Law," *Law and Human Behavior* 6 (1982): 379–98.

References

John L. Comaroff and Simon Roberts, *Rules and Processes: The Cultural Logic of Dispute in an African Context* (1981); John M. Conley and William M. O'Barr, *Rules versus Relationships: The Ethnography of Legal Discourse* (1990);

James M. Donovan and H. Edwin Anderson, *Anthropology and Law* (2003); Peter Just, "History, Power, Ideology, and Culture: Current Directions in the Anthropology of Law," *Law and Society Review* 26 (1992): 373–411; Laura Nader and Barbara Yngvesson, "On Studying the Ethnography of Law and Its Consequences," *Handbook on Social and Cultural Anthropology*, ed. J. J. Honigmann (1973), 883–921; Marie Reay, "Changing Conventions of Dispute Settlement in Minjarea," *Contention and Dispute: Aspects of Law and Social Control in Melanesia* (1974), 198–239; Francis Snyder, *Law and Anthropology: A Review* (1993); J. van Velsen, "The Extended-Case Method and Situational Analysis," *The Craft of Social Anthropology* (1967), 129–49.

CHAPTER 12

O'Barr and Conley and Studying Up

L EGAL ANTHROPOLOGY is well represented by more than its share of scholars and writers deserving individualized attention in a text surveying the field, however briefly. William O'Barr and his longtime research partner John Conley have been selected as the second example of postclassic ethnographers because their jointly produced work illustrates several trends in the discipline.

First, their work focuses on the American legal system. Far from invoking their own legal traditions as an analytical system for the interpretation of others, as Bohannan accused Gluckman of doing, legal anthropologists now began studying the folk categories of their home settings: "studying up," in Laura Nader's term. Western law has now become a focus for study rather than a standard for analysis, and O'Barr and Conley's research into the patterns of language in the trial setting have been both provocative and precedential.

The second reason O'Barr and Conley have been highlighted in this, the last chapter of the ethnographic overviews, has to do with the element of joint authorship. As a discipline defined by the overlap of the two independent fields of intellectual study law and anthropology, a legitimate issue is how the appropriate expertise can be brought to bear on a project of legal anthropology. Not infrequently, workers in the field are anthropologists with an amateur's grasp of law or a lawyer with a dilettante's understanding of anthropology. One way to bring to the table the full expertise of both disciplines is through collaboration by an anthropologist and a lawyer. O'Barr and Conley represent that combination and, as such, stand as one possible example for the field.

Ethnography at Home

Prompted in part by the urgings of Laura Nader, contemporary legal anthropologists have led the way in altering both the locus and the methods of anthropology. In the early 1970s, she agitated for an anthropology that "studied up" as well as the more traditional "studying down" (Nader 1972). Although anthropology had a long tradition of studying peoples who were "down" the ladder of social and political power, the time had come, she insisted, "to study the colonizers rather than the colonized, the culture of power rather than the culture of the powerless, and culture of affluence rather than the culture of poverty."

To no small extent, this call to action requires American anthropologists to study themselves. "It is appropriate that a reinvented anthropology should study powerful institutions and bureaucratic organizations in the United States, for such institutions and their network systems affect our lives and also affect the lives of people that anthropologists have traditionally studied all around the world." In this light, the move for an ethnography at home becomes merely a further unfolding of the holistic perspective of anthropology generally. Understanding of a "primitive" culture in isolation can go only so far; at some point, account must be taken of the ways in which forces impinge on it from the outside.

Nader's advice cuts against one of the more deeply held pedagogical traditions in academic anthropology, namely, the requirement of fieldwork outside one's own society and preferably a non-Western site at that. Hugh Gusterson's opinion that "it is now increasingly permissible to do even one's first fieldwork at home" still rings premature. That the field has not yet reached that point can be seen from perusing the placement advertisements in *Anthropology News*, where few departments list the United States as a preferred field site for its candidate hires.

Both Nader and Gusterson realize that studying up problematizes the method of participant observation, another of anthropology's sacred traditions. How, after all, can one be a participant observer in a government agency or a high-power law firm? These "repatriated" ethnographies require new research techniques. Gusterson offers in the place of participant observation a strategy of "polymorphous engagement":

> Polymorphous engagement means interacting with informants across a number of dispersed sites, not just in local communities, and sometimes in virtual form; and it means collecting data eclectically from a disparate array of sources in many different ways.

Nader holds up Ruth Benedict's incomparable *The Chrysanthemum and the Sword* (1946) as an example of the way in which anthropology can be conducted "at a distance," without direct access to the higher echelons of power that are the focus of studying up.

For a variety of reasons—Nader's influence on her students, the social activism of the 1960s, the perception of the unprecedented influence of the

United States on a global scale, and the role that law plays in the American cultural ethos, to name a few—legal anthropology has quickly become a specialty that frequently studies up, turning the traditional consumers of anthropology into the objects of anthropological study. The writings of O'Barr and Conley, conducted in American courtroom settings, are therefore representative of this new trend within legal anthropology to turn an ethnographic eye onto the institutions of the practitioners' own cultures.

Ethnography of Legal Discourse

William M. O'Barr, an anthropologist at Duke University, and John Conley, a professor of law at the University of North Carolina, applied a methodology that easily reminds one of Gluckman's. Their primary data were transcripts of sessions in fourteen small-claims courtrooms in six cities, supplemented whenever possible by interviews both before and after the hearing. Unlike Gluckman's work among the Barotse that studied the problem from the judge's point of view, the team looked at the interactions of individuals with the legal system: what were their expectations, and how satisfied were they by their experiences?

The theoretical innovation represented by their body of work was the shift from looking at language within the legal process for what was said (the semantics) onto how it was expressed (the pragmatics). In their evocative image, instead of using language as a window to look through onto something else (legal procedure or rules of law), they believed much could be learned by looking at the window itself.

The conclusions of this project, reported in *Rules versus Relationships: The Ethnography of Legal Discourse* (1990), identified two types of legal discourse: **rule-oriented** talk, which evaluates "problems in terms of neutral principles whose application transcends differences in personal and social status," and **relational-oriented** talk, in which the speakers "predicate rights and responsibilities on a broad notion of social interdependence rather than on the application of rules." Rules-oriented talk aligns closely with the deductive reasoning of the judicial process itself, and therefore, even in courtrooms ostensibly designed to be informal, the judge can find arguments framed in this style easier to process. On the other hand, a party relating his side of the story in a relational mode will tend to include details of the underlying social relationships, with the unsurprising result that the rule-oriented courts "often fail to understand their cases."

Although in many jurisdictions a law degree is not required to preside over small-claims court, the court-preferred rules orientation is the style primarily of white, male, law-trained judges. This correlation leads Conley and O'Barr to suggest that rule-oriented discourse is "an acquired skill which is the property of the literate and educated business and legal class" serving a gatekeeping function of keeping the hoi polloi on the legal periphery. To find remedy in the court, the disadvantaged parties are forced either to hire a surrogate speaker trained in this technique of power or to edit their narrative structure to conform to the favored style, in essence denying the social relationships they believe to be the more important cause of the dispute.

The authors pursue this relationship between law talk and power in a subsequent work, *Just Words: Law, Language, and Power* (1998). Adding sociolinguistics and Foucaultian perspectives to their theoretical armory, Conley and O'Barr set out "to explore the microphysics of legal power by examining such events at the microlinguistic level. . . . At the end, we reach the conclusion that language is not merely the vehicle through which legal power operates: in many vital respects, language *is* legal power." Examining transcripts of rape trials, for example, they conclude that "the basic linguistic strategies of cross-examination are methods of domination and control. When used against the background of the rape victim's experience, they can bring about a subtle yet powerful reenactment of that experience."

Women are similarly disadvantaged, they find, during mediation: "Women, simply by virtue of the way they talk, may be more likely than men to pursue agreement as an end in itself," even when such agreement clearly acts to their personal detriment.

All their researches lead O'Barr and Conley to be critical of the received knowledge of legal anthropology from Malinowski and through even to Laura Nader. Despite the appearance of rich description, almost none of these earlier scholars detail fully the subtle interplay between social categories such as gender and class and the dispensation of justice. Whereas Malinowski had required fieldwork be conducted in the local language, O'Barr and Conley would raise this bar even higher. Not only should legal anthropologists speak the language, but they should be expert as well in the sociolinguistic variables involved. They speculate that "the whole discipline of legal anthropology stands on suspect terrain because of its practitioners' lack of linguistic skills":

> [The] core claim of sociolegal scholarship is that the law in practice does not live up to the ideal of fairness. Justice is contingent, and the critical contingencies are such categories as gender, race, and class. What has been missing from much sociolegal research, in our view, is a detailed explication of what injustice looks like as it happens.

By "happens," they mean as it emerges out of discourse.

Interdisciplinarity and Balanced Reciprocity

The holism that leads to "studying up" has further ramifications for this discipline's methods. One of the consistent strengths of anthropology as an intellectual project has been that holistic perspective. Anthropology is not simply one academic discipline among so many others; it is the meeting place of all disciplines, where they can come together to create a complete picture of the human world. The Scottish philosopher David Hume could observe "that all the sciences have a relation, greater or less, to human nature; and that however wide any of them may seem to run from it, they still turn back by one passage or another." Human nature has been posited in the introduction as the principal object of study of anthropology, in which case, if Hume is correct, all the fields of intellectual activity ultimately contribute to anthropology. The virtue of such an array of perspectives, however, becomes a liability during the actual execution of anthropological research.

The likelihood that any one researcher could master such diverse subject matter is small, even given that the typical anthropology graduate student already takes an average of ten years to complete her doctoral program. The obvious alternatives seem undesirable: she can either include materials she is not fully equipped to understand, or she can master some small slice of the intellectual spectrum, achieving deep insights on that issue to the neglect of the true spirit of the holistic anthropological project. While one or the other of these options may be appropriate for some selected problems, at some point she is likely to be drawn to a third option: collaborative research with specialists outside anthropology. It is the work that must be holistic, not always the worker.

As anthropology becomes more commonly characterized by the collection of "anthropology of" and "anthropology and" specialties, the occasions to ally with a disciplinarian on the other side of the "of" become more frequent. This is perhaps especially true in the field of the anthropology of law, or legal anthropology.

At various points, these chapters have asked whether legal anthropologists need to go to law school in order to pursue this line of inquiry, a question that it is appropriate to consider here in more depth. It is not uncommon for a single practitioner to have formal training in both anthropology and law—that was frequently true among the classic legal ethnographers, and several prominent scholars today, such as Sally Falk Moore, hold that dual qualification. Karl Llewellyn, in fact, had concluded perhaps with some regret that "there was no rainbow bridge between the social sciences and jurisprudence, that only dual practitioners would be able to move back and forth between the two kinds of disciplines" (Hull 1997).

Still, the system of American legal education does not encourage this approach. While one can easily learn biology without going to medical school or religion without attending a seminary, it is not always feasible to study law without enrolling in law school. Because law schools in the United States are designed solely for the formation of practitioners, deep knowledge *about* the law rather than *of* the law is correspondingly difficult to acquire for anyone not intending to pass a bar and become a certified attorney. We should note that this lacuna has been alleviated somewhat by the creation of "law and society" and "law and justice" programs at a few institutions. In a recent count by Austin Sarat in 2004, however, that option was available at only sixty colleges and universities, a number that was unchanged in another tally two years later, as compared to almost two hundred accredited schools of law.

One can speculate about the degree to which the lack of formal legal training among the majority of legal anthropologists has influenced the direction of the specialty. This gap might, however, explain why legal anthropologists frequently look outside law to explain legal phenomena. We seem to have forgotten one of Maine's primary theoretical points, which is that law develops in large measure because of the needs of the legal institutions themselves. Many contemporary legal anthropologists, however, begin from Montesquieu's position that extralegal forces such as economics or power differentials provide a complete account for the development of law. While these variables certainly have some contribution to make to the understanding of law, it remains an open question how much we learn about "law" when we turn immediately for understanding outside of law.

Anthropologists, like all persons, employ the categories of thought they have been trained to favor, and lacking the excruciating three-year immersion of law school, those categories tend not to be drawn from law. Bohannan might argue that this lack is a good thing, and perhaps he is correct. But it should not be assumed to be an unmixed blessing if it predisposes anthropologists to underestimate the inertial forces within law itself. We may turn too quickly to economics or politics to explain what are inherently legal phenomena.

To avoid such errors, collaborative anthropologist and lawyer teams make good sense for legal anthropology. While O'Barr and Conley represent one such team, two others have appeared already within these pages. *Rules and Processes*, the book that argued influentially for the new processual perspective in legal anthropology, represents the collaborative output of anthropologist John Comaroff and lawyer Simon Roberts. But perhaps the most famous anthropologist–attorney combination has been E. Adamson Hoebel and Karl Llewellyn, authors of *The Cheyenne Way* and advocates for the adoption of legal realism and the trouble-case method as tools within legal anthropology.

Not all legal anthropologists are supporters of the field's interdisciplinary nature. Laura Nader (2002) insists that she has

> never sought to make an interdisciplinary field out of law and anthropology (although my work is informed by other disciplines), nor have I hoped to amalgamate the work of lawyers and anthropologists (although we inform each other's work). . . . [My] current perspective

> on the contemporary cacophony in legal and anthropological scholarship on law and in society prompts me to argue for separate but equal arenas: we do different things. We have much to learn from each other, but if we try to do each other's work, the work suffers from our naïveté and inexperience.

The second part of her claim is indeed true. Law and anthropology must be, at points, "separate but equal arenas." Legal anthropology on its face is unable to meet that standard, however, because in its name as in its practice, law is subordinated to the interests of anthropology, violating the goal of equality between the two. The relationship she describes has elsewhere been termed **balanced reciprocity**, defined as the state wherein "neither discipline is independent of, parasitic upon, or subordinate to, the other. Anthropology, to fully realize its own vision, needs a collateral discipline of jurisprudence; law, in order to achieve its goal of justice and social order, requires the theoretical grounding and empirical conclusions of anthropology" (Donovan and Anderson 2003). Balanced reciprocity resides as the philosophical core of a related but different specialty: "anthropology and law." In contrast with the ethnographically centered legal anthropology, which asks questions about the place of law in society and its use by group members, anthropology and law examines the intersection of the independent practices of law and anthropology, such as the ways in which legal processes should recognize the findings of anthropology and, reciprocally, the benefits that the legal institution can confer on the discipline of anthropology.

There are, however, points at which balanced reciprocity should not pertain, and that would include the whole of legal anthropology. Here, law is not a subject equal to anthropology but rather is the object of the anthropological gaze. In such contexts, the two fields are neither separate nor equal. That fact alone should encourage an interdisciplinary project design. The quality of any anthropological study, however, can be expected to be limited by the clarity of understanding of the object, which may be beyond the personal command of a given anthropologist. The desirability of an interdisciplinary approach to legal anthropology seems overdetermined.

Summary and Conclusions

As a discipline, anthropology's special contribution to intellectual life is that its perspective is holistic rather than compartmentalized. That standard demands that its practitioners consider the full wealth of collected human knowledge and not only that formally labeled as anthropology. By implication if not by design, then, the realization of anthropology's goals requires that its workers adopt a stance of interdisciplinary cooperation with experts in all the subfields that contribute to the larger picture of the human condition. "Indeed, it is fair to say that anthropology has contributed a very great deal to the recognition of interdependence among the specialties and to the development of what is called interdisciplinary research—a theoretical contribution of some importance" (Bohannan 1959). This necessity for cooperation across disciplinary boundaries applies at least as much to legal anthropology, if not more so, given the institutional obstacles to acquiring deep familiarity with legal concepts outside the law school.

Anthropologist and lawyer teams are one method of achieving the balance of expertise often required to obtain more than a superficial grasp of the operations of any legal system. John Conley and William O'Barr represent one such team, and their work demonstrates the productivity of interdisciplinary pairings.

As they have shown, law is nothing if not language. Disputes are typically heard rather than seen, and the interaction of litigants' and judges' speech encodes the power relationships within the society. Although anthropology has customarily demanded linguistic competence of the fieldworker, the purpose of that requirement has been to understand what the informant was talking *about*, with less attention paid to the manner in which it was said. Conley and O'Barr tell us that this has been a mistake, one that legal anthropology should immediately correct.

We can, finally, note that a principal finding of their ethnography of discourse has been that "from the litigant's perspective, the opportunity for unconstrained narrative is an important component of informal court procedure." Many litigants expect to use the judicial process at least as much to validate their social positions, relationships, and worth as to resolve a specific and bounded dispute. This common use of the legal system is at odds with a sanction-focused understanding of law, showing us again the limited utility of those traditional definitions.

BOX 12.1

Law and Language

It bears repeating, to put a new spin on Oliver Wendell Holmes's realist maxim that "the life of the law has not been logic; it has been experience," that the life of the law is language. Whether one chooses to define law in terms of norms or sanctions or commanding authority, they all imply the essential element of language, either to communicate the content of a norm, to adjudicate the necessity for a sanction, or to promulgate the wishes of the sovereign.

(Continued)

BOX 12.1
Law and Language (Continued)

In addition to the sociological dimensions of legal discourse, lawyers have themselves displayed a serious interest in all matters linguistic. For them, the primary problem was how to construe the meanings of laws.

An early theorist on interpretation of statutory language was Francis Lieber. His text *Legal and Political Hermeneutics* (3rd ed., 1880) "not only introduced the term 'hermeneutics,' it broke 'new ground as the first substantial American work on legislation and on the doctrine of precedent. It can fairly be said to be the first American book applying techniques of literary criticism to legal institutions" (Herz 1995).

An essential lesson of Lieber's study pertained to the inherent ambiguity of language. In fact, the effort to increase clarity by adding detail has the opposite effect: "The more we strive in a document to go beyond plain clearness and perspicuity, the more we do increase, in fact, the chances of sinister interpretation." Interpretation will always be necessary, and statutes particularly must be *construed*. **Statutory construction** refers to "the drawing of conclusions respecting subjects that lie beyond the direct expression of the text, from elements known from and given in the text—conclusions which are in the spirit, though not within the letter of the text." The science of establishing the rules for interpretation and construction is **hermeneutics**. Lieber's *Legal and Political Hermeneutics* outlines many of these rules.

Of particular interest is his insistence that the quest for linguistic precision is infinitely recursive. In the famous example he offers of a housekeeper telling the maid to "fetch some soupmeat," Lieber identifies eight assumptions that are required to interpret and comply with this request.

> Suppose, on the other hand, the housekeeper, afraid of being misunderstood, had mentioned these eight specifications, she would not have obtained her object, if it were to exclude all *possibility* of misunderstanding. For, the various specifications would have required new ones. Where would be the end? We are constrained then, always, to leave a considerable part of our meaning to be found out by interpretation, which, in many cases must necessarily cause greater or less obscurity with regard to the exact meaning which our words were intended to convey.

Semantic ambiguity is ineliminable. Moviegoers became familiar with this idea in the film *I, Robot* (2004), in which the "three laws" meant to guide robot behavior and to safeguard humans had been overconstrued, allowing the opposite result to be attained without formally breaking any of the laws.

This discovery of an inescapable need for statutory construction attained cross-cultural depth in the work of Max Gluckman. He identified as "probably true of all legal concepts" that they be general, unspecific, flexible, permeable, and absorbent. The "'uncertainty' of legal concepts has social value in maintaining the 'certainty' of law." The flexibility of the concepts allows the judges to adapt the existing law to fit new circumstances while giving the appearance of merely enforcing the established and unchanging traditions. To pin down the concepts with any binding precision would ultimately lead to the deterioration of the system because it would then be unable to adapt to novel facts.

Both law and anthropology are enormously interested in the details of language. Their studies on the subject represent a particularly clear example of how their works combine to bring a fuller understanding to the problem than either could achieve alone.

Suggestions for Further Reading

A recent interview with O'Barr and Conley offers interesting insights into both their process for collaborative research and their often critical views on the current state of anthropological research and writing: Jason Cross, "Language, Power, and Law: An Interview with John Conley and William O'Barr," *PoLAR* 29 (2006): 337–50.

For an overview of the place of language within legal processes, one may begin with D. Brenneis, "Language and Disputing," *Annual Review of Anthropology* 17 (1988): 221–37; see also Tom Baker, Alon Harel, and Tamar Kugler, "The Virtues of Uncertainty in Law: An Experimental Approach," *Iowa Law Review* 89 (2004): 443–94; Chris Heffer, *The Language of Jury Trial: A Corpus-Aided Analysis of Legal-Lay Discourse* (2005); Roger W. Shuy, *Linguistics in the Courtroom* (2006). The best place to start for a familiarity with sociolinguistics is perhaps Peter Trudgill's *Sociolinguistics: An Introduction to Language and Society* (2001). Microanalysis of discourse can be a labor intensive, yet surprisingly enlightening project. For one example, see Michael Moerman, *Talking Culture: Ethnography and Conversation Analysis* (1988).

The Conley and O'Barr study is usefully compared with Sally Engle Merry's *Getting Justice and Getting Even: Legal Consciousness among Working-Class*

Americans (1990), which conducts more traditional extended case analyses of working-class New Englanders and their interactions with criminal, small-claims, and juvenile courts and their associated mediation programs.

Annelise Riles has voiced a skeptical view of the current state of inter-disciplinary cooperation between law and anthropology while remaining hopeful about the future in "Representing In-Between: Law, Anthropology, and the Rhetoric of Interdisciplinarity," *University of Illinois Law Review* 1994 (1994): 597–650; see also William Twining, "Law and Anthropology: A Case Study in Inter-Disciplinary Collaboration," *Law and Society Review* 7 (1973): 561–84. For a follow-up to Sarat's article about law and society programs at the undergraduate level, see Katherine Mangan, "Law for Laypeople," *Chronicle of Higher Education*, July 28, 2006, at A6–A8.

References

Paul Bohannan, "Anthropological Theories," *Science* 129 (1959): 292–93; James M. Donovan and H. Edwin Anderson, *Anthropology and Law* (2003); Max Gluckman, *The Judicial Process among the Barotse of Northern Rhodesia* (2nd ed., 1967); Hugh Gusterson, "Studying Up Revisited," *PoLAR* 20 (1997): 114–19, at 116; Michael Herz, "Rediscovering Francis Lieber: An Afterword and Introduction," *Cardozo Law Review* 16 (1995): 2107–34; N. E. H. Hull, *Roscoe Pound and Karl Llewellyn: Searching for an American Jurisprudence* (1997), at 170; David Hume, *A Treatise of Human Nature* (1739–1740); Laura Nader, *The Life of the Law: Anthropological Projects* (2002), at 72–73; Laura Nader, "Up the Anthropologist—Perspectives Gained from Studying Up," *Reinventing Anthropology* (1972), 284–311; Austin Sarat, "Legal Scholarship in the Liberal Arts," *Chronicle of Higher Education*, September 3, 2004, at B20.

IV

Highlights of
Comparative Anthropology

PART IV TURNS from the problems of describing local law norms to the challenges associated with comparison of those systems. The hope is to identify general principles of legal institutions in human societies.

Comparison presumes the equivalence of the terms to be compared on the relevant variables. The problem of language and categories, therefore, already present in the ethnographic context, multiplies in importance when comparing those local results with one another. Chapter 13 looks at two of those problems: the Gluckman–Bohannan debate over acceptable vocabulary to describe the indigenous folk system and, relatedly, the prospects of the development of value-free units of legal primitives similar to those successfully applied in kinship analysis.

Chapters 14 and 15 provide an overview of the only two areas in which comparative anthropology of any quality has been conducted in legal anthropology. Dispute resolution has risen in contemporary American legal anthropology not only to be one topic in the field but perhaps to subsume it entirely. One benefit of this development is that much work of high quality has been—and continues to be—achieved in this one area at least.

Europeans tend to have a different view of the discipline, however, privileging questions of legal pluralism. Excellent results have been achieved in this subject as well—and for similar reasons. Attention is given to the emergence of these divergent intellectual traditions.

CHAPTER 13

Cross-Cultural Comparison

ONLY AFTER THE ethnographies have been collected can the work of anthropology proper begin. As Paul Bohannan (1959) observed, documentation of the folk system is but the first step in the process toward "generalization or broad comparison among cultures." Comparative legal anthropology has as its goal the identification of patterns that are both general enough to apply to a broad number of distinctive cultural contexts but specific enough to be intellectually interesting.

The extreme difficulty of these tasks should not be underestimated. Fundamental to the project is the basic question of how one talks about law stuff. The labels given to data exert extraordinary influence over what can then be done with them (a phenomenon first noticed by Benjamin Whorf in relation to how people behaved around "empty" gasoline drums). It should come as no surprise, then, that considerable attention has been expended on this problem. Following a brief overview of comparative work generally, the remainder of this chapter is given over to a review of the field's landmarks.

Reflections on the Comparative Method

The goal of comparative anthropology is—or should be—rarely to find a rule or "law" that rises to the level of universal validity on the model of physical laws of the natural world. The more modest and achievable goal intends to derive not laws but generalizations that require only minor corrections or qualifications in order to capture the essential elements of any particular case. Comparison allows the special features of the local context to be more readily and meaningfully identified. One virtue of such a process is that fewer resources are expended attempting to account for phenomena through invocation of culturally idiosyncratic variables when all things being equal a more generic explanation will perform just as effectively (i.e., **Occam's razor**— the philosophical principle of theoretical parsimony repeatedly invoked in the film *Contact* [1997]—in this case advises that one hypothesis capable of explaining data relating to law norms in multiple contexts is preferable to multiple hypotheses, one for each setting. Occam's actual statement was that "entities should not be multiplied beyond necessity.").

Obstacles to realizing this ideal are not negligible. Some, frankly, may even be insurmountable. For example, unlike laboratory scientists who can manipulate their variables to control the different combinations and interactions or sample their phenomena randomly, anthropologists are limited to natural or **quasi experiments,** which depend on natural occurrences of the phenomena. To study how a cognitive ability is distributed between sexes, for instance, one cannot perform a true experiment that manipulates ability and sex of subject, but one can study the ability as it occurs naturally in subjects of both sexes. As Laura Nader and Harry Todd point out, it is the "world [that] provides us with a laboratory of experiments in its forums for dispute." While anthropology can strive to be more scientific in its methodology, it can never be an experimental science. This incompatibility helps explain the disconnect between Pospisil's scientific vision and the inability of his field data to challenge his hypotheses in the way expected of truly experimental design.

The tree in figure 13.1 modifies Bohannan's parsing of cross-cultural comparison into its respective types, with some illustrative examples of each class. *Casual comparison* is a method of exposition and not a true research technique, a device to ease comprehension of other cultures by the reader. The examples and counterexamples invoked to illustrate a point can come

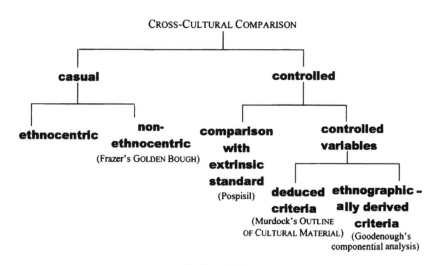

FIGURE 13.1
Bohannan's Typology of Comparison across Cultures

from the common cultural background of the writer and the reader (the ethnocentric technique) or can range freely over the ethnographic literature,
picking examples for their power of illumination in that specific context.
One thinks here, perhaps, of the free-ranging comparative style of James
Frazer's *The Golden Bough* (1890). Although offering a broader sample than
the ethnocentric approach, the selections do not represent a coherent picture of any phenomena.

Controlled comparison includes all methods intended to generate conclusions of general validity rather than merely pretty illustrative points.
The evaluation of ethnographic data by an extrinsic standard can refer to
the invocation of a general theory of law. Bohannan cites as examples
Pospisil's *Kapauku Papuans and Their Law* and sections of his own *Justice
and Judgment*.

Comparison by controlled variables can be by deduced criteria, such as
those in George Murdock's *Outline of Cultural Materials* (1945), or by variables deduced ethnographically, as with Ward Goodenough's technique of
componential analysis.

No single variety of comparative analysis is appropriate for every need.
Although the casual method may seem insubstantial for a scientific discourse, it can more than satisfy the need for a compelling counterexample to
dispel some widely held conclusion based on induction from other
instances. The report of a black swan anywhere will suffice to disprove the
belief that all swans everywhere are white. Margaret Mead's *Coming of Age
in Samoa* (1928) represents this use of the comparative method. Against the
widely held assumption that the angst of adolescence was a human universal, she offered a report of a society where this was—purportedly, given the
later challenges to her conclusions—not the case. The question we must ask
is not whether one or another of the approaches to comparison is good or
bad but whether it is appropriate to the task at hand.

Isaac Schapera made this very point when, in his own reflections on
comparative methodologies, he recognized that "method must be determined largely by problem, and where the problem is relatively limited in
scope the data required may also be limited." In the end, however, he
remained extremely negative about the promise of comparative work in legal
anthropology:

Comaroff: Does that mean a comparative anthropology is impossible?
Schapera: Unless you go to the extent of eliminating everything but the low-
    est common denominators—and then you miss everything worthwhile,
    don't you?
Comaroff: What, then, do you think was the lasting value of such comparative
    exercises—to which you contributed—as *African Political Systems* and
    African Systems of Kinship and Marriage?

Schapera: None. . . . The only relevance of comparison is that, unless you look at other societies, you cannot know what is unique. It is rather like Malinowski thought, although not as he would have put it: you are rarely aware that there is a problem at all until you look *outside* [your field of inquiry]. . . . That's the only time comparison is useful and valuable.

Although legal anthropologists need not surrender to Schapera's skepticism, we would benefit from his tone of caution. Better to have no comparison, perhaps, than bad comparison, but that should motivate us to improve techniques rather than to succumb to despair.

Certainly a step in the right direction is not to make comparative analysis more difficult than it needs to be. One way to avoid unnecessary complications is to collect and present field data in a manner that facilitates reasonable cross-cultural comparisons or that at least does not preclude at the outset such efforts.

Although the conundrum of cross-cultural comparison is common to all of anthropology, this chapter looks at two efforts within legal anthropology to confront and solve this dilemma. First, in a famed exchange of opinions, Max Gluckman and Paul Bohannan traded criticisms about the suitability of English legal vocabulary to convey the meanings of indigenous local systems. Although Gluckman's use of this approach may have been extreme, so too may have been Bohannan's apparent refusal to tolerate such a practice.

But if not English, is the better or even only choice to rely primarily on the terminology of the local system? One alternative to using the natural language of any culture to describe the system of another would be to create a value-free, context-neutral vocabulary to characterize the raw data. This approach has seemingly worked well within kinship studies, suggesting that a similar solution is possible within legal anthropology. The second section of this chapter reviews the most prominent proposal in this category, the legal primitives of Wesley Hohfeld.

The Gluckman–Bohannan Debate

The disagreement between Max Gluckman and Paul Bohannan was initially sketched as we considered their individual ethnographic achievements. To review, Gluckman liberally employed a technical legal vocabulary from the Roman and English legal traditions to describe the practices of the Barotse. Bohannan, on the other hand, retained the local terminology of the Tiv.

The difference between the two fieldworkers' method was not simply a matter of style. It reflected a deep theoretical divide over the very nature of the ethnographic project. Bohannan believed that to use such language as Gluckman's was to fundamentally confuse the analytic system of the anthropologist's theory with the folk system of the informants. This lapse was exacerbated when the analytic system applied was not some form of value-free interpretive scheme but merely the folk system of the fieldworker's own culture. This process smacked of the worst kind of ethnocentrism in that it made the Western local categories the universal standard by which all others would be evaluated—and this was the caustic criticism of Gluckman, who did use at least some local terminology. More extreme was Isaac Schapera (1938), who deliberately avoided any indigenous vocabulary in his *Handbook*. In the process, the rich detail of what the locals were actually doing becomes lost as their reality is forced into ill-fitting preconceived categories as if into a Procrustean bed.

Bohannan's solution was not without its own faults. Overreliance on indigenous vocabulary could, when taken to the extreme, produce a form of cultural solipsism. It is a matter of debate whether Bohannan's own work approached this point; unquestionably, his primary points are subtler than he is often given credit for. In principle, even if strict use of indigenous terms yielded greater insights at the local level—which is arguable, given the welter of foreign terms the reader needed to control—it complicated the true goal of the anthropology, which is comparison, not mere description. If data from disparate field sites are not reducible to a common conceptual scheme, comparison across data sets becomes impossible, putting out of reach the discovery of broader patterns of legal behavior. We are then studying not humans in some broad sense but only a catalog of sui generis collectivities of *Homo sapiens*.

Neither party was prepared to agree to disagree, and thus ensued one of the saltier exchanges within the discipline. Bohannan (1967) conceded that "all legal ideas can be expressed in any language" but insisted that the proper method is to translate *from* the local language *into* the analytical language. He accused Gluckman of translating "'backwards,' by starting with the English rather than the Lozi, [thereby obscuring] the Lozi distinctions and meanings by going in the wrong direction."

For his part, Gluckman (1967) shared with Bohannan a view of the desired goal to "present a folk-system in its purity" but disagreed over how that should be done. "[One] cannot escape from the use of one's own language." With perhaps a bit of irony, he points out that

there is no difference between using the language of Western social anthropology and using the language of Western jurisprudence in tackling these sorts of problems. Theoretically, both are equally distorting even while they may be illuminating. It is mere prejudice for social anthropologists to consider that the scheme which jurisprudents have used successfully for the analysis of Western law, cannot be applied to clarify the law of another "folk-system." It is particularly prejudice, if in fact their own systems of analysis can be reduced to almost exactly the same logical procedures.

The outcome of this debate depends on whom you ask. Laura Nader sensibly suggests that the truth lay somewhere in between the two polarized (and, by that time, caricatured) positions. John Conley and William O'Barr, however, concluded that "in hindsight, most contemporary legal anthropologists might say that Bohannan had 'won.' In subsequent decades, anthropology in general and political and legal anthropology in particular have become increasingly focused on the local." While inarguably true, this has perhaps been a Pyrrhic victory. The intellectual goal of anthropology is not the mere description of the local or even, as Bohannan (1959) himself recognizes, the documentation of the folk system. This is but the first step in the process toward "generalization or broad comparison among cultures." Fetishistic devotion to cultural particularism has made Bohannan's position engender a most un-Bohannanian outcome. Attention to the local that does not lay the groundwork for a shift in perspective to the nonlocal arguably dissolves the very purpose of anthropology.

If this debate appears to be over mere quibbles, it is largely because the terms in which it was conducted mask the more fundamental issues involved. Sally Falk Moore convincingly analyzed the episode. An apparent disagreement about the how and when of translating local terminology obscured the deeper division over the ultimate use of the referents of those terms:

> Gluckman sees the concepts and principles of law as *part* of legal systems, whereas Bohannan is most interested in studying the concepts *themselves*, because he considers them a reflection of the whole organization of the legal system.
>
> To Gluckman, these concepts and principles are manipulable tools within legal systems, part of their equipment, not reflections of their organization. . . . The total pattern of thought condensed into key words is what Bohannan is after as an ideal ethnographic aim. . . . Gluckman has an entirely different ultimate aim in mind when he approaches legal materials. The large pattern he is inquiring into is the inter-relationship between the legal system and its social and economic setting.

Bohannan (1959) indeed viewed the word as the unit of study: "The folk organization of social and cultural activity, in other words, is in terms of concepts and the word tags by means of which people identify them." He identified the locus of the primary significance of the legal system within the local worldview as being contained, whole and intact, within the categories of thought. No further evidence is required beyond his statement in *Justice and Judgment* that "I cannot translate *jir* by one English word; to translate it with several is to dissipate its force and truth." That he would identify the word as the locus for "truth" tells us much about the privileged status he accorded this symbol. Premature translation would taint—or, as he says of Gluckman's work, "irrevocably spoil"—the data set.

Gluckman, however, as a structural functionalist, was more concerned with relating the institutions together into a coherent whole. While striving for as much fidelity as possible to the folk system, this objective required only that the legal concepts be up to the task of indicating the social relationships that were the true meaning of the legal system. Given the irreconcilable differences of perspective over the proper path to understanding the legal system, it is no wonder he and Bohannan talked at cross-purposes to one another.

Two lessons should follow from this episode. First, there can be no such thing as an "ideal" method, dwelling apart from any specific application. Methodology should match purpose so that suitable data are produced to answer the questions posed by the research. In this case, neither Bohannan or Gluckman appears to be "wrong" in any absolute sense; each was applying the method that suited his research interests. The disagreement arose because each thought that the other should forgo his own approach and apply that of the other, perhaps in the mistaken belief that their projects were identical.

Still, the Gluckman–Bohannan debate sensitizes the legal anthropologist to the issue of language in general (see chapter 12). The second lesson should be that it makes a great deal of difference how anthropologists talk about their data and then relate that data to theory. While some points can be discussed in elaborate detail, others are presented without any justification at all. Why translate this word but not that one? How was the translated equivalent chosen? Failure to explain these choices instills in the reader a false sense of natural inevitability about the discussion on the page when in fact it is a contrivance of the highest order.

Having raised these issues, the inevitable question becomes, all things being equal, What *is* the best way to talk about legal phenomena? Perhaps neither Gluckman nor Bohannan was on the right track.

Hohfeldian Legal Primitives

How one talks about the data of legal anthropology influences what can be said about legal norms. The debate between Paul Bohannan and Max Gluckman revolved around the terminologies used in ethnographic discourse. Should the fieldworker restrict herself to local terms, or are those derived from English common law and Roman civil law acceptable?

An altogether different approach looks to design a value-neutral vocabulary to speak about law wherever it appears. Armed with such a code, the concerns of Bohannan and Gluckman vanish. One can choose to gloss data by whatever labels one prefers so long as the basic meaning is given in the terms of the value-neutral language.

The model for such a strategy could be the technique of kinship analysis. One can label a particular social relationship in the vernacular terms of the language shared by the writer and reader (e.g., "mother") or by the jargon of the specialty ("Hawaiian" or generational systems). The relationships underlying any such uses, however, are graphically represented according to a standardized key (see figure 13.2).

The connotations of any labels used to name this particular kinship system will not distract from the underlying denotation assigned by the coded relationships. The chart tells us that what we would call our "uncle" on our mother's side—mother's brother, or MoBr—is called by the same term as "father." Kin relations can be extremely complicated, but any confusion can be clarified by use of the code (MoBr) or the chart. If legal relationships could be similarly encoded, then much of the fear igniting the Gluckman–Bohannan dispute evaporates.

A lawyer, Wesley Hohfeld, attempted just this feat, parsing legal relationships into what he termed the "fundamental legal conceptions." These were to prove immensely influential. Gluckman regretted that he was unfamiliar with Hohfeld's system when he did his fieldwork, recognizing the value of these distinctions for the anthropologist called on to characterize unfamiliar legal interactions. Hoebel was a particularly aggressive advocate for general adoption of the Hohfeldian system.

Hohfeld built his system on four fundamental concepts, each of which had an opposite and a correlative:

> For every *right*, there is the opposite (no-right), and a correlative duty;
> For every *privilege*, there is the opposite (duty), and a correlative no-right;
> For every *power*, there is an opposite disability, and a correlative liability;
> For every *immunity*, there is an opposite liability, and a correlative disability.

Hohfeld characterized these categories as sui generis and thus irreducible to any of the other terms. In theory, any legally significant relationship could be deconstructed and described using only these terms.

Attempts have been made to refine Hohfeld's basic scheme. Max Radin, for example, in addition to tweaking some of the terminology, argued that what Hohfeld had conceived as correlatives were no such thing:

> A's demand-right and B's duty . . . are not correlatives because they are
> not separate, however closely connected, things at all. They are not even
> two aspects of the same thing. They are two absolutely equivalent state-

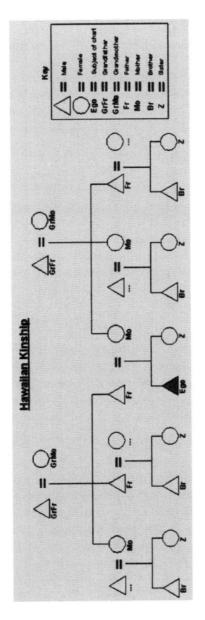

FIGURE 13.2
Graphical Representation of the Hawaiian Kinship System

ments of the same thing. B's duty does not follow from A's right, nor is it caused by it. B's duty *is* A's right.

Both Radin and Hoebel attempt to provide demonstrations of how Hohfeldian analysis improves and clarifies otherwise obscure claims about "primitive" law. Ownership offers a particularly fruitful concept, as claims about who owns what were often unclear. By deconstructing the concept of ownership into the fundamental concepts involved, one is able to state with perfect precision the rights, duties, and privileges involved with, say, ownership of a canoe. This ability to think clearly about such matters would significantly ease other problems, such as those surrounding intellectual property rights over cultural knowledge (see chapter 17).

Despite such earnest efforts, Hohfeld's legal primitives did not attract wide popularity among anthropologists (or lawyers, for that matter). While simply overlooked by most, Sally Falk Moore's rejection was more principled:

> Despite having been brought up, as Hoebel was, in the Hohfeldian religion by Karl Llewellyn, I would reject Hohfeld's terminology for ethnographic description for the following reasons. First, it is hopelessly clumsy. Second, it cuts up all legal relations into dyads, which is sometimes a very artificial and distorting procedure. Third, it cuts up legal relations into analytically distinguishable, but not always pragmatically distinct, qualities, until sight is lost of the relationship as a whole.

It is not immediately obvious that Hohfeld's system is any more "clumsy" than many another descriptive system widely employed by anthropologists, such as that used to describe kinship patterns. Her ultimate judgment is harsh indeed: "In my opinion legal anthropologists should read Hohfeld and then, cheerfully, should do without him."

Perhaps, as Moore claims, Hohfeld's own formulation is flawed (a conclusion that has not been demonstrated with any logical finality; at the very least, since a literature exists demonstrating its productive insights on otherwise intractable problems, critics might show how Hohfeld's primitives can lead the anthropologist into error). It is an entirely different matter whether his goal of a standardized value-free vocabulary to describe legal data does not remain one toward which future students should aspire. Moore offered candidate terms of her own that she believed would fill the need for neutral legal terms. She suggests that terminology used by Anglo-American judges in their recitation of the facts includes suitably generic "blank-check words": transaction, obligation, interest, understanding, concurred, binding agreement, accord, mutual assent, and transfer. Given that many of these terms are themselves the subject of litigation (e.g., what does it mean to be "mutual," and at what point does a transfer of ownership actually occur? On payment or physical possession?), it is not clear that her solution is any improvement on Hohfeld's. Bohannan (1960), on the other hand, expected that "the 'whole new independent language without national home' [Gluckman's phrase] will probably be Fortran or some other computer language," a suggestion explicitly rejected by Pospisil (1985).

One should perhaps not be so quick to dismiss the ultimate utility of Hohfeld. Given the acknowledged need for a value-neutral language to describe cross-cultural legal interactions, his approach remains the most promising of all those that have been suggested. Granting the importance of this problem, however, surprisingly little energy has been expended on its solution.

Berkeley Village Law Project, Part 1

The problems of the comparative method discussed in the previous sections of this chapter weigh particularly heavy on the solitary fieldworker who must conduct research and write up results that are fruitful not only for the personal objectives of that anthropologist but also for audiences unforeseen. The units selected for analysis and the terminology applied to describe phenomena ideally anticipate the theoretical interests of years to come. Perhaps for clear reasons, this ideal is so rarely realized, leaving most ethnographies, even the most gifted, to be criticized by somebody at some point because of what it failed to include. Indeed, in Nader and Todd's (1978) eyes, "the work was becoming more redundant than cumulative." As recounted by Francis Snyder,

> A more fundamental weakness of anthropological approaches concerns the relative absence of comparative research. Anthropologists have often proclaimed their discipline to be inherently comparative. Except in the very limited sense of concentrating on groups or societies other than one's own, however, very few anthropological studies are genuinely comparative, and therefore they offer only implicit contrasts with our own state and its law.

The closest legal anthropology has come to realizing a truly comparative methodology was during the Berkeley Village Law Project. Students of Laura Nader collaborated on fundamentals of a research method and the core questions to be asked while in the field. The results of this long-term collaboration have been presented in *The Disputing Process* (1978) although the project itself continued on, with the last published report in 1992. Participants—including future luminaries such as June Starr—conducted fieldwork from 1965 to 1975 in fourteen locations. Although allowed to select their own sites, "the data had to be collected in as systematic a way as possible, which meant that prior to departure for the field the fieldworkers needed to agree upon what they would collect and within what framework the collection of data would be undertaken."

Because of the standardized data collection methodology, the aggregated reports provided the strongest empirical support for generalized findings in the field of legal anthropology. The specific results are taken up in the next chapter. Our interest here is on the project as an exercise in comparative method.

The first point to be made is that, because of its method, the comparison is very real and not at all illusory. This judgment *cannot* be made for edited volumes that to the casual reader appear to offer much the same approach, situating topically related reports from disparate cultures. But because these data were collected idiosyncratically and not collaboratively, any similarity to the Berkeley Village Law Project is only superficial. The qualitative advance in method represented by *The Disputing Process* should not be undervalued.

Despite its unquestioned value, however, the text is comparative without truly comparing. Although using a standardized data collection protocol—or as near to such as practically possible—the chapters of *The Disputing Process* are still largely self-contained local studies. The reader never sees the comparison actually taking place. The locus of the comparison resides at least as much in the mind of the reader as in the pages of the book. One might recall that this is the same location where the adversarial legal system of the Berkeley Village Law Project participants' home culture situates truth and wonder if the correspondence is wholly coincidental.

Summary and Conclusions

The second of the three levels of anthropological study, following the first phase of ethnographic description, is cross-cultural comparison. Of the three levels, comparative legal anthropology is by far the most difficult and the most underdeveloped. This condition is especially ironic given the general understanding that the special project of anthropology as a discipline is just such comparative analysis.

Obstacles to successful cross-cultural comparison exist at every step. While ideally the results of ethnographic fieldwork feed their local data into more general analyses, most are conducted by methods that frustrate that intention. Extended description has been given to the problems of language that contribute to this difficulty, but others exist, not least among them a strong feeling among some anthropologists that comparative work should not be pursued. This lack of unanimity concerning the merits of the undertaking can make it difficult to acquire the necessary funding and support for a long-term comparative project.

Despite these reservoirs of pessimism, solid achievements in comparative legal anthropology have been accomplished, such as the Berkeley Village Law Project initiated by Laura Nader. While the project can be criticized for falling short of some Platonic ideal of cross-cultural comparison, it stands as a challenge to today's legal anthropologists to aspire at least as high if not higher.

Suggestions for Further Reading

Comparative Methods: Sally Falk Moore, "Comparisons: Possible and Impossible," *Annual Review of Anthropology* 34 (2005): 1–11; Gopāla Śarana, *The Methodology of Anthropological Comparisons* (1975); Henk Vinken, Joseph Soeters, and Peter Ester, eds., *Comparing Cultures: Dimensions of Culture in a Comparative Perspective* (2005).

Hohfeldian Analysis: Stephen Husak, "Legal Rights: How Useful Is Hohfeldian Analysis?" *Philosophical Studies* 37 (1980): 45–53; Giovanni Sartor, "Fundamental Legal Concepts: A Formal and Teleological Characterisation," *EUI Working Papers Law 2006/11* (2006).

Gluckman–Bohannan Debate: D. Brenneis, "Language and Disputing," *Annual Review of Anthropology* 17 (1988): 221–37.

References

Paul Bohannan, *Justice and Judgment among the Tiv* (1957); Paul Bohannan, "Anthropological Theories," *Science* 129 (1959): 292–93; Paul Bohannan, "Ethnography and Comparison in Legal Anthropology," *Law in Culture and Society*, ed. Laura Nader (1960), 401–18; Paul Bohannan, "Review of *The Ideas in Barotse Jurisprudence*," *Kroeber Anthropological Society Papers* 36 (1967): 94–101; Jean Comaroff and John L. Comaroff, "On the Founding Fathers, Fieldwork and Functionalism: A Conversation with Isaac Schapera," *American Ethnologist* 15 (1988): 554–65; John M. Conley and William M. O'Barr, "A Classic in Spite of Itself: *The Cheyenne Way* and the Case Method in Legal Anthropology," *Law and Social Inquiry* 29 (2004): 179–217, at 211; Max Gluckman, "Reappraisal (1966)," *The Judicial Process among the Barotse of Northern Rhodesia* (2nd ed., 1967); Ward Goodenough, "Yankee Kinship Terminology: A Problem in Componential Analysis," *American Anthropologist* 67, suppl. 1 (1965): 259–87; E. Adamson Hoebel, "Fundamental Legal Concepts as Applied in the Study of Primitive Law," *Yale Law Journal* 51 (1942): 951–66; Wesley Newcomb Hohfeld, "Some Fundamental Legal Conceptions as Applied in Judicial Reasoning," *Yale Law Journal* 23 (1913): 16–59; Sally Falk Moore, *Law as Process: An Anthropological Approach* (1978), at 143–44, 142; Laura Nader, "The

Anthropological Study of Law," *American Anthropologist* 67, no. 6, pt. 2 (1965): 3–32; Laura Nader and Harry F. Todd, *The Disputing Process—Law in Ten Societies* (1978), at 40; Leopold J. Pospisil, *The Ethnology of Law* (2nd ed., 1985); Max Radin, "A Restatement of Hohfeld," *Harvard Law Review* 51 (1938): 1141–64, at 1150; Isaac Schapera, *A Handbook of Tswana Law and Custom* (1938); Isaac Schapera, "Some Comments on Comparative Method in Social Anthropology," *American Anthropologist* 55 (1953): 353–62; Francis G. Snyder, "Anthropology, Dispute Processes and Law: A Critical Introduction," *British Journal of Law and Society* 8 (1981): 141–80, at 162–63.

CHAPTER 14

Dispute Resolution

THE FIRST PART of this chapter looks specifically at a recurring theme in this narrative about legal anthropology: the story of how legal anthropology morphed from the study of law into the more limited examination of disputing. Review of historical developments in the discipline will show that this outcome was overdetermined by method, philosophy, and theory, most particularly the long-term influence of legal realism. While the restriction of study to the topic of disputing can be criticized on many points, it cannot be faulted as unproductive. It remains one of the few topics that has enjoyed serious comparative study. The subsequent parts of the chapter consider some of the comparative exercises in the topic of dispute resolution.

But because legal anthropology is *not* reducible to the study of dispute resolution, we would anticipate some strands of the discipline to have adopted a different emphasis. The next chapter looks at legal anthropologies with interests outside dispute resolution, most notably in the problem of legal pluralism.

American Disputology

American legal anthropology, with very few exceptions, is the study of disputing. Nondispute topics within the field of legal anthropology receive less attention on this side of the Atlantic. As we shall see in the next chapter, this situation reverses when looking at legal anthropology outside the confines of the American university.

On the surface, it is not immediately clear what conclusions can be drawn from this limited practice. If legal anthropology refers to the anthropology of *law*, one implication of the restriction of the field to disputing is that law and disputes become interchangeable. Another interpretation has legal anthropologists functioning as "disputologists," one subset of a larger enterprise of the anthropology of law, without any necessary conclusion that the two domains are coterminous.

Arguably, legal anthropologists are themselves of two minds about this issue. They do occasionally rhapsodize about the wide scope of law, one far broader than disputing alone:

> The law has many functions. It serves to educate, to punish, to harass, to protect private and public interests, to provide entertainment, to serve as a fund-raising institution, to distribute scarce resources, to maintain the status quo, to maintain class systems and to cut across them, to integrate and disintegrate societies—all these things in different places, at different times, with different weightings. (Nader and Todd 1978)

Having recognized the large range of functions that law performs within society, however, they then go on to look at only one, the settlement of disputes, or conflict resolution. The contrast may arise out of the tension between the commonsense understanding of law as a multifaceted social institution and the technical understanding of law that is rooted in the philosophical premises of the field's methodology.

Karl Llewellyn and E. Adamson Hoebel introduced their trouble-case method to settle some of the problems that had vexed the anthropological study of law up to that point. The early philosopher-scholars had pondered what law *is* and whether every society has it. Just as they equated religion with rituals and overt references to supernatural entities, they construed law according to a Western model of enactment by legislatures, enforced by policing agencies, and adjudicated by courts. Accordingly, they found little law among the world's societies. Functionalists beginning with Malinowski successfully rebutted this parochial perspective and found that law existed in every society, even those lacking intricate legal institutions.

Shorn of the easy indicators of institutional machinery, however, law became a problematic field concept. Where does the anthropologist look to find it? The solution offered by Llewellyn and Hoebel and taken up by others committed to legal realism was to concentrate on the trouble case, or settlement of disputes and altercations within the community. One learns the content of a legal system not by collecting disembodied rules, however "known and clear in words," but through the study of "case after case in which the rules have come into question, or have been challenged or broken." Law, according to the legal realism they represented, was ultimately only what the adjudicator said it was, and therefore the only place to look for a society's law was in the cases ruled on by the judge (or the cultural equivalent).

The rationale for this focus on disputing necessarily denies to law any other locus than the sanctioning of troublemakers for breaches of the peace.

While perhaps not the original intention, the locus and the function merged over the decades: law is not merely *revealed* in dispute resolution, but its *purpose* is dispute resolution. Rules that fall into the category of the law are simply those that adjudicators apply to resolve conflicts. No room is left for the study of the role of law in *preventing* breaches. What then of the rule that prevented rule breaking and was therefore never adjudicated? If, as legal realists have argued, law was to be found only in the decisions of the courts, no decision means no law. Laws that are *obeyed* become essentially nonlaw. The case method predisposed not merely an emphasis on disputing but also a limitation to that topic: "Disputing displaces law as the subject of study" (Snyder 1981).

As previously discussed, the case method in turn became the extended case method, which looked to follow the dispute from the perspective of the disputant rather than the intervener and on the negotiated navigation of the litigant through the culturally available justice-dispensing forums. This modification of the case method did not, however, fundamentally alter the intellectual inheritance it received from its methodological predecessor. The life of the law, to again modify Nader's phrase, is still the case, although the focus has shifted onto the litigants, and the development of the conflict over time has become the prime interest.

The incremental quality of the transition between the case and extended case methods can be directly illustrated by an examination of their respective material products. While legal anthropology has outgrown a rigid application of the case method, it has not yet left wholly behind the format designed to promote that methodology, the casebook. Even Laura Nader arranges her ethnographic materials in a method indistinguishable from Llewellyn and Hoebel: numbered cases, embellished with appropriate elaboration and development to serve the purposes of the particular theoretical point its introduction was designed to further. While the selection criteria may have changed over time, along with the theoretical apparatus to extract the precious insights, the discipline continues to favor that style of presentation.

Although postclassic legal anthropology successfully argued that attention to the case was too limiting, their solution—the dispute—has proven equally restrictive because of that unit's conceptual descent from its predecessor. Only an incremental improvement on the original case method, the extended case method imported in toto the philosophical foundation that supported it. Thus, extended case studies too have little room for, or conceptual recognition of, functions of law not directly related to disputing.

John Conley and William O'Barr have grown uncomfortable with this seeming obsession for conflict as the central topic within legal anthropology. The "most pernicious problem of all [in legal anthropology] may be the assumption inherent in the very conceptualization of legal anthropology as the cross-cultural study of conflict and its resolution. Where is the subfield that studies social accord?" In response to their lament over the lack of a systematic legal anthropology of peace, we can say that legal anthropology's current approach strongly inhibits exactly those studies. We focus on disputes because that is where our tradition tells us to look for law. If law can exist outside that context, we shall need a new theory that can tell us where to look and why; otherwise, the discipline becomes again as adrift conceptually as it was before *The Cheyenne Way*. Disputes were chosen as the unit of analysis because it offered one way around the vexatious problem of defining what "law" was. Everyone could agree both that disputes bore some relationship to what was ordinarily referred to by "law" and that they were much easier to identify reliably cross-culturally. The result, although few have realized it, has been an unintended definition by implication.

The problems with the narrow focus on the dispute have practical implications as well as the theoretical ones already mentioned. While chapter 12 argued that when legal anthropology turned its attention away from law and toward disputing, losing the rationale on which to draw conclusions about its self-denominated focal phenomenon, the methodological transition to processualism also erected a more pragmatic limitation. Many of the pressing issues of the day, in which legal anthropologists should be expected to assume a commanding role, may not be reducible to the disputing model.

Since the 1960s, when Nader first gave voice to the interests of legal processualism, the significant problems toward which legal anthropology might be expected to make a useful contribution have changed. Of particular importance among the emerging challenges are the issues of human rights and intellectual property.

Certainly, much of what goes on within intellectual property rights (IPR) does conform to the model of disputing. But the majority (like violations of human rights) does not always fit that model because there is no "resolution" possible. Victimized groups cannot be compensated for genocide; likewise, indigenous peoples from whom valuable resources have been taken out of their control have been denied their right to self-determination as defined in Article 1(2) of both the International Covenant on Economic, Social, and Cultural Rights and the International Covenant on Civil and Political Rights. Losses incurred through such "commercial exploitation of cultural property can become irreversible and can contribute to the loss of people's autonomy" (Posey and Dutfield 1996). The lesson appears to be that if the situation has devolved to the point of a "dispute," not only are the indigenous peoples likely to lose because the IPR system is by design tilted against them, but whatever the outcome, they have already suffered an irremediable harm.

If one goal of dispute resolution is to restore the status quo (by either compensating the victim for damages or returning the victim to her previous condition), the dispute paradigm cannot serve where the status quo cannot be restored. The peoples have been exterminated, or the knowledge has been given forever to the public domain. For these kinds of problems, the only worthwhile goal is to prevent the violation rather than to rely on post facto responses to them. This need compels the reconsideration of the positive functions of law identified by Malinowski that stand beyond the conceptual techniques of a dispute-centered legal anthropology.

Berkeley Village Law Project, Part 2

To critique the disputing orientation is not to deny that within its realm of influence it has been extraordinarily productive. Chapter 13 reviewed the design and goals of Laura Nader's Berkeley Village Law Project. Beginning in 1965, the project served multiple purposes. A training ground for students who would later become some of the most influential specialists in legal anthropology, its published output constitutes one of the few genuinely comparative efforts in the field.

The volume *The Disputing Process* contains a decade's collaboration between Nader and her graduate students who conducted fieldwork in a wide variety of field settings. The chapters represent the group's interest in "social morphology—the forms used for disputing processing and their concomitant interrelation with specific forms of social groupings." At its conclusion, "the known range of types of remedy agents" had been examined.

As an early work in the newly announced processual theory, the Berkeley Village Law Project was able to turn its attention not only to the dispute and its resolution but also to the life cycle of the conflict as a whole, offering "a more dynamic approach that treats the dispute as but one event in a series of events linking persons and groups over time and possibly involving other disputes." Perhaps the conceptual key to their method was the realization that "disputes are social processes embedded in social relations," all of which required explication.

The Berkeley Village Law Project yielded meaningful patterns thought to be valid cross-culturally. The attention of the participants to the process of disputing led the fieldworkers to document the structure of the events. They identified "components" that "universally such cases share . . . depending on what stage the dispute is in":

- *Object* of the dispute: is it over property, relationships, honor?
- *Parties* to the dispute and their sociological elements, such as age, sex, and relative status
- *Presentation* of the respective arguments about the dispute to relevant decision makers
- *Procedures* for handling the dispute
- *Outcomes* of the dispute, including the *termination* of the grievance and the *enforcement* of the decision

When looking at a dispute longitudinally, the project's students were able to isolate three distinct phases of its life cycle:

- The *grievance* or *preconflict* stage "refers to a circumstance or condition which one person (or group) perceives to be unjust, and the grounds for resentment or complaint."
- The *conflict* stage occurs when "the aggrieved party opts for confrontation."
- The *dispute* stage "results from escalation of the conflict by making the matter public."

Finally, the variables the project identified as influencing the course of an individual dispute included the following:

- *Structure* of the social relationships involved
- Whether the dispute involves contesting control over *scarce resources*
- Relative *power* of the disputants
- *Goals* of the disputants in pressing the complaint
- What *forums* the parties have access to
- How much *time and money* the complainant is willing to invest in pursuing the case
- What the *cultural and symbolic factors* are that accompany an escalation of a complaint into an open dispute

The Berkeley Village Law Project stands as one of the outstanding accomplishments of legal anthropology. If it has a failing, it was in not inspiring similar projects on other topics. When the project's organizer, Laura Nader (2002), later reflected on its legacy, she concluded,

> Our most important findings centered on conditions under which different forms or styles of dispute management occur. For example, mediation between parties of greatly unequal power does not work. Again, context provided clues as to why styles of conflict decision-making varied within each culture, as well as between cultures.

The form assumed by the disputing process between parties of unequal power would become the evolving focus of Nader's legal anthropology.

Alternative Dispute Resolution

Michael Freeman credits anthropology for having "taught lawyers something about dispute resolution and [for helping] spawn the ADR [**alternative dispute resolution**] movement." Little reflection is needed to see the truth of Freeman's conclusion. What can be questioned is whether anthropology should be proud or ashamed for its role as intellectual progenitor of this nonlegal form of dispute resolution.

While several of the ethnographies we have considered dealt with societies possessing formal court apparatus (e.g., Gluckman's Barotse and Bohannan's Tiv), others studied conflict resolution in more informal contexts, such as among Pospisil's Kapauku. A hybrid circumstance would include Nader's work among the Zapotec: although official organs of government were available to resolve disputes, these occasions as frequently served as a venue for a moderated settlement as for adjudicated outcomes.

Nader has sharply criticized the ADR movement that has emerged within the United States. It gained popularity under a growing perception that Americans were becoming overly litigious, clogging the courts with "garbage cases" that were felt to be essentially minor complaints about socially insignificant issues. The proposed solution sought to redirect these cases into alternative settlement venues.

Philip Gulliver culled the ethnographic literature in order to construct a typology of dispute resolution processes. His identified procedures included the **duel, violent self-help, avoidance, supernatural redefinition,** and **negotiation and adjudication.** Adjudication involves a third-party decision maker who has received his authority either from society (as in a courtroom) or from the parties themselves, who can submit themselves to a process of binding arbitration. Many westerners are much more familiar with arbitration than they realize because that is what they witness when they watch a reality television program like *Judge Judy* or *The People's Court.* Although the shows can have the appearance of being a legal proceeding, in actuality they are not. Participants have waived their right to have their complaint heard in a court and agreed (usually for consideration) to abide by the outcome of the hearing of arbitration, which is not bound by codes of procedure.

Negotiation lacks any kind of third-party decision maker, the outcome being instead "a joint decision" among the parties to the dispute. "Each party can only obtain what the other is in the end prepared to allow":

> At least one party, but usually both, must move toward the other. Although there may be a compromise of some sort, this is not inevitable since one party may be induced to move altogether to his opponent's position or, alternatively, there can be the joint, integrative creation of something new that is acceptable to both parties.

As Gulliver paints the contrasting processes, the differences between adjudicated and negotiated disputes ultimately involve more than the locus of the decision-making powers:

In adjudicating, there is more likely to be concern for values and a definition of disputes in terms of values, an emphasis on the application of
norms, and a concern for all-or-nothing decisions, for acts (rather than
actors) and past behavior, and for less multiplex relationships. In negotiation, there is more likely to be a concern for interests and a definition of
disputes in terms of interest, an emphasis on the making of norms, and
a concern for the personal qualities and dispositions of disputants, for the
future of their and others' rights and responsibilities, and for multiplex,
persisting relationships.

The contrasting trends within each of the two resolution techniques easily
permit prediction of the contexts in which a style would predominate. Adjudication tends to act as a social *leveler*: the judge looks at the "facts" of the specific acts rather than the web of social relationships in which they occurred
(recalling the distinction that Conley and O'Barr made between rule-oriented
and relational-oriented discourses as well as the one that Gluckman observed
in the Lozi courts between suits between strangers and those among friends
and relatives). This impersonal application of the law functions best in large,
complex societies in which power disparities can be significant.

On the other hand, negotiated settlements that look to the interests of
the parties rather than the impersonal application of existing norms would
thrive in situations where the parties have both a prior history before the
conflict and expect as well to have enduring interaction afterward. Nader's
Talean courts illustrate that context exceptionally well, and she documents
in detail the use of mediated negotiations in that Mexican village.

Despite her warm regard for mediation within the village, she argues
convincingly that we should be skeptical of its encouraged use in the United
States: "Law in face-to-faceless societies characterized by highly unequal
distribution of power [like the United States] does not always lend itself to
the same solutions for handling disputes used in small face-to-face communities, where power differentials are more transparent" (Nader 2002).
Accounting for this difference requires application of her theory of harmony
ideology (discussed in chapter 11).

The immediate link between harmony ideology and ADR occurs in
Nader's (1988) analysis of the language Chief Justice Warren Burger invoked
to champion the cause of ADR. He argued that "alternative fora were more
civilized" and "that our litigious society was in need of peace and harmony.
. . . [Burger] was encouraging people to avoid legal action, and also constructing a social order that exercised injunctions against conflict and against
voicing disputes. The ADR movement could also be interpreted as a license
to violate or ignore law, and could be construed as both anti-legal and a
powerful control for enforcing harmony."

Characterizations of Americans as overly litigious occur against a background of the *declining* use of courts by the public. Judge Patrick Higginbotham, in fact, argues that there are not *enough* civil trials. Federal district court judges are hearing only an average of between fourteen and twenty trials per year. While filings from 1970 through 1999 rose by 152 percent, actual hearings fell by 20 percent. Called on so infrequently, judges will have little need of specialized skills and few opportunities to exercise them. This sociological change will impact the kind of person drawn to the profession, he worries, most likely to the detriment of the administration of justice. Marc Galanter reports similar declines in the use of courts. His research concluded that from 1962 to 2002, the proportion of federal cases settled by civil trial fell from 11.5 to 1.8 percent. These analyses "leave the reader to wonder how it came about that a vast reform movement could be built on folk sociology" (Nader 1988).

The solution, according to Nader, lies in the convergence of interests between "Chief Justice Burger's rhetoric and the ethic of Christian harmony as well as the interests of corporations [who would prefer a private negotiation to a public trial], psychologists [who understand conflict as an expression of individual pathology rather than sociological influences] and other vested interest groups." The true problem was not an overuse of the American legal system but rather who was attempting to use it.

> ADR was in essence an anti-law movement, an anti-1960s rights movement. They called the environmental, consumer, women, and minority cases 'garbage cases.' ADR procedure was to follow consensual, harmonious styles. . . . [Just] as at the conference on peace making in Africa where no one mentions arms dealing, multinationals, colonial legacies, or mercenary armies, so too in Oakland anger managers do not mention inequalities or hunger. Power differentials are not part of the ADR agenda. (Nader 1999)

"An intolerance of conflict," she says, has "seeped into [our] culture; the goal was to prevent not the *causes* of discord but the *expression* of it" (Nader 2002). The ADR agenda is not to solve the problem per se but only to placate the individual complainant in a private forum that can provide no precedential value to any other person with the same difficulties.

Chief Justice Burger can be presumed to have had only the best of intentions when he advocated—ultimately successfully—for the creation of ADR venues (e.g., many contracts now require submission of a complaint to binding arbitration, and signing the contract or buying the ticket constitutes waiver of a right to have the dispute heard in a court before a jury). The analytical tools created in large part by the Berkeley Village Law

Project, however, provide the means by which the deep structure of this new institution can be analyzed and its full impact on society recognized.

Summary and Conclusions

While an important dimension of legal anthropology's intellectual history, the methodological collapse of law into disputing and its theoretical consequences should not be exaggerated. Our attention here is on broad patterns rather than exceptionless generalizations.

With that caveat, other workers such as Francis Snyder have expressed a similar concern that "a particular weakness of many recent anthropological approaches is the tendency to reduce law to dispute settlement." This reduction, as we have seen in the foregoing pages, is not illusory, and it emerges out of the discipline's historical and theoretical foundation in legal realism.

It would be ridiculous to argue that dispute resolution has no or only a small role to play within legal anthropology. Yet this attention to the dispute has obscured other portions of what falls within the scope of the ordinary understanding of "law" as well as the range of social phenomena recognized by legal anthropologists themselves in their more visionary passages.

The major shortcomings can, in the end, be sorted into two groups. The theoretical limits follow from the underdescribed relationship of disputing to law, with particular gaps appearing when attempting to use data about the former to draw conclusions about the latter. The practical limits arise because many of the future key issues for the field are not reducible to the disputing paradigm, thus leaving legal anthropology not as well equipped as a discipline—apart from the meritorious contributions of specific individuals—to contribute to those debates as it might otherwise be.

Suggestions for Further Reading

Richard L. Abel, "A Comparative Theory of Dispute Institutions in Society," *Law and Society Review* 8 (1974): 217–347; Simon Roberts, "Law and Dispute Processes," *Companion Encyclopedia of Anthropology*, ed. Tim Ingold (1994), 962–82; June Starr, "Mediation: Anthropological Perspectives," *ALSA Forum* 6 (1982): 221–62.

The results of the Berkeley Village Law Project did not, of course, emerge out of a void but were presaged by earlier influential studies, including Laura Nader and Duane Metzger, "Conflict Resolution in Two Mexican Communities," *American Anthropologist* 65 (1963): 584–92.

In addition to the Berkeley Village Law Project, Laura Nader organized another collaborative effort with her students, the Berkeley Complaint Project, which also culminated in an influential edited volume, *No Access to Law:*

Alternatives to the American Judicial System (1980). The volume looks at consumer complaints (many of which they learned about through letters written to her brother, Ralph Nader) and how corporations deal with them, a theme explored also in her film *Little Injustices* (1981). Contrary to the claim that Americans are overly litigious, Shawn J. Bayern discusses reasons behind an observed reluctance to go to court in "Explaining the American Norm against Litigation," *California Law Review* 93 (2005): 1697–719.

The lack of a substantive anthropology of peace is relative rather than absolute. One place to begin reading in that area might be *The Anthropology of Peace: Essays in Honor of E. Adamson Hoebel* (1992).

References

John M. Conley and William M. O'Barr, *Rules versus Relationships: The Ethnography of Legal Discourse* (1990); Michael Freeman, "Law and Science: Science and Law," *Science in Court* (1998), 1–9; Marc Galanter, "The Vanishing Trial: An Examination of Trials and Related Matters in Federal and State Courts," *Journal of Empirical Legal Studies* 1 (2004): 459–570; Philip H. Gulliver, *Disputes and Negotiations: A Cross-Cultural Perspective* (1979), at 5, 21; Patrick E. Higginbotham, "Judge Robert A. Ainsworth, Jr. Memorial Lecture, Loyola University School of Law: So Why Do We Call Them Trial Courts?" *SMU Law Review* 55 (2002): 1405–23; Karl N. Llewellyn and E. Adamson Hoebel, *The Cheyenne Way* (1941); Laura Nader, "The ADR Explosion—The Implications of Rhetoric in Legal Reform," *Windsor Yearbook of Access to Justice* 8 (1988): 269–91; Laura Nader, "Pushing the Limits—Eclecticism on Purpose," *PoLAR* 22 (1999): 106–9; Laura Nader, *The Life of the Law: Anthropological Projects* (2002), at 39; Laura Nader and Harry F. Todd Jr., *The Disputing Process—Law in Ten Societies* (1978), at 1; Darrell A. Posey and Graham Dutfield, *Beyond Intellectual Property: Toward Traditional Resource Rights for Indigenous Peoples and Local Communities* (1996), at 7; Francis G. Snyder, "Anthropology, Dispute Processes and Law: A Critical Introduction," *British Journal of Law and Society* 8 (1981): 141–80, at 145.

CHAPTER 15

Legal Pluralism

Disputing and Pluralism

If legal anthropology in the United States is characterized by its singular attention to disputing processes, elsewhere the situation is markedly different. According to Norbert Rouland, writing primarily for a French audience, it is "legal pluralism [that] is the issue presently concentrating the minds of legal anthropologists."

An original presumption underlying the earliest studies was that law is a product of the state. Although the work of Malinowski showed definitively that this relationship was far from exclusive, it did not directly address a corollary: if law is the product of state activity, then each state has only one legal system. **Legal pluralism** challenges this assumption. Encompassing a number of variants, the general idea is that a society can contain multiple legal systems in addition to any "official" legal rules at the level of the state. Contentious arguments surround the nature of these alternative legal systems, their hierarchical arrangement within the society as a whole, the manner in which they articulate with each other, and finally how the person navigates through and between the often conflicting normative demands that she is obliged to observe.

This divergence of national intellectual traditions between disputing and pluralism is rooted in the respective political histories. As mentioned in part III, many of the classic ethnographies of legal anthropology were produced under the impetus of colonial pursuits (often but not exclusively British) around the world and especially in Africa (accounting for the preponderance of ethnographies of African systems in table III.1). The problems this situation creates are well known from Western history, as we saw earlier in the brief account of natural law (chapter 3). In addition to the civil law that governed Roman citizens, a separate legal tradition arose to settle disputes involving non-Roman aliens. Likewise, British officers sought to govern their far-flung colonies by attending only to the matters that served their own interests; the rest could be regulated according to the local practices presumably in effect when the Europeans arrived.

The need to record those indigenous legal traditions became an urgent priority that warranted state-funded anthropological research. Schapera's *Handbook* represents the clearest example of this intimate association between anthropology and colonial interests. By design, the colonies were structured to include multiple legal systems broken down much as the Romans had solved the problem: one rule of law applied to Europeans and another to cultural outsiders.

Legal pluralism became a real-world concern for these anthropologists in a way that it did not for Americans, who to that point had lacked a colonizing imperative. Even their experience at home has been different. While the British solution to the colonization of Africa adopted a theory of *personal* jurisdiction (which body of law applied to settle a specific dispute depended on who the parties were), when the British colonized the "New World," they applied the common law doctrine of *territorial* jurisdiction, meaning that the question of criminal jurisdiction depended on *where* the crime occurred and not *who* committed it (Kawashima 2001). This difference prevented a legally plural environment from arising out of the contact between the British and the colonies' original inhabitants. Not being immersed in legal plural environments, American legal anthropologists have been free to turn their theoretical attention to other topics, such as dispute resolution.

Variant Structural Pluralisms

Because of the colonial contexts in which many of them worked, anthropologists have always possessed a pragmatic awareness of legal pluralism. The concept did not receive a fuller theoretical description, however, until Leopold Pospisil offered his theory of the legal levels (outlined in chapter 10). He postulated that no human society possesses "a single consistent legal system, but as many such systems as there are functioning subgroups. Conversely, every functioning subgroup of a society regulates the relations of its members by its own legal system." Although some critics insist that it is unhelpful to call these lower-level norms "law," Pospisil is able to use this label because they possess all four attributes that he had defined as essential to the category: sanctions, obligatio, intention of universal application, and authority.

Within this scheme, the individual "is subject to all the different legal systems of the subgroups of which he is a member," leading to potential normative conflicts. What one subsystem can require, another might forbid. While such dilemmas put strain on the individual, the crosscutting network of interests created by every member's membership within multiple legal subsystems would contribute to the summed group cohesiveness.

As the idea of legal pluralism has gained currency, it has been the beneficiary of wider theoretical refinement, some of which are graphically modeled in figure 15.1. **Legal centrism** (A) represents the ideology that "law is and should be the law of the state, uniform for all persons, exclusive of all other law, and administered by a single set of state institutions" (Griffiths 1986). Refuting this posture is simple in today's environment. Given that "everyone in the world today is formally subject to a national legal system" (Fuller 1994), all are also subject to *inter*national legal rules. This means that there are always at least *two* legal systems governing the actions of every individual, preventing any situation from satisfying the condition of legal centrism. The question is not *whether* there is legal pluralism but rather what form it takes.

The simplest arrangement of the subsystems is for them to be embedded within the official system but autonomous from both it and the other subsystems (B). In theory, this may describe the idealized colonial context, where the locals had "their" law while the Europeans had another. It could also describe situations where the binding norms change as one moves between roles and settings. What is inappropriate behavior at home may become routine at the office.

Type C offers the more commonly envisioned relationship between the many legal systems contained within a society. Any single person simultaneously occupies multiple identities, roles, and statuses, each with its own normative system. Instead of "switching" one off and the next on, the individual informs her choices in one setting on the basis of the internalized values from many others. Likewise, the systems themselves, far from being isolated from wider social forces, come to reflect the prevailing normative standards within the society at large. This can result in both convergence and divergence of

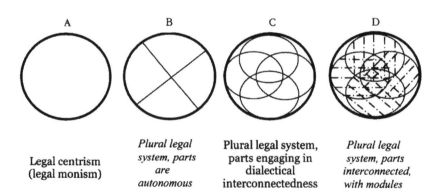

FIGURE 15.1
Varieties of Legal Pluralisms

the subsystems, as some values are absorbed but others rejected as being incompatible or in order to preserve a distinct subcultural identity.

Finally, the cacophony of interacting subsystems becomes still more complex if each is viewed as comprised of distinct modules, such as one set of norms for procedures and different for substantive rules (D). The discrete norms may interact with the norms of surrounding subsystems differently.

As one moves further along the progression, the questions become less purely structural and more interrelational. With the deflation of the myth of legal centrism, a critical issue becomes the formal relationship of the legal subsystems to the official (often state-level) law. **Weak** (or **juristic**) pluralism occurs "when the sovereign (implicitly) commands different bodies of law for different groups in the population" (Griffiths 1986). For example, federal systems are formally plural in that a federal government coexists with permitted state governments. Such an arrangement is not the kind of pluralism social scientists would find particularly interesting. Ironically, although colonial contexts may have first sensitized anthropologists to the possibility of multiple and simultaneous legal systems embedded within a single official one, those settings are not the ones generally investigated.

More challenging are the instances of **strong** legal pluralism. This type of pluralism, according to Griffiths, "refers to the normative heterogeneity attendant upon the fact that social action always takes place in a context of multiple, overlapping 'semi-autonomous social fields,' which, it may be added, is in practice a dynamic condition":

> A situation of legal pluralism—the omnipresent, normal situation in human society—is one in which law and legal institutions are not all subsumable within one "system" but have their sources in the self-regulatory activities of all the multifarious social fields present, activities which may support, complement, ignore or frustrate one another, so that the "law" which is actually effective on the "ground floor" of society is the result of enormously complex and usually in practice unpredictable patterns of competition, interaction, negotiation, isolationism, and the like.

Under this image "the" law of society emerges not from the official dictates of governing bodies but out of the collision and intermixing of all the legal systems contained within the social body.

In this vein, Sally Falk Moore (2001) lists five senses of "pluralism" she finds present within legal anthropology today. Pluralism can refer to the following:

> (1) the way the state acknowledges diverse social fields within society and represents itself ideologically and organizationally in relation to them [weak pluralism];

(2) the internal diversity of state administration, the multiple directions in which its official sub-parts struggle and compete for legal authority [e.g., when the executive branch challenges the legislative branch for ultimate authority];

(3) the ways in which the state itself competes with other states in larger arena (the EU, for one instance), and with the world beyond that [international pluralism];

(4) the way in which the state is interdigitated (internally and externally) with non-governmental, semi-autonomous social fields which generate their own (non-legal) obligatory norms to which they can induce or coerce compliance [strong pluralism]; and

(5) the ways in which law may depend on the collaboration of non-state social fields for its implementation [reverse weak pluralism].

Moore authored the theory of the **semi-autonomous social fields** mentioned earlier by Griffiths. Whereas Pospisil's legal levels had been defined in terms of social groups, Moore's social fields can arise independently of stable groups. Rather than the picture of discrete organizations as "mini-states," here the image is of normative regulation emerging out of the processes of interaction. Any situation that "can generate rules and coerce or induce compliance to them" satisfies the criteria to identify a social field (see figure 15.2). A field is semi-autonomous in that while it possesses rule-making capacity, it remains "simultaneously set in a larger social matrix which can, and does, affect and invade it, sometimes at the invitation of persons inside it, sometimes at its own instance." She uses this conception to explain why official legislation does not always have the effect intended by its creators.

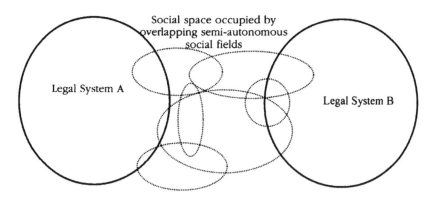

FIGURE 15.2
Structure of Social Space according to Moore (Griffiths 1986)

In a certain sense, we have moved from a strict association of law with the state (legal centrism) to a theoretical position where law might exist independently of any stable group at all, emerging out of interaction processes wherever they occur. That certainly would shed light on the problems of intractability of the designed social engineering so attractive to legal realists, if the locus of lawmaking adheres not in people but in processes, which are much less amenable to control.

Moore's represents the most significant contribution to the problem of legal pluralism in recent years. Griffiths believes that it is sufficiently robust to serve as the basis for a definition of law: law is "the self-regulation of a semi-autonomous social field." Most social fields will fail this test—and therefore not be "law" in the strict sense—because they are too permeable to other social fields to enable them to be self-regulating. In this sense, one could argue on principle (for the first time) that only the state has law because only the state creates sufficient power to regulate its own field of influence. That, however, remains an empirical claim that requires adequate study.

Problems with Pluralism

Although the senses assigned to the concept of legal pluralism can vary significantly, the generic idea encapsulated in the label strikes many as uncontroversial. But not everyone is convinced.

Brian Tamanaha is an especially ardent legal positivist. "Law is," he flatly states, "the law of the state." This is where he *begins* and is not the conclusion of any study as that envisioned in the preceding paragraphs. Given his premise, any claim that there exist nonstate legal systems is self-refuting:

> Legal pluralists insist that the state does not have a monopoly on law. This is the core credo of legal pluralism: there are all sorts of normative orders not attached to the state which nevertheless are *law*. . . . [So] generous a view of what law is slippery slides to the conclusion that all forms of social control are law.

As a review of the claims of legal pluralism, Tamanaha could not be more wrong. Pospisil originally defined the multiple levels as "legal" when they possess all four of the attributes of law. Additional methods to distinguish law from other norms of social regulation can conceivably be constructed (see chapter 19). Forms of social control that fail to rise to the level of law are easily found, contrary to Tamanaha's fears.

The error Tamanaha makes is that he insists on seeing state law as qualitatively rather than quantitatively different from nonstate law. In all likelihood, what makes state law different is a nonnormative element, an excess of coercive power (e.g., such that it is able to self-regulate its social field, as Griffiths suggests). Great power may make state law more pervasive, but it need not make state-level norms in any way distinctive from lower-level norms. One of the cumulative contributions of legal anthropology from Malinowski to the present has been the demystification of state law. It may serve as the prototype for "law" in the way that Christianity serves for Western academics (and the U.S. Supreme Court) as the prototype for "religion," but that use does not restrict the category to that exemplar. As law can exist without states, in refutation of Tamanaha's positivistic equation, then law can exist within states that is not the progeny of the state.

On one point, though, Tamanaha touches close to a truth. Pospisil and Tamanaha apply exactly the same method to reach their contrary conclusions about legal pluralism. Both begin with a definition of "law" and then look to see what social phenomena fit that definition. For Pospisil, that process generates a very large set that constitutes his legal levels. Tamanaha finds an empty set excepting only the original prototypical instance of state law, leading him to argue that there is no legal pluralism.

The issue of the "reality" of legal levels, then, reduces to a simple matter of one's definition of law. Again we see that despite the discipline's distaste for the task of definition, it cannot be avoided.

Summary and Conclusions

Sally Engle Merry observed that "the literature in [legal pluralism] has not yet clearly demarcated a boundary between normative orders that can and cannot be called law." Because the types of norms of social regulation are continuous rather than discrete, one should not expect black-letter sorting rules. At most, we can hope to find criteria for the central characteristics of the type of norm identified, thereby providing conceptual tools to achieve the discrimination among kinds that Merry and other legal anthropologists desire.

One of the many benefits of the study of legal pluralism is that it "facilitates the move away from an exclusive focus on situations of dispute to an analysis of ordering in nondispute situations" (Merry 1988). It provides a vocabulary—in the way that studies of disputing processes never could—for the anthropology of peace that Conley and O'Barr had wished for.

Suggestions for Further Reading

Baudouin Dupret, Maurits Berger, and Laila al-Zwaini, *Legal Pluralism in the Arab World* (1999); M. B. Hooker, *Legal Pluralism: An Introduction to Colonial and Neo-Colonial Laws* (1975); Hanne Petersen and Henrik Zahle, eds., *Legal Polycentricity: Consequences of Pluralism in Law* (1995); Simon Roberts,

"Against Legal Pluralism: Some Reflections on the Contemporary Enlarge-ment of the Legal Domain," *Journal of Legal Pluralism and Unofficial Law* 42 (1998): 95–106; Herman Slaats and Karen Portier, "Legal Plurality and the Transformation of Normative Concepts in the Process of Litigation in Karo Batak Society," *Anthropology of Law in the Netherlands: Essays on Legal Pluralism*, ed. Keebet von Benda-Beckmann and Fons Strijbosch (1986), 215–39; Warwick Tie, *Legal Pluralism: Toward a Multicultural Conception of Law* (1999).

References

Chris Fuller, "Legal Anthropology: Legal Pluralism and Legal Thought," *Anthropology Today* 10 (1994): 9–12; John Griffiths, "What Is Legal Plu-ralism?" *Journal of Legal Pluralism* 24 (1986): 1–55, at 39; Yasuhide Kawashima, *Igniting King Philip's War: The John Sassamon Murder Trial* (2001); Sally Engle Merry, "Legal Pluralism," *Law and Society Review* 22 (1988): 869–96; Sally Falk Moore, *Law as Process: An Anthropological Approach* (1978); Sally Falk Moore, "Certainties Undone: Fifty Turbulent Years of Legal Anthropology, 1949–1999," *Journal of the Royal Anthropologi-cal Institute* 7 (2001): 95–116; Leopold Pospisil, "Legal Levels and Multiplic-ity of Legal Systems in Human Societies," *Law and Conflict Resolutions* 11 (1967): 2–26; Norbert Rouland, *Legal Anthropology* (1994), at 42; Brian Z. Tamanaha, "The Folly of the 'Social Scientific' Concept of Legal Plural-ism," *Journal of Law and Society* 20 (1993): 192–217.

V

Issues in Applied
Legal Anthropology

PART V CONSIDERS prominent instances where the insights of legal anthropology (as derived from ethnography and comparative anthropology) have been or could be productively applied to serious problems confronting the peoples of today's complex world. As Sally Falk Moore phrased it, applied anthropology is where "small-scale fieldwork" is used to "comment on large-scale issues."

Chapter 16 not only addresses the concept of the "human right" (what it means and what rights the category includes) but also presents a specific case study. Many would regard the ability to control one's cultural patrimony as one of those fundamental human rights. Chapter 17, accordingly, offers an overview of the conflict of indigenous legal values with that of the culturally hegemonic West on the global stage of intellectual property rights. Whether there is a need or a justification for the "culture defense" is considered in chapter 18: should a local legal system (in this case, the United States) consider a person's cultural background when determining guilt or levying punishment? Finally, one of the predominant topics of vital concern is that of international terrorism. What this term means and how it is invoked are among the questions in chapter 19 that a socially aware legal anthropology can usefully address.

CHAPTER 16

Human Rights

EMERGING OUT OF legal anthropology's historical dependence on legal realism and its associated emphasis on the dispute as the relevant unit of analysis are the beginnings of a different kind of legal anthropology. Sally Engle Merry's most recent work, *Human Rights and Gender Violence: Translating International Law into Local Justice* (2006) avoids most of the pitfalls mentioned thus far. For example, she does not rely on the casebook model to present a collection of discrete and numbered episodes but instead tells an ongoing story of the interrelationship between universal, exceptionless human rights standards and local policies that reflect the understandings and histories of each specific group. Her "deterritorialized ethnography" is a beautiful balance of both "studying up" that documents how international law is created and debated at the United Nations and the more traditional "studying down" that records how these standards are appropriated and transplanted into local communities. In addition to offering a substantive contribution to her particular subject, the book can hint at what form legal anthropology may take in its future.

Merry's book continues legal anthropology's record of solid contribution to the area of human rights literature. Anthropology cannot usefully contribute to every debate, but it certainly has much to offer any topic that invokes terms and concepts that anthropology not only uses but controls. Thus, if an argument arises that X is a "right," the outcome of the debate depends largely on philosophical or legal premises. But if the argument concerns a claim that X is a "universal" right or one from "time immemorial," then anthropology can step in not only to support or refute but also with an authority that should terminate the quarrel. Neither philosophy nor law can contradict fact.

So it is with the debates of human rights. What kinds of rights are these and what are those rights are questions that can be best answered by anthropology.

Anthropology and Human Rights

The relationship of anthropology to the promulgation of international human rights is decidedly complex. On the one hand, anthropologists were instrumental in bringing to the world's attention the wide variety of cultures extant on the planet we all share. Yet when the United Nations endeavored to articulate its Universal Declaration of Human Rights, the Executive Board of the American Anthropological Association (AAA) publicly expressed its skepticism that such a laundry list was either possible or desirable.

The 1947 Statement on Human Rights reasons the following:

1. The individual realizes his personality through his culture; hence, respect for individual differences entails a respect for cultural differences.
2. Respect for differences between cultures is validated by the scientific fact that no technique of qualitatively evaluating cultures has been discovered.

These claims are variants of the then-prevailing doctrines of cultural determinism and cultural relativity, respectively. The premises that cultures are both different and incommensurable led the board, under the guiding pen of Melville Herskovits, to conclude the following:

3. Standards and values are relative to the culture from which they derive so that any attempt to formulate postulates that grow out of the beliefs or moral codes of one culture must to that extent detract from the applicability of any Declaration of Human Rights to mankind as a whole.

In hindsight, the concerns of the AAA that Western-rooted human rights would wear poorly on the rest of the world were not wholly unwarranted. While some of the enumerated rights contained within the Declaration intuitively capture the intention behind the concept of the universal human right (e.g., Article 5: "No one shall be subject to torture or to cruel, inhuman or degrading treatment or punishment"), others veer much closer to the kind of ethnocentric projection of parochial concerns onto a global stage that was feared. Article 23(4) ("Everyone has the right to form and to join trade unions for the protection of his interests") and Article 24 ("Everyone has the right to rest and leisure, including reasonable limitation of working hours and periodic holidays with pay"), for example, point to issues that—whatever their importance to citizens within industrial societies—probably do not much concern traditional hunter-gatherers. Rights like these that are a function of technological and economic development rather than flowing from one's "humanness" seem poor candidates for "human rights."

Cultural relativism is the first of five reasons that Ellen Messer lists to explain the perception of disengagement of anthropologists from the wider human rights discourse. The second refers to the sympathies of the fieldworking anthropologist with the rights of the group and not with the individual who was the unit for the "first generation" of political and civil human rights.

She describes the ironic influence of applied anthropology as her third explanation for why anthropologists played little role in formulating human rights principles. At first, anthropologists were not involved enough, fearing that "such policy-oriented or interventionist activities" would be deemed "inconsistent with scientific rigor." Later, the pendulum swung in the other direction, as the now fully involved anthropologist had become too impatient to fritter her time "in political discussions of abstract rights or in the time-consuming process of drafting declarations," a process vividly described in Merry's book.

Fourth, the "political sensitivity of doing fieldwork" held back many anthropologists from confronting the abuses they witnessed among the world's indigenes. So long as their presence required the formal permissions of state agencies, the rationale was that they could not risk alienating such powerful authorities.

Finally, Messer admits that the "predominantly legal approach" of human rights discussions tended to shut anthropologists out. Lacking the sufficient technical background in international law and other law-related areas, anthropologists could not actively participate.

That last obstacle would tend to be comparatively unproblematic for the law-trained anthropologist. This has been one way in which times have changed, finding legal anthropologists no longer afraid to tread into these turbulent waters. Among the valuable contributions to be made are perspectives on some of the issue's most fundamental questions: What, exactly, is meant by the term "human rights"? And how are they to be identified?

Rights Human and Universal

When chapter 3 discussed natural law theories, it was mentioned that human rights pose a special problem. While persuasive reasons exist to eschew natural law approaches—not the least being that they are usually tied to theological perspectives and are difficult to fill with any specific content—it can also be challenging to adopt a positive law position while crediting the notion of universal human rights.

To better see the problem, we need to clarify what implications are commonly embedded in the label of a claim as a "human right." A common contrast is with a mere civil right. If human rights are rights one possesses by virtue of one's status as a "human," civil rights in turn are rights that inhere with one's status as a citizen. As such, they flow from the positive order of the state rather than from a natural order of the world. Although the two categories are often confused, that imprecision is rarely to the benefit of any discussion. While civil rights can in principle be revoked (by constitutional or statutory amendment), human rights can only be denied.

In the strict sense, then, positive law can create only civil rights, not human rights. But the problem with that arrangement is exactly what we have seen: civil rights are revocable. The revocability of fundamental rights made the Holocaust possible and in turn necessitated the creation of the category of the human right.

German military officers were tried at Nuremberg for "crimes against humanity" committed against civilians, even though most of the acts were legal under the laws of that nation. Whence the authority for those trials? People today forget how unprecedented the Nuremberg trials were at the time, leaving their legal authority unclear. Granting that one can be prosecuted for transgressing only laws in force at the time of the commission and granting also that many of the Nazi acts were formally legal under German law, whose laws had they broken such that they were now on trial? The answer to this question invoked "unwritten laws of humanity" (Wronka 1998). The theory is that some acts are absolutely wrong regardless of the legal circumstances. The conceptual repository for these transcendent standards would become what we know today as human rights.

Born of legal expediency, the human rights idea emerges from the ashes of natural rights theory, bringing with it all the shortcomings of that pedigree. Two problems immediately present themselves: what kind of entity can claim these rights (i.e., what does it mean to be "human"), and what are the specific contents of the category (what, exactly, are those rights)? These twin concerns are definitional and substantive, respectively. Leaving the identification of the human rights to the next part, we take up here the problem of universality.

In practice, the term "human" is intended to indicate both the source of the rights (from the being's status as human) and the scope of the right (belonging to every human). These meanings are not equivalent, however. It is possible for a human right to have a different extension than a universal right, with the universal right being the more restricted:

> In drafting the Beijing Declaration and Platform for Action [at the Fourth World Conference on Women], some states proposed the insertion of the term "universal" in the text in such a manner that it could be interpreted as a restrictive modifier. For instance in the sentence "the Platform seeks to promote and protect the full enjoyment of all human rights" (§2), the insertion of "universal" before "human rights" would in the eyes of those states limit the scope of the expression to the rights accepted by all states without exception. (Brems 2001)

Another way to parse the difference continues to recognize that human rights are, in Jack Donnelly's words, "the rights one has simply because one is a human being." Universal rights, on the other hand, can be claimed by anyone in the appropriate position. In Aristotle's terminology, human rights treat "unlikes alike" (everyone, regardless of age, sex, class, nationality, etc., can claim the same rights), while universal rights treat "likes alike": everyone similarly situated possesses the same rights. Accordingly, protection against torture (Article 5) is a true human right, but a guarantee of paid vacations (Article 24) is universal without being human since it applies only to some economic systems but not others. The claim is universally valid against capitalistic societies, for example, but not against agrarian. So while "universal human rights" is arguably redundant, having the same extension as "human rights" alone, the phrase "universal and human rights" is not, being the concatenation of both human *and* universal rights.

Identifying the Cross-Culturally Salient Human Rights

Eva Brems has cataloged exhaustively the many senses in which human rights can be claimed to be universal. She identifies no fewer than sixteen ways that a human right can be judged universal, only one of which being that it applies to all human beings. Other readings look to the manner of acceptance as a standard in international law, or the historical origins of the ideas reflected in the right.

The fifth category, however, looks to the right's "anthropological or philosophical acceptance":

> UNESCO sponsored several projects aimed at strengthening the universality of human rights by demonstrating that human rights have been expressed by all cultures, religions and ideologies at all times. The initiator of one of those explains that the results of their search for universality depend on the level of language that is taken into consideration: the concept of human rights itself, at the level of explicit theories, legal rules or objective ethnological description is not universal. Yet the existential roots of human rights, the fundamental requirement that a certain respect is due to human beings, can be found across the world.

Assuming that to be true, we are still left with the problem of translating that generic "respect" into enforceable rights. Alison Dundes Renteln offers a promising method to achieve that goal.

She seeks the "homeomorphic equivalent" of human rights in the world's cultures. Noting that "to date negligible progress has been made in the direction of establishing that human rights are universal or even that certain moral principles are widely shared," she presents one case study showing how that demonstration might be accomplished.

Renteln does not survey the world's literature in hopes of extracting a list of universal human rights. She instead works backward, beginning with the principle of "retribution tied to proportionality," which might be correlated with the content of the UN Declaration's Article 5 prohibition against torture and cruel and inhuman treatment and punishment (as well as other tenets of international documents). The challenge is to identify the cultural extensiveness of this principle.

Surveying the ethnographic, religious, historical, and legal literatures, she concludes that "all cultures have mechanisms which are intended to limit violence and to prevent needless killing." That result does not translate into a claim that the right against excessive punishment is a cross-cultural universal, but it supports a pragmatic reliance on the preexisting indigenous ethos to "provide a foundation for human rights." It is that ethos, according to Sally Engle Merry, that can provide a "frame" for the translation of universal principles of human rights into "specific local cultural narratives and conceptions," making programs appropriated from one setting acceptable to the targeted population in another.

Conceivably, Renteln has offered a way for anthropology to ground human rights discourse in cross-cultural empiricism. For a right to earn the label of either "universal" or "human," certain facts should be first established. Under this method, the list of recognized human rights would be far shorter than the lists currently generated by political organizations. That fact should not discourage the creation of those lists but rather foster recognition of their status as aspirational rather than enforceable.

Ongoing Criticisms

Contrary to claims asserting the universalism of human rights, some continue to believe that these legal endowments reflect the ethnocentric values feared by the 1947 AAA Statement. The argument is that, far from articulating principles of "human" living, the Declaration and its progeny are exercises in cultural hegemony by the West. For some, this is not an unattractive proposition. Yehoshua Arieli sounds quite pleased when he claims that "in the West, and only there, did develop secular cultural, intellectual, moral and technical trends, attitudes and capacities which would claim universal significance and validity."

Others who are less sanguine complain that the recognized human rights emphasize the Western liberal ideal of the solitary, independent individual as well as Western forms of government (Article 21 [3]: "The will of the people shall be the basis of the authority of government; this will shall be expressed in periodic and genuine elections which shall be by universal suffrage and shall be held by secret vote or by equivalent free voting procedures") and economics (Article 17: "Everyone has the right to own property alone").

Missing in the **first generation** of political and civil human rights are any referring to the *group* as an entity owed duties despite the importance of these and other values outside the West. In addition to the individualism reflected in the initial documents, non-Western societies (most of them African, Islamic, and Asian) would recognize other values of significance. It is not immediately clear, for example, that the right to be free from hunger should rank lower on the list of human rights priorities than the right to paid vacations.

When examining human rights documents such as the British Human Rights Act and the European Convention on Human Rights, Adam Tomkins notes the glaringly skewed interests to be protected. These instruments

> represent a particular political—and party political—vision of what it is that society should privilege and prioritize. In the ECHR, and thereby in the HRA, for example, we find the paradigmatic right of liberal political theory (freedom of expression) but not the core of republican philosophy or deliberative democracy (freedom of information, open government, and guarantees of full participation). Property is protected for those who possess it, but the homeless have no right to be housed. Religious freedom is protected, but not the right to an adequate standard of health care. And so on, and on.

Not only Europe fails to fully grasp the true burdens of its claims to be the guardian of human rights around the world. The United States, which likewise protects the property of the propertied, guarantees no right to education but only equal access to any education it chooses to make publicly available, in contravention of UN Declaration Article 26(1). The new constitutions of other countries, such as South Africa, have adopted a more expansive understanding of what are the human rights (Woods 2003).

These gaps led to the articulation of a **second generation** of economic, social, and cultural rights that seeks to protect participation in the community's cultural life. Further still, as described by Ellen Messer, "Third World nations, especially in Africa, added a '**third generation**' of *solidarity* or *development rights* to peace, a more equitable socioeconomic order, and a sustainable environment. . . . Indigenous peoples are now in the process of adding a '**fourth generation**' of *indigenous rights*, which will protect their rights to political self-determination and control over socioeconomic development—rights that are currently threatened within state frameworks." On September 13, 2007, the United Nations concluded over twenty years of debate with overwhelming approval of a nonbinding declaration on the rights of indigenous peoples. This statement urges nations to allow tribal peoples as much control as possible over land and other resources they traditionally possessed and even to return confiscated territory or pay compensation. Only four nations voted against the document: Australia, New Zealand, Canada, and the United States.

The need for these additional instruments in international law (most of which the United States has declined to join) suggests that the problem of cultural relativity is not an illusion. Cultures hold distinct, different, and at points even contradictory beliefs about what should be the inviolable rules of conduct and to what extent any sovereign must yield to achieve and protect them.

On the one hand, perhaps the most fundamental human right is to be able to choose one's own way of life. But some will make choices that others do not approve. What happens then, and what contributions can legal anthropologists make to the discussion?

Case Study: Female Genital Cutting

The confluence of issues involved in human rights discourse can be illustrated by a brief look at the controversial practice of female circumcision/genital mutilation. The rhetorical opposite of global, universal human rights that respect the dignity of the person, including women, are those traditional practices that invoke cultural customs. Sally Engle Merry points out that for those walking the halls of the United Nations, "culture" is something "out there" in the uneducated, backward rural areas rather than something belonging to everyone, including diplomats. "Female genital cutting is the central issue around which the conception of harmful cultural practices or harmful traditional practices has coalesced."

This practice involves one of four types of alteration of the female genitals. *Sunna* can involve as little as the nicking of the clitoris, while *clitoridectomy* describes the removal of all or part of the clitoris. Where this removal extends to the labia minor, an *excision* has occurred. The most extreme form, however, is called *pharaonic* or *infibulation*, in which both the clitoris and the labia minor are completely removed as well as the labia majora. "The cut edges are stitched together so as to cover the urethra and vaginal opening, leaving only a minimal opening for the passage of urine and menstrual blood. A small stick is commonly inserted to maintain the opening, and the legs of the girl are bound together to promote healing" (Shell-Duncan and Hernlund 2000). Although the pharaonic method accounts for only a small minority of cases, it is the more widely disseminated image of the practice outside the African continent.

Many if not all of the "civilized" states have denounced the practice, setting the stage for airing the values within human rights discourse. Assuming that the parents and even children approve of the practice—if everyone, participants and observers, agrees that the practice should be abolished, there is no longer a point to a debate over "whether" but only over "how"—should it still be allowed? Do people have a right to lead a life that others have judged to be contrary to human dignity?

> The universalist stance holds that certain individual rights are so fundamental to humankind that they should be upheld as universal rights whose breach is subject to condemnation and, in certain instances, punishment through legislative force. Through a series of UN conferences, "female genital mutilation" has increasingly been conceptualized as a human rights violation. (Shell-Duncan and Hernlund 2000)

United States federal law requires the government to

> oppose any loan or other utilization of the funds of their respective institution, other than to address basic human needs, for the government of any country which the Secretary of the Treasury determines (1) has, as a cultural custom, a known history of the practice of female genital mutilation; and (2) has not taken steps to implement educational programs designed to prevent the practice of female genital mutilation (22 U.S.C. § 262k-2)

The particularist perspective appears in the very name of the phenomenon. Those who refer to it as "female circumcision" are accused of trying to normalize an uncivilized oppression of women, while those preferring the label "female genital mutilation" display their antagonism at their first words.

Far from being a straightforward example of national and international pressure to reform barbaric practices, female genital cutting better illustrates culturally relative standards that have been raised to universal ethics by those with the power to enforce them. According to Fuambai Ahmadu,

> The aversion of some writers to the practice of female "circumcision" has more to do with deeply imbedded Western cultural assumptions regarding women's bodies and their sexuality than with disputable health effects of genital operations on African women.

Not all African women, it seems, agree with the assessment by Western feminists that cutting is the most pressing of problems that they face. They offer a potent argument that the lesser forms of cutting inflict no worse damage on the human body that the forms Western women exalt, such as breast augmentation and liposuction or the ubiquitous circumcision undergone by almost all American males (Grande 2004). Nancy Ehrenreich and Mark Barr point out that the criticisms of female genital cutting may be especially problematic given our own society's reflexive submission of those born intersex to "corrective" surgery. Given these practices in our own culture, why do human rights advocates target only the African practices and in such strident tones?

Anthropological research can establish how the women at issue themselves feel about the tradition. Any argument to extinguish it gains strength to the extent that those most concerned also desire its abolition. Often, in this case and in many another, study will reveal that the alleged victims do not see themselves in that light and may even ardently support the practice. If people have a right to choose their own way of living and all within that group are satisfied with their cultural traditions, can outsiders disrupt and criminalize those practices on the ground that doing so is in the local's best interest or to satisfy an abstract standard of "human rights"? While the local attitudes remain an empirical question, the Western human rights agendas have rendered such opinions moot and have effectively removed from the local women the right to choose their own course of life. This condition also represents a topic of investigation for the fieldworking legal anthropologist: what have been the ramifications on the desuetude of such targeted practices on other cultural institutions, such as gender roles and marriage preferences?

These issues cannot be settled without specific local information concerning the practices at issue. As such, no debate on human rights worth having can fail to begin from the ethnographic foundation generated by legal anthropology.

Summary and Conclusions

Although Messer began her review of the relationship between anthropology and human rights on a negative tone, she concludes by listing the many ways in which anthropologists, despite their initial misgivings, can now contribute to formulation and enforcement of human rights principles:

1. In the analysis of human rights rhetoric as this penetrates local parlance and governance and informs advocacy, social organization, and practice
2. In the expansion and explication of socioeconomic and cultural rights, which are likely to be much more culture specific in formulation and monitoring but are still in need of universal human rights protection
3. In the historical and cultural analysis of the conditions under which particular rights or responsibilities and notions of the community deserving rights or assuming accountability expand or contract

To this list should be added the challenge to identify which rights most of the world's societies are prepared to recognize as universally binding. In her pursuit of this goal, Renteln offers a complete application of the three levels of anthropological research outlined in chapter 2. She begins by collecting ethnographic descriptions of the behavior of interest and by comparison and contrast is able to generate a conclusion that is both broadly applicable yet specific enough to inform the original problem. She would apply this outcome to create a better fit between human rights conventions and preexisting indigenous ethical standards, offering a methodological technique to achieve the outcomes described by Sally Engle Merry as already arising out of local practice. Renteln uses each phase of legal anthropological inquiry and in correct order.

Although anthropology offers meaningful input to the full range of human rights discussions, its special contribution is to the recognition of indigenous rights, or the "fourth generation." Legal anthropology plays a valuable role in translating the legal precepts of local societies into the vernacular of the dominating cultures. One arena in which this battle is fought, the intellectual property rights over traditional culture, is reviewed in the next chapter.

Suggestions for Further Reading

Human Rights: Lynda S. Bell, Andrew J. Nathan, and Illan Peleg, *Negotiating Culture and Human Rights* (2001); Jane K. Cowan, Marie-Bénédicte Bembour, and Richard A. Wilson, eds., *Culture and Rights: Anthropological Perspectives* (2001); Mark Goodale, "Toward a Critical Anthropology of Human Rights," *Current Anthropology* 47 (2006): 485–511; Kirsten Hastrup, ed., *Legal Cultures and Human Rights: The Challenge of Diversity* (2001); Theodore E. Downing and Gilbert Kushner, eds., *Human Rights and Anthropology* (1988), offering an extensive bibliography on literature published to that date; Jeremy Firestone, Jonathan Lilley, and Isabel Torres de Noronba, "Cultural Diversity, Human Rights, and the Emergence of Indigenous Peoples in International and Comparative Environmental Law," *American University International Law Review* 20 (2005): 219–92; Micheline R. Ishay, *The History of Human Rights: From Ancient Times to the Globalization Era* (2004); Randall Peerenboom, "Beyond Universalism and Relativism: The Evolving Debates about 'Values in Asia,'" *Indiana International and Comparative Law Review* 14 (2003): 1–85; Neus Torbisco Casals, *Group Rights as Human Rights: A Liberal Approach to Multiculturalism* (2006). Richard Wilson, in addition to additional volumes on the subject—including *Human Rights in Global Perspective: Anthropological Studies of Rights, Claims, and Entitlements* (2003)— has written an article that brings together two themes of this text: "Reconciliation and Revenge in Post-Apartheid South Africa: Rethinking Legal Pluralism and Human Rights," *Current Anthropology* 41 (2000): 75–98. The broader perspective of human rights that includes social and cultural rights can be found in Jeanne M. Woods and Hope Lewis, eds., *Human Rights and the Global Marketplace: Economic, Social, and Cultural Dimensions* (2005).

Female Genital Cutting: Ellen Gruenbaum, *The Female Circumcision Controversy: An Anthropological Perspective* (2001); Stanlie M. James and Claire C. Robertson, eds., *Genital Cutting and Transnational Sisterhood: Disputing U.S. Polemics* (2002); Rogaia Mustafa Abusharaf, ed., *Female Circumcision: Multicultural Perspectives* (2001); Anika Rahman and Nahid Toubia, *Female Genital Mutilation: A Guide to Laws and Policies Worldwide* (2000); Rosemarie Skaine, *Female Genital Mutilation: Legal, Cultural, and Medical Issues* (2005); Allen E. White, "Female Genital Mutilation in America: The Federal Dilemma," *Texas Journal of Women and the Law* 10 (2001): 129–208.

References

Fuambai Ahmadu, "Rites and Wrongs: An Insider/Outsider Reflects on Power and Excision," *Female "Circumcision" in Africa: Culture, Controversy, and Change*, ed. Bettina Shell-Duncan and Ylva Hernlund (2000), 283–312, at 284; American Anthropological Association, "Statement on Human Rights," *American Anthropologist* 49, no. 4, pt. 1 (1947): 539–43; Yehoshua Arieli, "On the Necessary and Sufficient Conditions for the Emergence of the Doctrine of the Dignity of Man and His Rights," *The Concept of Human Dignity in Human Rights Discourse*, ed. David Kretzmer and Eckart Klein (2002), 1–17; Eva Brems, *Human Rights: Universality and Diversity* (2001), at 9; Jack Donnelly, *Universal Human Rights in Theory and Practice* (1989); Nancy Ehrenreich and Mark Barr, "Intersex Surgery, Female Genital Cutting, and the Selective Condemnation of 'Cultural Practices,'" *Harvard Civil Rights-Civil Liberties Law Review* 40 (2005): 71–140; Elsibetta Grande, "Hegemonic Human Rights and African Resistance: Female Circumcision in a Broader Comparative Perspective," *Global Jurist Frontiers* 4, no. 2, article 3 (2004); Sally Engle Merry, *Human Rights and Gender Violence: Translating International Law into Local Justice* (2006), at 27; Ellen Messer, "Anthropology and Human Rights," *Annual Review of Anthropology* 22 (1993): 221–49, at 241; Alison Dundes Renteln, *International Human Rights: Universalism versus Relativism* (1990); Bettina Shell-Duncan and Ylva Hernlund, eds., *Female "Circumcision" in Africa: Culture, Controversy, and Change* (2000), at 4, 27; Adam Tomkins, "Introduction," *Sceptical Essays on Human Rights*, ed. Tom Campbell, K. D. Ewing, and Adam Tomkins (2001), 1–11, at 10; Jeanne M. Woods, "Justiciable Social Rights as a Critique of the Liberal Paradigm," *Texas International Law Journal* 38 (2003): 763–93; Joseph Wronka, *Human Rights and Social Policy in the 21st Century* (1998).

CHAPTER **17**

Intellectual Property Rights

IN 1999, *Anthropology News* published a letter in which anthropologist Gilbert Herdt was accused by clan representatives from his pseudonymous field site, the "Sambia," of "breach[ing] . . . the intellectual property rights to our custom and . . . contracts he made with us not to publish materials without our approval" (Dariawo 1999). In the course of his reply, Herdt surmises that "the accusers . . . would like to extract compensation from [his field informants] either directly through the courts or, more likely, through blackmail or extortion," presumably as payment for divulging cultural secrets.

This short exchange encapsulates the primary issues of intellectual property in applied legal anthropology: the rights of the informants, the ability of the society to enforce those rights on the world stage, as well as the very concept of a "property right" to cultural knowledge. Laura Nader (2002) suggested that these would be the central issues of the coming years: "A commonwealth of 'resistance' is emerging in which the biggest battles will be over property rights, the anthropology of ownership, of nature, of commercialism." It remains to be seen what role anthropologists will play in that discussion.

The debate over intellectual property rights structurally falls out much as that over human rights. In both cases, the unavoidable fact is that the principal terms of the discourse have been dictated by Western society under the leadership of the United States (in this context the primary oppositions are not between the West and everyone else but between the Northern Hemisphere and the South). The uniformity of the "North" should not be overstated, however. Significant differences remain; for example the "moral rights" in copyrighted works that are deemed inalienable by the author in England are generally not recognized in the United States. As compared to human rights, however, in this case there has not been even the veneer of pretense that the end product represents multicultural viewpoints. The rest of the world's peoples have been left to accommodate their own interests to this legal order as best they can, within the interstices of the law not pre-empted by the economic interests of the developed nations.

Nothing would be easier than to become mired in the legal technicalities of national and international intellectual property law. A few anthropologists, such as Mary Riley and Michael Brown, have accepted the formidable challenge to monitor this discussion. For our own purposes, we can limit our attention to specific illustrations of the contributions legal anthropologists particularly can offer.

The obstacles faced by indigenous groups are of two kinds. First, their own understanding of property generally and of intellectual property specifically can significantly vary from that contained within the emerging global standard. Second, even when that law might favor their claims, many societies do not have access to the venues where their complaints can be heard and their rights enforced. Legal anthropologists can offer assistance in both these areas.

The Idea of Ownership

The legal category of **intellectual property** contains three different entities: patents, copyrights, and trademarks. **Patents** are legally enforceable monopolies over new inventions for a limited term (twenty years in the United States). **Copyrights** protect an author's expression but not the idea being expressed. Although the level of protection given copyright is less than what is offered to a patent, it lasts longer. Works published after 1977 are protected for the life of the author plus seventy years. **Trademarks** grant an exclusive use of a mark or label in commerce and last as long as they are in use.

Underlying this entire legal edifice is the idea of property that can be owned by (and thus potentially alienated by) identifiable individual persons. As Mita Manek and Robert Lettington describe the situation,

> In this Northern paradigm [of a Cartesian divide between mind and matter], knowledge and technology are things—objects which can be valued and traded. To allow for this valuing and trading, knowledge and technology must be regarded as property, and orthodox intellectual property rights are the rules for the ownership of this property. . . . Traditional communities, in contrast, see knowledge and technology as integral parts of their existence. . . . Northerners may debate the relative valuation of rights in material things, while for indigenous and local communities these discussions often involve the very meaning of life.

When multinational corporations extract valuable cultural resources from a traditional society—be those a plant variety that has been cultivated for its desirable properties for generations, an artistic motif for use in commercial products, and sometimes even the bodies of locals from whom genetic material has been harvested and patented—not only are the members deprived of valuable economic resources they could turn to their own advantages but, more important, as described in chapter 14, they can lose control over their ability to define their way of life.

A desirable goal is improved understanding on both sides of the cultural presumptions of the other. Less technologically advanced groups cannot deny the hegemonic influence of the North's legal system of intellectual property; the North, on the other hand, can be presumed to be operating in a good-faith belief that its methods are to the ultimate benefit of everyone and that, where this can be shown to not be the case, it may find a way to ameliorate the harmful impact of its rules. The North's focus on the material dimension of the world is neither good nor bad, but it is an unavoidable element of the intercultural relationships involved. Similarly, the meanings attached to tangible objects that transcend their economic value will not always be obvious to the cultural outsider. While these matters will remain fraught with tension and potential for abuse, what troubles as can be avoided should be, and there is no reason to presume that either side is inherently uninterested in that dialogue.

At the core of this debate is the concept of property and ownership. What can be owned? Who can own what? What rights does ownership confer upon the right holder? For example, what the North might see as being in the "public domain" and thus free for appropriation without compensation the locals might consider patrimony of the entire group, belonging to no single individual and inseparable from the community. As reported by Duane Suagee, "Most indigenous peoples do not regard their heritage in terms of *property* but rather in terms of individual and community *responsibility*, and that heritage is more appropriately seen as a bundle of relationships rather than a bundle of economic rights."

Even on this one issue, legal anthropologists have much insight to offer. We have already seen one example. During the review of Hohfeld's legal primitives (chapter 13), Hoebel demonstrated the improved clarity that can be brought to the label of "ownership" over items both tangible (a Yurok canoe) and intangible (Plains Indian songs). Legal anthropology could further pursue this line of investigation, and develop more refined ways of thinking about the blunt concept of "ownership." This would not, of course, resolve all the difficulties of indigenous intellectual property rights, but it would constitute a needed contribution.

In addition to the owner, property presents its own conceptual difficulties. Pospisil, in the final chapter of *Anthropology of Law*, executes a "formal analysis of substantive law." He conducts what is essentially a componential analysis of land tenure rules. The resulting matrix distributes the

Kapauku terrain types according to their "contrastive legal correlates," including such dimensions as what rights various parties have with regard to that category of land. Another analysis of similar method is performed on inherited property.

The end result is actually quite elegant. These analyses again demonstrate the heightened clarity that legal anthropologists can bring to indigenous concepts of ownership and property. The next step would be to apply these to the categories of specifically "intellectual" properties and then to translate the results into terms compatible with the legal regimes of the North. The benefit would be that the local ideas of property would be correctly represented to outsiders, with the expectation that from greater understanding would follow increased cooperation and sensitivity. Of course, it should go without saying that the folk systems of the North would be similarly scrutinized.

"Translation of indigenous concepts of 'ownership' into national and international law," conclude Sandra Pinel and Michael Evans, "will require a sustained effort." What is perhaps surprising is that we are no further along on this project than we currently are. Christopher May and Susan Sell, in their history of the idea of intellectual property rights, make the observation that "definitions of what constituted property depend upon time, place, the constellation of interests and degree of competition present, stage of economic development, and political economic power." Floyd Rudmin sharpens these intuitions, finding that the concept of private property ownership correlates cross-culturally with "the practice of agriculture, the use of cereal grains, and the presence of castes and classes." That list suggests the limited extent to which private property would arise among the world's communities and hints at the kinds of fundamental restructuring of other basic institutions that would be involved in its forced introduction. Thus, we find the Chinese—whose failure to comply with copyright restrictions U.S. trade representatives have found particularly problematic—did not develop their own form of intellectual property, "whatever the economic and technological factors, for a specifically political philosophical reason: Confucianism. The valuing of the past within a complex pattern of social relations led the Chinese to value unencumbered access to the knowledge of the past from whatever source" (May and Sell 2006, discussing the work of William Alford).

The peoples involved, however, have not been idle, instead working to articulate their own vision of intellectual property rights and how they articulate with others of their concerns:

> In attempts to formulate indigenous theories of property, Native scholars and artists have insisted on the cultural aspects of cultural property

that legitimize Native claims—as in oral histories (stories), collective assertions of identity, and the point taken up here: that Native title to cultural property and art forms is not only inextricable from land-based claims to sovereignty, but its legal reach grasps the embedded relationships of land, art, and indigenous knowledge systems more firmly than copyright protections over creative works. (Berman 2004)

The joining of the issue of cultural property to that of land and sovereignty recurs throughout the literature that includes the viewpoints of the local people. It suggests one reason why Northern countries—many of whom occupy territories taken from these groups' ancestors—are hesitant to recognize the forms of control over culture for which they advocate.

Representation on the World Stage

Aside from whether indigenous peoples "win" in the game of intellectual property rights, a few words should consider what it means to play the game at all. Assuming that one wishes an outcome that does not merely capitulate and mirror the North's legal system regarding intellectual property, these are not issues that can be resolved at the local level. To press their claims, to lobby for the adoption of their own version of rights protecting cultural property (e.g., the concept of **traditional resource rights** as opposed to intellectual property rights; see Posey and Dutfield 1996), requires access to the international venues where such discussions are conducted.

Legal anthropologists can facilitate this exchange of views in two ways. First, they can perform much the same function as they would for the culture defense (chapter 18), as an expert witness helping to educate each side to the point of view of the other. If a feasible middle ground is to be achieved at all, it will be only when all parties have an accurate understanding of the positions of the others; a solution can be found only if everyone is agreed on the problem. Experts in both viewpoints, legal anthropologists are uniquely poised to productively foster this exchange.

Second, the groups most negatively impacted by the global schemes of intellectual property will be precisely those that are least accustomed to operating in these international settings. Legal anthropologists have a role to play not only as advocates, helping to inform local groups about the options available to them, but also in their more traditional role as descriptive ethnographers. As Sally Engle Merry discovered concerning human rights (discussed in chapter 16), there is a hermeneutic relationship between the local and international levels. International norms shape local discourse, and local practices impact international obligations. This holds true equally for other types of tribunals where these two levels confront one another:

Transnational tribunals affect the normative development of domestic legal systems. As such, they hold a promise and a peril for societies in the midst of political and social change. On the one hand, transnational tribunals may be used to help protect rights when it may be difficult for the nascent domestic courts to do so. Yet, because of their ability to change the domestic distribution of power, they may also allow "outsiders" such as multinational corporations to have a significant voice in the legal evolution of a State. (Borgen 2005)

Close watch should be kept on the ways in which the mere fact of attempting to negotiate formal recognition, in an attempt to preserve one's cultural lifeways, itself winds up fundamentally altering those same lifeways. Legal anthropologists can track such influences and, by making these observations available to the affected populations, allow them a heightened degree of self-determination over their own cultural development.

Summary and Conclusions

Intellectual property issues offer perhaps one of the richest fields of application for the skills of the legal anthropologist. If any area of study would benefit from intimate knowledge of both the law and the anthropology, this will be the one.

Complex issues of intellectual property impact the routine work of all anthropologists. This is one area of legal expertise with which every fieldworking academic should have at least a superficial familiarity. As one example of the kinds of troubles that can be created for a community who cooperates with an ethnographic project, a published account of some medicinal herb would qualify as *prior art* that may move that use into the public domain, preventing the community from reaping any economic benefit from its possible exploitation on the commercial pharmaceutical markets. Such *defensive publication* may in some circumstances be precisely what the group may wish since it prevents another entity (such as a multinational drug company) from patenting and controlling the resource. But this should be a decision left to the community and not taken out of their hands through the anthropologist's carelessness.

Suggestions for Further Reading

Stephen B. Brush, "Indigenous Knowledge of Biological Resources and Intellectual Property Rights: The Role of Anthropology," *American Anthropologist* 95 (1993): 653–86; Rosemary J. Coombe, *The Cultural Life of Intellectual Property: Authorship, Appropriation, and the Law* (1998); Alain Pottage and Martha Mundy, eds., *Law, Anthropology, and the Constitution of the Social: Making Persons and Things* (2004).

In keeping with many of these chapters' interest in the use of language to achieve sociolegal ends, the reader's attention can be drawn to Paul J. Heald, "The Rhetoric of Biopiracy," *Cardozo Journal of International and Comparative Law* 11 (2003): 519–46. The Duke Center for the Study of the Public Domain has initiated an entertaining series of graphic novels explaining aspects of intellectual property law, the first of which is *Bound by Law? Tales from the Public Domain* (2006).

References

Tressa Berman, "'As Long as the Grass Grows': Representing Indigenous Claims," *Indigenous Intellectual Property Rights: Legal Obstacles and Innovative Solutions*, ed. Mary Riley (2004), 3–25, at 9; Christopher J. Borgen, "Transnational Tribunals and the Transmission of Norms: The Hegemony of Process," St. John's University Legal Studies Research Paper Series #08-0024 (August 2005), at 57, available at http://www.ssrn.com/abstract=793485; Michael F. Brown, "Can Culture Be Copyrighted?" *Current Anthropology* 39 (1998): 193–222; Michael F. Brown, *Who Owns Native Culture?* (2003); Ben Dariawo et al., "Breach of Contract?" *Anthropology News* 40 (October 1999): 4; Mita Manek and Robert Lettington, "Indigenous Knowledge Rights: Recognizing Alternative Worldviews," *Cultural Survival Quarterly* 24, no. 4 (2001): 8–9; Christopher May and Susan K. Sell, *Intellectual Property Rights: A Critical History* (2006), at 105, 73; Laura Nader, *The Life of the Law: Anthropological Projects* (2002), at 214–15; Sandra Lee Pinel and Michael J. Evans, "Tribal Sovereignty and the Control of Knowledge," *Intellectual Property Rights for Indigenous Peoples: A Sourcebook*, ed. Tom Greaves (1994), 43–55, at 53; Darrell A. Posey and Graham Dutfield, *Beyond Intellectual Property: Toward Traditional Resource Rights for Indigenous Peoples and Local Communities* (1996); Leopold Pospisil, *Anthropology of Law: A Comparative Theory* (1971); Mary Riley and Katy Moran, eds., "Culture as Commodity: Intellectual Property Rights," *Cultural Survival Quarterly* 24, no. 4 (Winter 2001); Floyd Webster Rudmin, "Cross-Cultural Correlates of the Ownership of Private Property: Two Samples of Murdock's Data," *Journal of Socio-Economics* 24 (1995): 345–73; Duane B. Suagee, "Human Rights and Cultural Heritage: Developments in the United Nations Working Group on Indigenous Populations," *Intellectual Property Rights for Indigenous Peoples: A Sourcebook*, ed. Tom Greaves (1994), 193–208, at 203.

CHAPTER 18

The Culture Defense

CHAPTER 15 introduced the concept of legal pluralism, the condition that arises when a given political entity contains within its borders more than one discrete system of law. Although such a situation can arise as a stable feature of the community's permanent arrangements, a related structure can emerge out of the more general operation of multiculturalism.[1]

For example, as a formal state expands beyond its original boundaries, it encompasses other groups whose systems of law may differ. The problem of social regulation then becomes how to manage these distinct legal traditions. The most obvious solution—the imposed conformity on all people of the legal institutions of the controlling group—is not always available for several reasons. First, the dominant culture may, out of a parochial ethnocentrism, doubt that the subordinated people are sufficiently elevated or civilized to learn and comply with the lofty nuances of its own law. More probably, though, the groups to be governed are simply too many, too diverse, too dispersed, and ruled by simply too few to make imposition of a radically different set of legal expectations an effective option. The imposition of a significantly different rule of law would require sizable police forces and judicial systems that are not always available.

In such a circumstance, the more efficient solution may be to let the conquered conduct their daily affairs according to their traditional practices and apply foreign law only to matters that directly impact the interests of the alien governors. Yet even if the dominant power allows subordinate groups to maintain their local practices for most matters (e.g., as was Alexander's approach as well as that of the administrators of the British Empire, as discussed in chapter 15), the difficult issue remains concerning

---

1. This chapter profited immeasurably from discussions with John Stuart Garth and contains several themes from our article "Delimiting the Culture Defense," *Quinnipiac Law Review* 26 (2007): 109.

actions involving parties—whether two individuals in private dispute or one person in conflict with the civil authorities—who do not share the same legal background. What law applies?

Romans—members of the original Western multicultural society—recognized that each jurisdiction had its own *ius civile* whose specific demands may be unfamiliar to a visiting foreigner. Infractions of such local regulations would tend to be treated tolerantly. Indeed, because Roman citizenship was as much a status symbol as a status, the "civil law [i.e., the law of citizens] was the proud possession of Roman citizens and could not be extended indiscriminately to peregrines [foreigners]" (Stein 1999). The *ius civile* thus formally applied only to Roman citizens. As that citizenship would not be extended to all free members of the empire until 212, we can imagine the extended period for which problems arising from the intersection of legal systems and multiculturalism would vex the empire.

Aliens, however, were hardly permitted free license in their actions. Although not answerable to the *ius civile*, all persons were subject to the *ius gentium*, or the law of nations. As discussed in chapter 3, this body of rules focused on those that Romans believed were not locale specific but could instead be recognized by all rational beings. As a general principle, then, when faced with the growing multiculturalism of their expanding empire, the Romans considered the cultural backgrounds of the various parties for matters that were solely the concern of the civil law but not for those that fell within the universal law of nations.

Our own society has become equally multicultural, and thus one would expect to arise similar problems of conflict of legal systems. Whether American courts should recognize an appeal to culture remains a contested issue to which legal anthropologists have much to offer. The "culture defense"—characterized as a claim that when ascertaining guilt or setting a penalty the court should consider relevant features of the defendant's cultural background—arises inconsistently during both criminal and civil proceedings. Individual judges may rule the argument extraneous to the issues, while different courts confronting similar facts find the culture defense relevant to the case. Anthropologists can help articulate a reasonable ground for the defense as well as its limits.

A first step in this project of clarification is to examine the terms involved. The culture defense refers to the mitigation or negation of "criminal responsibility where acts are committed under a reasonable, good-faith belief in their propriety, based upon the actor's cultural heritage or tradition" (Goldstein 1994). Although the usual terminology in the literature refers to the "cultural defense," that label is unnecessarily misleading. All defenses are intrinsically cultural in that their embedded logics and presuppositions draw on the shared background of the group. In fact, that is precisely why there is argued to be a need in the first place for the culture defense, which seeks to draw the court's attention to the role of the defendant's nondominant culture in his decision to commit the charged crime. In principle, it serves as a counterbalance to the cultural presumptions of the majority already embedded as defaults in the legal system itself, most nakedly in the standard of the so-called reasonable man. The nuances of this distinction are better preserved by the use of the noun rather than the adjective.

Alison Dundes Renteln, who suggested the method for a productive contribution in human rights discourse (see chapter 16), has also been preeminent in articulating the justification for a culture defense. Her support for the defense builds on the presumption "that culture shapes the identity of individuals, influencing their reasoning, perceptions, and behavior." Because the culturally embedded predispositions run deep within a person's psyche, judicial systems should take them into account either when apportioning responsibility or when determining punishment. The alternative, she argues, is the enforcement of an ideology of complete assimilation of all who come within U.S. borders.

Illustrative Cases

A few examples of actual cases should illustrate the problem to which Renteln is drawing our attention (additional samples are offered in table 18.1):

- A man originally from Afghanistan was charged with "gross sexual assault" after he kissed the penis of his nine-month-old son. Kargar admitted the action but denied that this was a "crime" within the intention of the criminal statute under which he was charged. Witnesses testified that such demonstrations were "considered neither wrong nor sexual under Islamic law and that Kargar did not know his action was illegal under Maine law" (Wanderer and Connors 1999). The court accepted this argument and held that Kargar was not guilty under Maine's de minimis statute, which allows a court to dismiss a prosecution if "it finds the defendant's conduct . . . [presents] such other extenuations that it cannot reasonably be regarded as envisaged by the Legislature in defining the crime" (*State v. Kargar*, 679 A.2d 81 [Maine 1996]). In this case, the court accepted the culture defense to *negate* the allegation, in part because the legal scheme of Maine had a preexisting category into which such arguments would fall.
- Renteln and Deirdre Evans-Pritchard discuss an unreported 1985 case, *People v. Moua*, in which "Kong Moua, then twenty three years old, believed he was following Hmong customary marriage practices when he engaged in sexual intercourse with Seng Xiong. But Seng Xiong, then nineteen years old, apparently rejected this tradition and believed

TABLE 18.1 Culture Conflicts in the Courtroom (synopsizing representative cases collected in Renteln 2004)

Context	Case	Description
HOMICIDE		
Excuse defenses		
—Insanity	*People v. Kimura*, Defense Sentencing Report and Statement in Mitigation; & Application for Probation. Case No. A 091133 (1985)	Woman attempts *oyako-shinju* (parent–child suicide), but only children drown. Illegal but not unknown in Japan. Homicide charge reduced to voluntary manslaughter and sentenced to one year in jail.
—Automatism	*People v. Wu*, 286 Cal Rptr 868 (1991)	Chinese woman strangles son and attempts suicide "because her lover did not return her affection [and treated] their son poorly." Defense argued cultural motivation "to save her son and herself from shame and abuse and to be reunited in the afterlife." Convicted of voluntary manslaughter.
—Battered woman defense	*Nguyen v. State*, 505 SE 846 (Ga App 1998); rev'd 520 SE2d 907 (Ga 1999)	Woman from Vietnam shot disrespectful husband and stepdaughter when informed of his wish to divorce. Trial court refused to allow cultural testimony; overturned by GA Supreme Court.
—Culture-bound syndromes	*State v. Ganal*, 917 P2d 370 (Haw 1996)	Filipino man shot relatives after "running amok" brought on by humiliation over failing marriage. Convicted of first-degree murder.
—Diminished capacity	*People v. Poddar*, 103 Cal Rptr 84 (1972)	Member of Harijan caste killed woman after romantic rejection. Court excluded

(Continued)

TABLE 18.1 Culture Conflicts in the Courtroom (synopsizing representative cases collected in Renteln 2004) (Continued)

Context	Case	Description
		testimony about cultural stress of untouchables attending American universities. Conviction for second-degree murder overturned on unrelated grounds.
—Provocation	*People v. Aphaylath,* 502 NE2d 998 (NY 1986) See also *Chen* case in discussion	Laotian refugee stabs wife in jealous rage. Culture-based defense regarding culture shock and shame-related infidelity was disallowed. Conviction of second-degree murder over-turned because of exclusion of culture shock testimony.
Justifications		
—Self-defense	*People v. Croy,* 42 Cal3d 1 (1985)	Native American kills police officer during chase over dispute in liquor store. Cultural argument that Croy, as a result of past discriminations, "had been conditioned not to trust white authorities." The jury acquits of all charges.
Sentencing mitigation		
—Death penalty	*Siripongs v. Calderon,* 133 F3d 732 (9th Cir 1994)	Thai national admits to being present at robbery of store but denies killing two clerks. After conviction and death sentence was upheld, argued that refusal to name accomplices was culturally motivated. Court skeptical "because Siripongs seemed too Americanized." Executed in 1998.

Children

—Discipline	*Dumpson v. Danial M.*, *NY Law Journal*, October 16, 1974, p. 17	Nigerian father is accused of excessive corporal punishment resulting in the removal of the children. The court recognizes diverse child-rearing practices but decided on the basis of "the applicable legal standards of the dominant culture."
—Touching	*Krasniqi v. Dallas Cty Child Protective Services*, 809 SW2d 927 (Tex Ct App 1991) See also *State v. Kargar*, 679 A2d 81 (Me 1996) in discussion	Albanian Muslim man lost parental rights after accusations of sexual molestation of four-year-old daughter. While cultural testimony won acquittal in the criminal case, it proved irrelevant to the custody battle: the "two children were legally adopted by their foster parents and forced to convert from Islam to Christianity."

Marriage

Types of marriage

—Child marriage	*People v. Benu*, 385 NYS2d 222 (1976)	Father convicted of child endangerment for arranging, with her consent, the marriage of his thirteen-year-old daughter with the seventeen-year-old father of her unborn child. "Regardless of conformity or lack of conformity to Moslem ritual, the fact is that Fatima was thirteen years old at the time of marriage, and thus, the marriage was voidable."

(Continued)

TABLE 18.1 Culture Conflicts in the Courtroom (synopsizing representative cases collected in Renteln 2004) (Continued)

Context	Case	Description
—Marriage-ability	*Marks v. Clarke*, 102 F3d 1012 (9th Cir 1996)	During an illegal search, Spokane police officers conducted body searches of unmarried Rom girls, leaving them "polluted," or *marime*, in the eyes of the community. Suing for $19 million, after eleven years the family agreed to a $1.43 million settlement.
—Capture	See *Moua* case in discussion	
—Polygamy	*People v. Ezeonu*, 588 NYS2d 116 (1992)	Nigerian national prosecuted for rape in the second degree of his second wife who was thirteen years old, a charge defined as "when, being eighteen years old or more, he or she engages in sexual intercourse with another person to whom the actor is not married less than fourteen years old." The defendant argued that as he was legally married to the girl, he was innocent of the crime. Although the marriage was valid in Nigeria, the court held that bigamy was no defense to the charge of rape.
—Temporary	*In re Marriage of Vryonis*, 248 Cal Rptr 807 (1988)	Iranian woman, after entering into a temporary marriage (*mut'a*), filed for spousal support after it failed. The man denied a marriage existed. Although the trial court ruled that she had a good-faith belief in the validity

of the marriage, the appeals court held that such belief was not grounded on an objectively reasonable basis because the ceremony lacked the "usual indicia of marriage."

Divorce

—Child support	*Uboh-Abiola v. Abiola,* *NY Law Journal,* June 12, 1992, p. 1A	Twenty-fifth wife of Nigerian chief sues for divorce and child support. Although unwilling to recognize the polygamous marriage, the court ordered $15,000 per month in support.
—Spiritual custody	*In re Marriage of Weiss,* 49 Cal Rptr 2d 339 (1996)	Baptist former wife had written commitment pledging to rear children of the marriage in former husband's Jewish faith. After the lower court denied husband's request that wife be enjoined from engaging in certain religious activity with child, the court of appeal held that wife's antenuptial promise to raise child in husband's religion was unenforceable.

herself to have been raped." Both parties were born and raised in Laos and immigrated to the United States after reaching their teens.

Moua's charge of rape was complicated by the Hmong practice of "marriage by capture," whereby "the man is required to take the woman to his family home and keep her there for three days in order to consummate the marriage. The woman is supposed to protest, 'No, no, no, I'm not ready,' to prove her virtue." To the external observer, the marriage ritual would be indiscernible from an actual sexual assault.

The criminal justice problem grows more complex with the realization that rape, to the extent the Hmong have an equivalent concept, refers to sex with a classificatory inappropriate woman rather than sex with a woman who withholds her consent. This raises the question whether, even if Kong has believed Seng's protests to be sincere, that realization would have led him to think he was doing something wrong.

In this case, Kong was sentenced to three months in jail, and fined $1,000, $900 of which were given to Seng as "reparation." Although the culture defense did not completely negate the allegation against Kong, it did mitigate the punishment handed down.

Homicide offers the most difficult context for the cultural defense. While many might accept that the outcomes for Kargar and Moua were appropriate, few would like to see a murderer escape punishment, either completely or even with diminished sanctions, by invoking a justification that appeared to be an attempt to escape responsibility.

- Goldstein relates the circumstances of *People v. Chen*, a 1989 case in which Dong Lu Chen, after learning that his wife was having an affair, "left the room, returned with a claw hammer, knocked her onto the bed, and hit her on the head eight times until she was dead." Again the culture defense was successfully invoked to mitigate Chen's punishment. Instead of a conviction for second-degree murder, he received the lightest sentence possible for second-degree manslaughter.

  The information the court accepted (offered by an anthropologist in the role of expert witness) concerned the cultural appropriateness of this response in reaction to infidelity. The episode resulted in a death because, unlike what typically occurs in China, the community failed to intervene to prevent the tragic outcome. The dysfunctional element, we are told, was not Chen's outburst but the dissociation of the Chens from other Chinese who would play their own parts within this cultural script.

The Reasonable Man Redux

The three sample cases demonstrate the usefulness of a culture defense from the defendant's perspective. According to Renteln, the role of the legal anthropologist in this process would include the demonstration of the embeddedness of cultural assumptions within legal systems. An illustration of that project highlights the topic of the reasonable man.

While the presence of the reasonable man standard within the Barotse judicial process may remain controversial (as reviewed in chapter 8), no such uncertainty surrounds its use in the American legal system. Chen's punishment was reduced because he was able to invoke a provocation defense. Provocation defenses, Renteln explains, are among "the most ancient doctrines in criminal law" and are commonly known as "the heat of passion rule":

> The "provocation/passion" formula, which can reduce a murder charge to one of manslaughter, is based on the idea that a person who is pro-

voked to kill does so without the malice aforethought required for the crime of murder and is, therefore, less culpable.

For the defense to be successful, the claim must satisfy a four-prong test:

> (1) There must have been a reasonable provocation. (2) The defendant must have been in fact provoked. (3) A reasonable man so provoked would not have cooled off in the interval of time between the provocation and the delivery of the fatal blow. And (4), the defendant must not in fact have cooled off during that interval. (LaFave 2003)

The reasonable man standard is an "objective" test, meaning that the defendant's state of mind and personal beliefs are not relevant. Under that rule, it becomes the idealized *observer's* state of mind and personal beliefs that determine the outcome, hence Renteln's conclusion that "this 'objective' being is simply the persona of the dominant culture." The reasonable man test therefore becomes a proxy for a culture-appropriateness test: did Chen behave in a way that a stereotypical *American* would behave under like circumstances?

As a matter of fact, quite probably. According to LaFave (who authored a textbook used by first-year law students), while the law "practically everywhere" allows a husband (and *perhaps* also a wife) to be reasonably provoked when catching the spouse in flagrante delicto, some "cases have held that a reasonable man may be provoked upon suddenly being told of his wife's infidelity." The culture defense offered by Chen, therefore, was only bolstering a claim that at least some U.S. courts had already allowed rather than asserting a wholly new claim along the lines of Moua's.

The use of the reasonable man standard to evaluate a defendant's actions illustrates the broader principle that legal systems have a tendency to reify their own cultural assumptions and to objectify these as being "normal" and even "natural." For full members of the majority group, this heuristic may even be roughly valid since they do tend to hold the beliefs and understandings that the law projects onto them. The difficulty is consequently not with the process of legal rationalizing itself but rather with its collision with other demands of a functioning system of law.

A fundamental component of the "rule of law" is that all similarly situated persons are treated equally before the law. If the law affords males the privilege of being judged according to the typical male behaviors, then females deserve the right to be evaluated according to a measure that reflects their own modal tendencies and experiences. That same principle requires that, just as the majority are allowed to be judged by their own cultural standards, the minority has a right to have its considered as well. For "litigants to be treated equally under the law [they must be] treated differently" (Renteln 2004).

Addressing the Objections

The move toward the culture defense has not been universally welcomed. Legal anthropologists can assist the debate by demonstrations that many legal standards are not self-evident but are instead culturally specific and by addressing some of the most pointed objections to this rule of evidence.

Damian Sikora conveniently catalogs the objections preventing recognition of the culture defense: "cultural defenses may promote stereotypes; immigrant women and children's rights are undermined by the defense; it would be impossible to draft legislation that defines when, where, and how the defense can be used; and the defense would cause a balkanization of the criminal justice system." Our discussion here focuses on the question of whether the boundaries of the defense could be rationally identified and applied.

The fear is that if criminal law recognizes a defendant's cultural imperatives when assigning guilt or meting out punishment, this becomes a license for chaos. Good social order requires a certain commonality of behavioral standards that as a general rule apply equally to all. Simply migrating from another culture should not be a sufficient excuse to commit acts criminalized in the new setting.

Few argue that persistent unwarranted disparate treatment of defendants charged with identical crimes would be good for any system grounded in a respect for the fundamental fairness and justice of the rule of law. The challenge, then, becomes to respect the value of culture as a powerful motivation for action while keeping the impact of such considerations from undermining the bonds of social cohesion.

The Culture Concept

Central to any satisfying resolution of the problem stands the concept of the culture. As the label itself suggests, the culture defense relies heavily on the basic anthropological idea of discernible cultures. While the meaning of that term has varied over the years (an intellectual history insightfully outlined in Adam Kuper's *Culture: The Anthropologists' Account* [1999]), the core sense required here is that a relationship exists between the beliefs and ideas of the individual and the cultural milieu in which she lives. This tight relationship can be illustrated by the following passage from Robert Levy's *Tahitians: Mind and Experience in the Society Islands*:

> In part, being a Tahitian is having a "Tahitian mind," operating with assumptions and motives which have been shaped by various aspects of growing up and of everyday life in Tahitian communities. People act in a Tahitian way and "conform" to Tahitian culture because it is the natural thing for them to do.

Culture provides a template of default ways of being in a wide assortment of social and existential contexts. Culture is not determinative, but it does provide ready-made solutions to the most commonly encountered problems of living and especially of group living. To deviate from such whole-cloth assumptions requires "work" of a personal and anxiety-provoking sort, not least because of the lacuna typically inserted between rejection of the group model and the convinced formulation of the idiosyncratic solution (or, alternatively, the adoption of the cultural set of a new society). Few people, then, are likely to reject more than a small slice of the cultural array. In most environments, the person operates unreflectively in the mode of the default.

This summary highlights the ways in which culture can influence the actions of the individual. The theoretical question raises concerns about the details of how this person–culture bond is forged. This process, known as **enculturation**, has been characterized by Melford Spiro in these terms: "To learn a culture is to acquire its propositions; to become enculturated is, in addition, to "internalize" them as personal beliefs, that is, as propositions that are thought to be true, proper, or right." This internalization is so pervasive that even "the most deliberately unconventional person is unable to escape his culture to any significant degree" (Linton 1961).

Within this perspective, culture emerges as the core to the identity of an individual to such an extent that it is inextricable from that identity. This point has been argued by the cultural psychologists. According to Richard Shweder, for example, culture and psyche are mutually constituting. Neither exists independently of the other. Culture is inseparable from the individual, providing "the media for 'how to be' and for how to participate as a member in good standing of particular social contexts" (Fuhrer 2003).

This intimate relationship notwithstanding, it would be a mistake to assign every act that a person executes as attributable to her "culture." As elaborated, enculturation refers to the internalization of the normative values of the *group*. Culture, while perhaps the most influential, is not the only constituent of individual identity. Spiro names experience as another crucial element. Some motivations, consequently, are grounded in idiosyncratic rather than cultural values. The culture defense would look to the latter while excluding the former. It would be the task of the anthropologist as expert witness to help the court draw that line in a principled manner.

This sketch of the anthropological concept of culture, while incomplete, suffices for the present task to meet the critics' objection to the introduction of the culture defense into criminal court proceedings. To whom should this defense be available? Conviction of criminal charges in the American legal system requires proof of the defendant's "mens rea" when committing the deed. In its most general sense, this term of art refers to the state of mind of the person committing the crime and usually involves scrutiny of whether the act was committed "purposely" or "knowingly." The relevant argument here appears to be that while the defendant may have intended the act, he did not intend the *crime*, and thus he lacks the requisite "guilty mind" required. Kargar, for example, surely intended to kiss the penis of his infant son, but he did not thereby intend to break the law.

A distinction can often be drawn between someone who inadvertently commits a "crime" by observing a normative standard that he has been taught is expected of "a member in good standing" of his reference group and someone who perhaps performs the same deed but this time maliciously and in full knowledge of the act's criminal status within the local culture's legal system. While this latter person satisfies the mens rea requirement, the former arguably does not—this was the conclusion of the court regarding Moua.

The key claim here is that it would necessarily fall to the anthropologist to articulate which norms are demanded of the defendant's home culture and which are merely preferred but rarely observed or perhaps formerly required but today obsolete. In any situation but the first, the culture defense would be insupportable.

To what crimes should the culture defense be applied? Renteln's exhaustive survey documents the assortment of cases in which cultural evidence has been invoked, ranging from homicide, sexual abuse of varying degrees, drug use, animal cruelty, death, and marriage. If the critic's objection to the culture defense is to be met, some standard should be found that will control the opportunities for its invocation.

One approach to this challenge would again refer back to the anthropologically informed concept of culture as articulated earlier. Cultural norms as a whole tend to further the end of group living. The purely idiosyncratic would have its roots elsewhere, such as personal experience or perhaps even biological causes. The culture defense seeks to provide a mechanism for the court to consider the former but not the latter. Chen murdered his wife not solely because of his personal anger but because his wife's adultery was viewed as a shame to his ancestors as well as himself and his children. This shame is so harrowing that it becomes the man's duty, as schooled by his society and modeled by his fellows, to attempt to remove the tarnish by killing the adulteress.

The culture defense should perhaps be limited to acts that claim to have embedded within them the interests of the social group rather than those of the individual person. Conceivably, crimes involving theft, armed or unarmed robbery, and other presumptively self-serving crimes might fall outside the scope of a properly delimited culture defense.

These simple restrictions may prevent the culture defense from becoming the carte blanche for criminality feared by some skeptics. The defendant should come from the cultural background claimed rather than being merely associated with a more diffuse ethnicity. Even these persons would lose access to this defense if they cannot demonstrate that their acts relied on the normative practices of a specific culture and not on personal or non-normative interpretations of those standards. Answering both these questions would require the legal anthropologist's expertise as witness to the cultural facts.

Summary and Conclusions

The culture defense can be viewed as a special instance of a broader dictum. "Studying up," legal anthropologists should excavate hidden presuppositions within ostensibly unproblematic legal claims, defenses, and rules not only within the American legal system but within others as well. Especially where the judicial process advertises itself as being fair to all, any "stacking of the legal deck" that legal anthropologists uncover should provoke responses.

If the reasonable man standard is as freighted with the presumptions of the majority culture as has been claimed, the culture defense does not represent a special defense and type of legal exceptionalism feared by critics; rather, it makes available to cultural minorities the same presumptions enjoyed by the dominant population: to be judged by the standard of reasonableness expected of a person in his or her situation, extending even to the cultural presuppositions.

Renteln's hope is that more courts will be willing to listen to offers of culture-based evidence. She does not insist that these defenses should always prevail, as other considerations (such as public policy) may have higher priority in the court's decision-making process. Still, the routine openness of the court to hearing these arguments could be expected to effect cumulative changes that favor cultural diversity among persons appearing before the bench.

Legal anthropologists can work to make theirs an achievable goal by contributing on two fronts. First, they can provide the kinds of ethnographic analysis required to support the details of a specific claim of culture defense. Second, they can apply the force of the culture construct not only to justify the legal defense but also to map out defensible limits to its uses.

Suggestions for Further Reading

Culture Defense: William Y. Chin, "Multiple Cultures, One Criminal Justice System: The Need for a "Cultural Ombudsman" in the Courtroom," *Drake Law Review* 53 (2005): 651–65; James G. Connell and Rene L. Valladares, *Cultural Issues in Criminal Defense* (2001); Susan S. Kuo, "Culture Clash: Teaching Cultural Defenses in the Criminal Law Classroom," *St. Louis Law Journal* 48 (2004): 1297–311.

Anthropologist as Expert Witness: Anthony Good, *Anthropology and Expertise in the Asylum Courts* (2007); Randy Frances Kandel, ed., *Double Vision: Anthropologists at Law* (1992); Lawrence Rosen, "The Anthropologist as Expert Witness," *American Anthropologist* 79 (1997): 555–78.

References

Deirdre Evans-Pritchard and Alison Dundes Renteln, "The Interpretation and Distortion of Culture: A Hmong 'Marriage by Capture' Case in Fresno, California," *Southern California Interdisciplinary Law Journal* 4 (1994): 1–48; Urs Fuhrer, *Cultivating Minds: Identity as Meaning-Making Practice* (2003), at 82; Taryn F. Goldstein, "Cultural Conflicts in Court: Should the American Criminal Justice System Formally Recognize a 'Cultural Defense'?" *Dickinson Law Review* 99 (1994): 141–68; Adam Kuper, *Culture: The Anthropologists' Account* (1999); Wayne R. LaFave, *Criminal Law* (4th ed., 2003); Robert I. Levy, *Tahitians: Mind and Experience in the Society Islands* (1973), at 326; Ralph Linton, *The Tree of Culture* (1961), at 39; Alison Dundes Renteln, *The Cultural Defense* (2004); Richard A. Shweder, "Cultural Psychology: What is It?" *Cultural Psychology: Essays on Comparative Human Development*, ed. James W. Stigler, Richard A. Shweder, and Gilbert Herdt (1990), 1–46; Damian W. Sikora, "Differing Cultures, Differing Culpabilities? A Sensible Alternative Using Cultural Circumstances as a Mitigating Factor in Sentencing," *Ohio State Law Journal* 62 (2001): 1695–728, at 1708; Melford E. Spiro, "Some Reflections on Cultural Determinism and Relativism with Special Reference to Emotion and Reason," *Culture Theory: Essays on Mind, Self, and Emotion*, ed. Richard A. Shweder and Robert A. LeVine (1984), 323–46, at 326, 324; Peter Stein, *Roman Law in European History* (1999), at 12; Olga Tellegen-Couperus, *A Short History of Roman Law* (1993), at 48; Nancy A. Wanderer and Catherine R. Connors, "Culture and Crime: Kargar and the Existing Framework for a Cultural Defense," *Buffalo Law Review* 47 (1999): 829–73.

CHAPTER 19

Terrorism

N O TOPIC TODAY consumes a larger portion of today's public discourse than the threat of terrorism, both domestic and international. Among the ways in which legal anthropology can contribute to this discussion is by looking at the process of calling another a "terrorist." These labels involve the application of political power to remove another from the natural entitlements of human rights described in chapter 16: terrorists are not merely those who commit criminal deeds; they are deemed outside the norms of civilized society, a designation that parallels the distancing techniques employed in other contexts like colonialism. What follows are but two approaches to the problem of terrorism.

Terrorism and Political Process

The formal mechanisms that normally create international law have not yet settled on a workable definition of **terrorism**.[1] The obstacles are considerable: the term must identify which acts are prohibited in a way that does not tie the hands of one's self or any "friendly" nations. Various proposals have been tendered. Some wish to make terrorism definitionally inapplicable to states. That strategy would render all state actions never so bad as to rise (or fall) to the standard of actual terrorism—and thus triggering the censure that the label is meant to invoke—while any group working to overthrow a corrupt and oppressive dictatorship will always be the greater of two evils.

Another proposal looks not at the actor but at the deeds involved. The goal is to identify the sorts of acts that should be prohibited regardless of who commits them. Unlike the previous suggestion, here states can be

---

1. This section draws heavily on a previously published work, James M. Donovan, "Civilian Immunity and the Rebuttable Presumption of Innocence," *Journal of Law in Society* 5 (2004): 409–56.

recognized as terrorists. Little agreement, however, has been reached on the range of methods that should be completely outlawed. An illustrative example here might be the debate over whether land mines should be banned or whether there is ever a justification to explode nuclear weapons. Technologically advanced societies tend to favor eliminating weapons and strategies that they used in the past but no longer need, having replaced them with newer techniques. Those nations with less progressive tools of war may continue to need these methods in their legitimate defense. In practice, therefore, this definitional approach can demand heavy sacrifices from those least in a position to make them while asking little of those more favorably situated.

In chapter 1's review of definitional techniques, the claim was made that a good place to begin in thorny problems of this kind is to take seriously the way in which the term is ordinarily employed. A collection of examples using the term "terrorism" would quickly make apparent a third semantic element. Rather than (or in addition to) looking at the actor and the deed, acts consensually recognized as terrorism would look to the moral status of the victim. Specifically, a sense emerges that terrorism targets persons who are "innocent" in some importantly relevant sense.

An inquiry into just what it may mean to be innocent in this relevant sense is perhaps best left to philosophers of ethics. We cannot avoid, however, an initial foray into this field given the nature of the subject. The result of that investigation will likely assign a critical role to the concept of responsibility. As mentioned in chapter 9, a central task for law is the assignment of responsibility for a given action. The person found to be responsible becomes liable for punishment (if the deed was a criminal violation) or for damages (if it was a civil transgression). Joining these two observations, we can offer a suggestion that—whatever else it may be—terrorism is an act of political violence that targets the innocent in the sense that these are not the persons responsible for the political order being opposed. Per Bauhn has helpfully mapped out the necessary relationships that could support a charge of terrorism (see figure 19.1). When an opponent puts pressure directly on the state, these acts can be criminal or, depending on the circumstances, warfare. Terrorism occurs when the opponent puts pressure on the state indirectly by attacking its civilians. To threaten to kill a leader if she does not change a policy is criminal but not terrorism; to threaten to harm her family, however, is likewise criminal but now also terrorism. For this relationship to hold, the citizens must be distinguishable from the state government; otherwise, the lines of applied force collapse from the second condition into the first. As we will see, this can sometimes be a difficult threshold condition to satisfy.

It is at this juncture that legal and political anthropologists have an important contribution to make. Granting this operationalized definition of

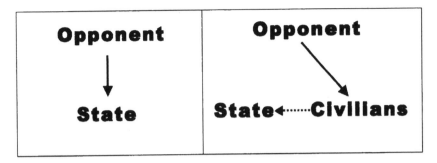

FIGURE 19.1

Relationships Distinguishing Terrorist from Criminal Acts

terrorism, it becomes an empirical ethnographic question as to the extent to which civilians can be held responsible for their government. Dictatorships and similar authoritarian systems might more easily satisfy this criterion, so that attacks on their citizens are terrorism, than do democracies and other "bottom-up" flows of authority.

The problem is confounded by contexts in which civilians believe they have an influential voice in governing when this may not be the case. All governments have reason to foster a belief in the collective responsibility of its peoples:

> First, it makes us feel good; instead of feeling outsiders, with "them" always doing things to "us," we can take pride in our society, identify with it, and feel at one with what is going on around us; corporate responsibility is ego-enhancing. Second, it gives us a good reason for obeying the law. If I feel that the law is our law, and that I am one of us, then I shall feel obliged to go along with it even when we have decided something against my own better judgment. Third, it encourages people to play an active part in their community, and to take initiatives and co-operate actively in carrying out public policy. (Lucas 1995)

While it may therefore be beneficial for a state to have its citizens believe that they share collective responsibility for its government, it stands as a separate question whether they are in fact responsible. Legal anthropologists are not satisfied to know the official views of legitimacy; they look deeper to identify how the state actually functions. What kinds of actions incur responsibility and liability that may remove a civilian's formal innocent status?

Karl Jaspers, an existential philosopher who examined the guilt Germans bore for the actions of their country during World War II, identified four kinds of guilt: *criminal guilt*, incurred by individuals for their own acts;

political guilt, shared by all citizens by virtue of that status; *moral guilt*, which is a personal liability following on specific acts of support; and *metaphysical guilt*, arising from a lack of empathy with the suffering of others. Criminal and political guilt are to be judged by others, moral guilt by ourselves, and metaphysical guilt by God.

Within Jaspers's typology, all citizens will incur political guilt because it is grounded in strict liability: "A people answers for its polity." Political guilt in this way converges with Joel Feinberg's **collective responsibility**, which, rooted in group solidarity, is comprised of three components: a large community of interest, a community associated with "bonds of sentiment directed toward common objects," and the degree to which the parties share a common lot. Moral guilt, in contrast, inheres in citizens "conveniently closing their eyes to events, or permitting themselves to be intoxicated, seduced or bought with personal advantages, or obeying from fear" (Jaspers 1947). People who wallow in the "unconditionality of a blind nationalism" are guilty in a sense beyond that attached to a simple political status.

Although all citizens must share political guilt for the actions of their government—one need look no further than the derivation of the word "citizen" itself—the special outrage over acts of terrorism suggests that the victims are supposed to be morally innocent apart from their portion of any political guilt without requiring that they have done anything specifically criminal. The hypothesis is that this presumption of civilian moral innocence might be rebutted if moral responsibility has accrued through mechanisms that legitimated the governmental actions the violence is intended to change. This liability, according to Jaspers, can be triggered only if the citizens had actual power to prevent those governmental actions or policies, power that they failed to exercise either willfully out of agreement with them or negligently from a failure to exercise sufficient oversight. The central research question becomes, from this perspective, whether the government has acted as the recognized **agent** of the citizenry or simply as its **ruler**. If indeed "responsibility goes with effective authority" (Lucas 1995), then some citizens will possess the requisite moral innocence to maintain the sufficient distance from political authority to be morally innocent of its actions—and thus attacks on them would be terrorism—while others will not, and attacks on them will be heinous and criminal but not technically terrorism. Legal anthropologists can trace these critical lines of political authority.

The preceding outlines of a research agenda assume that the desired goal is to bring clarity to the concept of terrorism so that this powerful label is applied in a manner that is consistent and reasonable. Even if the distinguishing feature that separates terrorist from nonterrorist acts proves to be something other than civilian innocence relative to their government's powers, this viewpoint takes for granted that a similar variable will be found that will accomplish the broader goal. That assumption, however, may be false.

The next section looks at some of the language invoked when applying such labels. The final conclusion may be that words like "terrorism" are not truly sociolegal categories but only terms of opprobrium used to stigmatize the "other" in the worst possible way (Magnarella 2003), perhaps filling the role within the modern imagination once held by the image of the "witch."

The Language of Capacity Preemption

Chapter 12 highlighted the need for legal anthropologists to consider language issues when working in their field, and the present topic of terrorism offers an exceptionally relevant illustration of their importance.[2] A recurring rhetorical theme when assigning to others the status of terrorist invokes the distinction between the civilized and the uncivilized. Terrorists are those who reject the methods of resistance expected of civilized nations and thereby show their bestial contempt for the lives of the innocent. Fears over what terrorists might do have led to calls to strike first. This section looks at this idea of **anticipatory self-defense**.

Unlike self-defense, which refers to the repelling of an actual attack as it occurs, anticipatory self-defense, also known as **capacity preemption**, has as its goal the elimination of another's ability to pose such a threat at any future time even when no such danger is currently present. Capacity preemption, never recognized by international law as a legitimate rationale for a state's use of force, was announced as official U.S. policy in George W. Bush's 2002 West Point speech.

The argument for an act of anticipatory self-defense would be bolstered to the extent the leader is able to convince the public—as well as the wider international community—that a theoretical capacity to inflict harm is tantamount to an imminent threat of actual attack. If having but not using a weapon is allowed to stand as an alternative scenario, then the needfulness of the planned attack can be questioned.

This necessary illusion of inevitability can be achieved by a process of rhetorical dehumanization. The enemy must be depicted as irrational and his actions therefore neither predictable nor foreseeable. In such circumstances, his plots cannot be defended against by traditional means such as diplomacy, negotiation, or containment. For people like "them," having a power to harm inevitably culminates in its exercise. The necessary psychology for such a portrait, however, suggests a creature radically different from the speaker representing "civilized" peoples who think logically and strategically and are open to compromise and bargaining. This depiction of the alien other as different

---

2. This section incorporates work more fully available at Jeanne M. Woods and James M. Donovan, "'Anticipatory Self-Defense' and Other Stories," *Kansas Journal of Law and Public Policy* 14 (2005): 487–523.

in kind returns us to the era before Malinowski's *Crime and Custom*, undoing the cumulative advances of modern legal anthropology.

The justification for capacity preemption, therefore, depends on portraying the enemy as unable to act in any way other than belligerently. That task, in turn, can be achieved only through dehumanizing him to the extent that he is shown to be unable to *choose* to act in any other way.

Rhetorical dehumanization can take at least three forms. First, *direct labeling* will simply equate the human target with some inhuman object, such as "animal," "beast," or "demon." Second, *denial of attributes* describes the target as lacking attributes that are deemed necessary to claim membership in the human family. Rationality has served as the hallmark for this function within Western thought, and therefore Western speakers tend to describe enemies as crazy or mad. A final strategy involves *denigration* of elements of the enemy's essential identity-forming institutions, such as his religion.

The run-up to the war in Iraq demonstrates a contemporary application of this dehumanizing technique in order to justify aggressive military acts that, under international law, would otherwise be of dubious status. In that pivotal 2002 West Point speech, in which the "Bush Doctrine" was

TABLE 19.1 Americans Compared with Enemies in "Bush Doctrine" Speech

Terms Describing Americans	Terms Describing America's Enemies
Power	Weak
Soldiers	Terrorists
Good	Evil
Hope	Deluded
Firm moral purpose	Radical
Defense	Blackmail
Innocent	Guilty
Liberty	Joyless conformity
Freedom	Totalitarian
Great	Small
Moral clarity	Unbalanced
Peace	Violence
Homeland	Dark corner of the world
Civilized	Brutal
Nations	Regimes
Right	Wrong
Justice	Cruelty
Noble	Lawless
Honorable	Ruthless

After Woods and Donovan, table 1

announced, President Bush employed the dichotomous oppositions shown in table 19.1. The anthropologist will recognize that the terms in the second column are simply the structural transformations of those in the first column. This pattern is not, however, the result of a gifted speechwriter's original application of the rhetorical strategy outlined earlier. Table 19.2 makes a similar comparison, only this time it concerns the 1675 preemptive conflict known as "King Philip's War." In that conflict the early Plymouth colonists initiated a war with the Wampanoag sachem Philip that proved devastating to his people and forever altered for the worse the relationship between the European colonists and the New World's original inhabitants.

The igniting conflict was a dispute over who had jurisdiction to try a Native American for the murder of another Native American: his own people or the British. Philip recognized that to concede this issue would be no small matter for the future of his people: "By insisting that the death of a Wampanoag Indian, supposedly at the hands of other Wampanoags, be resolved in a colonial court, the Plymouth magistrates . . . denied to the Wampanoags the last shreds of their sovereignty as a people and a culture" (Kawashima 2001). The crux of the dispute concerned ultimately the right to land: denied their sovereignty in legal matters, they were soon to be denied sovereignty over their ancestral territories. Contemporary apologists such as Increase Mather wrote to defend the Puritans' subsequent war with the Indians as one of anticipatory self-defense: "Whilst they and others that have been in hostility against us, remain unconquered, we cannot enjoy such perfect peace as in the years which are past." Others, however, have interpreted the history differently:

TABLE 19.2 America's Enemies Then and Now

Terms Describing America's Enemies Today (from table 19.1)	Terms Describing America's Enemies circa 1675
Brutal	Brutish
Terrorists	Savages
Ruthless	Merciless
Violent	Skil[l]ful to destroy
Cruelty	Delight in cruelty
Dark corner of the earth	Dark corners of the Earth
Deluded	Hatred for religion
Evil	Children of the Devil
Lawless	Perfidious
Radical	Profane
Unbalanced, mad	Quarrelsom[e] disposition

After Woods and Donovan, table 2

The few intelligent racists' problem was to put a good face on a war of intended conquest by the Puritans that was met with desperate resistance by the Indians. That they concocted elaborate rationalizations to present Puritan aggression as anticipatory defense—to borrow a phrase from the twentieth century—is not strange. Puritans had long known the power of propaganda presented as history. In their scheme of predestination, invention was the mother of necessity. Roger Williams had made the wryly proper assessment of a Puritan justification for aggressive war: "All men of conscience or prudence ply to windward, to maintain their wars to be defensive." (Jennings 1975)

The interesting point for the present discussion is the extent of the parallelism between Bush's language in 2002 and that of Mather in 1676. Their justifications for acts of anticipatory self-defense use essentially the same dehumanizing language to describe the targeted populations. The ends intended for this language should dishearten even those who may support the individual military actions proposed, for their effects linger far after their initial purposes have been achieved. Even after King Philip's War had ended with the complete submission of the Wampanoags, the elements to spin an unending tale of capacity preemption permanently entrenched themselves within the colonists' worldview. A pervasive belief emerged "that all Indians, because they embodied qualities deemed to be characteristically Indian, were too dangerous and different to be allowed to remain in contact with white society" (Johnson 1977). After the war, in an act of legislative capacity preemption, Massachusetts "passed an act confining all friendly Indians to a *cordon sanitaire* and offering bounties 'for every [hostile] Indian, great or small, which they shall kill, or take and bring in prisoner'" (Axtell 1972). The target of these sanctions was anyone with the status of "Indian"—and thus a potential challenger to land title—and not only those individuals or groups who had actually fought against the colonies.

This mythology of the inhuman Indian became immortalized in the Declaration of Independence, wherein the English King is indicted for "excit[ing] domestic insurrections against us, and . . . bring[ing] on the inhabitants of our frontiers, the merciless Indian Savages, whose known rule of warfare, is an undistinguished destruction of all ages, sexes, and conditions." As Jennings points out, "The net effect of all these policies in America has been the myth of the Indian Menace—the depiction of the Indian as a ferocious wild creature, possessed of an alternately demonic and bestial nature, that had to be exterminated to make humanity safe."

Looking beneath the surface of political and legal rhetoric to reveal hidden patterns like those described offers a special opportunity for the legal anthropologist to make a vital contribution to critical debates occurring on the global stage. We may not be able to alter every outcome that we might wish, but we can strive to equip all participants with a clearer knowledge about the influences involved and what are the foreseeable consequences for any imagined course of action.

Summary and Conclusions

It can be difficult to write about any topic as heated and vital as those involving the lives and possible deaths of real people. Emotions understandably run high when one's national honor and security are believed to be at risk. Legal anthropologists should not, however, shirk from studying these topics or fear that their conclusions will not always serve the self-interests of any specific faction. As scholars, we can only try our best to describe and understand in as truthful a manner as possible the events that unfold before our eyes.

Although terrorism has lurked in the American consciousness for several decades, perhaps most usually in relation to the Israeli–Palestinian conflict in the Middle East, it burned itself into our collective nightmares on September 11, 2001. The years since have witnessed dramatic changes on the world scene, as every nation has jockeyed to position itself relative to the issue of defeating "the terrorists." Legal anthropologists are particularly well positioned to critique applications of these terms, as some countries may seek to eliminate legitimate opposition under the aegis of combating terrorism. They can, in other words, shed light on just what it is that makes someone a terrorist and not simply a criminal. One potential criterion was described: the targeted civilian victims' lack of responsibility for the exercise of political power by their government.

Insight into this phenomenon is needed because the fear of terrorism is not impotent. It has justified legal acts such as the curtailment of civil liberties and the waging of wars. This chapter reviewed the related consequence of the felt need for capacity preemption, and the manner in which it defends its justification draws a visceral energy from the dehumanization of the intended enemy. Such strategies are not costless, however, and legal anthropologists, after documenting the techniques themselves, need to remind policymakers of the long-term consequences these choices may entail.

Suggestions for Further Reading

Definitions of Terrorism: Louis René Beres, "The Meaning of Terrorism—Jurisprudential and Definitional Clarifications," *Vanderbilt Journal of Transnational Law* 28 (1995): 239–49; Richard J. Erickson, "What Is Terrorism and How Serious Is the Threat?" *Legitimate Use of Military Force against State-Sponsored International Terrorism* (1989), 23–37; Igor Primoratz, "What Is Terrorism?" *Journal of Applied Philosophy* 7 (1990): 129–38; Ben Saul, *Defining*

Terrorism in International Law (2006); Andrew Strathern, Pamela J. Stewart, and Neil L. Whitehead, eds., *Terrorism and Violence: Imagination and the Unimaginable* (2005).

Collective Responsibility: Burleigh Taylor Wilkins, *Terrorism and Collective Responsibility* (1992); Alvin I. Goldman, "Why Citizens Should Vote: A Causal Responsibility Approach," *Social Philosophy and Policy* 16 (1999): 201–17; Richard Shelly Hartigan, *The Forgotten Victim: A History of the Civilian* (1982).

Capacity Preemption: Timothy L. H. McCormack, *Self-Defense in International Law: The Israeli Raid on the Iraqi Nuclear Reactor* (1996); Yoram Dinstein, *War, Aggression, and Self-Defence* (2001).

References

James Axtell, "The Scholastic Philosophy of the Wilderness," *William & Mary Quarterly* 29, 3rd ser. (1972): 335–66, at 344; Per Bauhn, *Ethical Aspects of Political Terrorism: The Sacrificing of the Innocent* (1989); Joel Feinberg, "Collective Responsibility," *Responsibility*, ed. Ellen Frankel Paul, Fred D. Miller, Jeffery Paul (1999), at 222; Karl Jaspers, *The Question of German Guilt* (1947), at 31–32, 61–73, 77; Francis Jennings, *The Invasion of America: Indians, Colonialism, and the Cant of Conquest* (1975), at 298, 213; Richard R. Johnson, "The Search for a Usable Indian: An Aspect of the Defense of Colonial New England," *Journal of American History* 64 (1977): 623–51, at 650; Yasuhide Kawashima, *Igniting King Philip's War: The John Sassamon Murder Trial* (2001), at x; J. R. Lucas, *Responsibility* (1995), at 233, 83; Paul J. Magnarella, "The What and Why of Terrorism," *Anthropology News* 44, no. 5 (May 2003): 6; Increase Mather, *A Brief History of the War with the Indians in New-England* (1676), at 49.

VI

Conclusions

WHAT DIRECTIONS might legal anthropology take in the future? The shortcomings inherited from the tradition of legal realism are beginning to be overcome, as we saw in the "deterritorialized ethnography" of Sally Engle Merry. Chapter 20 adds to the repertoire a new suggestion, one that approaches afresh the problem of demarcation between law and other institutional responses to the task of social regulation. The model will conclude that law is uniquely tasked to render palatable the structural inequalities of society by fostering appropriate perceptions of what is or is not "fair." This is not the only task that law performs, but, the argument goes, it is the special task of law. The final chapter more fully situates this proposal in the context of the long and productive history of legal anthropology.

CHAPTER 20

A Fairness-Centered
Legal Anthropology

EARLIER CHAPTERS outlined the historical contingencies that have
resulted in legal anthropology's current emphasis on the dispute as the
organizing concept, with a shift in the problem from that of law to the elucidation of dispute-resolution processes. This development was reasonable,
even needful when viewed in the context in which it unfolded. Still, this outcome has not been without costs. Principal among those identified are an
overemphasis on the negative functions of law, an undefended assumption
that disputing data unproblematically informs on questions about legal
norms and institutions, and a disadvantage when studying those of today's
problems that cannot be productively reduced to models of disputation.

These limitations flow intrinsically from the concept of the dispute itself
and thus are likely to endure so long as the specialty favors that focus. While
individual workers have made significant strides to surmount these limits,
this chapter outlines an alternative conceptualization of the project of legal
anthropology, one that avoids these shortcomings while also reorienting the
specialty again toward law.

The presentation builds on the earlier premise that law should be viewed
not in isolation but rather as one of a number of norms of social regulation
(see chapter 1). The challenge will be to identify those other forms and to isolate the unique contribution of law when situated within this global suite of
normative systems. The assumption here is that any unique quality identified
for law should serve as the foundation for an anthropology of law. Discussion
concludes with the proposition that the unique work of law is to foster perceptions of fairness, especially about structural social inequalities and the unfavorable outcomes of disputes. Reorienting the anthropological study of law
away from disputing and onto fairness issues would not eliminate interest in

disputes but would only make dispute analysis the means to a law-centered end rather than an end in itself.

Typology of Norms of Social Regulation

The sense of inevitability of the reduction of legal anthropology to dispute analysis arises because each step in the progression followed naturally from the phase that immediately preceded it. If the goal is to find an alternative that avoids that outcome, it seems advisable to begin anew. What is this thing called "law" that attracts the attention of social scientists, including legal anthropologists? Although the details vary between societies, law as it interests social scientists is closely associated with the ongoing social life of a community.

As described in chapter 1, the property to generate a predetermined field of behavioral expectancies places law within the category of *social norms*. In that discussion, norms of social regulation were depicted as needed to balance the centrifugal social forces with countervailing centripetal bonds. To achieve this end, rules governing both intra- and intergroup interactions are required. Law is but one variant of these normative rules of social regulation. Although a clear typology of such norms has not been accepted, a few broad observations may suffice for present purposes.

Allowing that greater social importance is assigned to the maintenance of intra- than of intergroup bonds and that intragroup relations will present a wider variety of problems requiring a diverse array of solutions, we expect more normative types to operate in this context. Assessments of intragroup behaviors can perhaps be aligned according to a simple trichotomy of whether they are ideal, typical or average, or minimal. These normative standards in turn map onto institutions roughly as morals and religion, custom, and law.

As a category, norms of morality foster standards of *ideal* social behavior, what people *ought* to do. Custom, as that term is usually understood, distills the summed observations of cumulative group experience, indicating what people are expected *typically* to do. *Minimal* norms are those behaviors members must observe if the group is to endure with a baseline level of functionality as a distinct and stable collectivity. Given the corporate costs of noncompliance, these are the rules that society is prepared to enforce with physical sanction if necessary, leading many social scientists to identify this category as "law." The members of this typology obviously overlap in practice. They are offered as Weberian ideal types, not as descriptions of social realities.

In contrast to the three types of norms of intragroup social regulation, the model anticipates only one that specifically targets intergroup behaviors. Yet another debt this discussion owes to Malinowski is his concept of

phatic communication, defined as "a type of speech in which ties of union are created by a mere exchange of words." This linguistic category is a species of "phatic communion," which "serves to establish bonds of personal union between people brought together by mere need of companionship and does not serve any purpose of communicating ideas" (Malinowski 1923 [1949]).

Behavioral acts other than the linguistic can serve equally well to establish phatic communion. Phatic norms are behaviors that seek to establish that both parties inhabit the same social reality for purposes of the immediate interaction. The norms embodied in these acts are primarily display rules used to show that one party—usually the subordinate member of the dyad—can interact meaningfully with the local community, the upper class, or whatever in-group the outsider desires to approach, with the goal, in Malinowski's words, to bring the parties "into the pleasant atmosphere of polite, social intercourse," within which more substantive exchanges can then occur.

These four types of norms—ideal, typical, minimal, and phatic—guide behaviors by different mechanisms toward the same end of regularizing interactions so as to foster group stability and efficiency. While no claim can be made that they exhaust the varieties of social norms, we shall take it as given that any final set shall include at least these.

Coordinating the Types of Norms

Max Gluckman believed that "'law' is to be grasped not by a single definition, but by being placed in relation to other forms of control by contrast, by refinement of vocabulary . . . and by examining its actual role at the head of a hierarchy of constituent concepts" (1967). In other words, to be useful to the social scientist, "law" does not require a definition of essential properties so much as an identified structural relationship to related concepts. This section attempts to meet Gluckman's challenge.

To investigate whether the identified types hide a deeper relationship, we must further parse the idea of social regulation. If we can identify the organizing dimensions of the category, we might be able to use these axes to arrange the four named species of norms into a meaningful associational network.

Recall from the generic summary of law that the ordinary extension of the category includes both rules that model and inculcate aspirational ideals and those that sanction behavioral infractions (i.e., Malinowski's positive and negative legal functions). Ideals are internalized, while behaviors are acts that may or may not reflect a concordant inner state. People often participate in communal religious rituals, for example, without really "believing." This distinction can be rephrased as a contrast between **social**

cohesion, which achieves social regulation on the basis of internalized values, and **social control**, which achieves social regulation through external enforcement.

The major contrast is that of *control* in the sense of containing people against their will, or at least against the personal desires of the individual, frequently by means of exercise of political powers, with *cohesion*, the binding of people into a collectivity through their own desires and actions. "'Cohesiveness' is the descriptive and technical term used by social psychologists to refer to the essential property of social groups that is captured in common parlance by a wide range of other expressions, such as solidarity, cohesion, comradeship, team spirit, group atmosphere, unity, 'oneness,' 'we-ness,' 'groupness,' and belongingness" (Hogg 1992). Unlike control, cohesion emphasizes "the attractiveness of the group—the extent to which the group is a goal in and of itself and has valence." Again, the distinction is ideal, not descriptive. One person may experience the norm against murder as a form of social control—but for her fear of punishment, she would commit the act—while her neighbor finds the rule expressive of her own inclination against killing and characteristic of the group's attitude about the value of life. But it seems possible to speak about systems of regulation that are experienced predominantly in one way rather than another.

A second dimension of social norms considers their content. Some norms describe *how* things are to be done; others mandate *what* is to be done. This contrast—suggested in the generic summary by the contrast between rules and metarules—can be described several different ways: process versus outcome or means versus ends, but that applied here shall be *procedure versus substance*. **Procedural norms** (the "how") determine matters such as who has authority to make rules and settle a conflict and the manner by which these responsibilities are assigned and penalties assessed. The primary purpose of **substantive norms** is to define which actions are transgressive within the group by either their commission or their omission.

In terms of these dimensions, law can be operationalized as a cohesive-procedural, minimal norm of social regulation. This is not a description of law's essential attributes but situates law within the context of its sister categories. Law as a distinctive normative category is concerned more with the "how" of social intercourse than with the "what." Moreover, it is distinguished primarily by its reliance on internalized acceptance of norms than by power-based control from external authorities.

This characterization of law in some ways contradicts those, such as Hoebel, for whom control and sanction are the hallmarks of law, although we needn't go so far as Rouland in saying that "to attempt to define law through the use of sanctions is . . . an abuse of language." Once one has surrendered Hoebel's insistence that sanction be physical and accepted Pospisil's conclusion that even social and psychological sanctions qualify, sanctioning becomes a property of every normative system and not of legal norms alone. Nor does sanctioning by "a staff of people holding themselves specially ready for that purpose" (Weber 1954) resolve the difficulty, given, as one example, that religious sanctions are also doled out by persons acknowledged to possess the requisite formal authority, be they priests or gods.

One advantage of the present exercise in structural coordination is that it suggests an alternative that can perform the theoretical work that sanctioning was expected to accomplish, namely, the identification of an attribute unique to law. The traditional yet unwarranted emphasis on sanctioning may have been a consequence of analyzing law apart from other norms. That which appears unique or of special value when contemplated in isolation fades in significance when considered comparatively not only across cultures but also between institutions within the same society.

The weakness of sanction as an essential element of law ultimately lies in its failure to offer a valid image of the ordinary relationships between law and the individual. An initial premise of the concept of "law" was that it fostered group living. From this follows the expectation that most people, most of the time, will comply with most laws without the intervention of external authorities as a consequence of their identification as part of the group. Often, observance of these norms helps establish the boundaries of the group and thus serves to reinforce identification with the group. Such compliance cannot then be reduced to a fear of possible punishment in the event of a breach. While that description may accurately apply to some specific instances, a technical analysis would parse the social condition as a political order cloaked in legal machinery rather than as a legal institution per se because group solidarity is not the goal of the enforced normative order. The distinction between power and norms is the sine qua non of the line between politics and law.

Accordingly, contrary to the literature's frequent control emphasis of law, cohesion appears to be the most usual phenomenological relationship of people to their legal systems. Most people, if asked why they comply with laws, would simply say that it is the right thing to do. Specialized policing agents may exist to enforce the occasional breach, but no society can rely on compliance with law only in the presence of such forces, at least over the long term. Tom Tyler tested this hypothesis in the American culture and found that

> people obey the law because they believe that it is proper to do so, they react to their experiences by evaluating their justice or injustice, and in evaluating the justice of their experiences they consider factors unrelated to outcome, such as whether they have had a chance to state their case and have been treated with dignity and respect. . . . This image differs strikingly from that of the self-interest models which dominate current

thinking in law, psychology, political science, sociology, and organizational theory, and which need to be expanded.

The position adopted here is that, instead of focusing on the unusual examples of law enforcement when sanction is required, as have some of the earlier theories in legal anthropology, the modal view of law emerges from the more ordinary examples of the role of law in daily life wherein people want to abide by these norms. It is in this sense that law has here been characterized as a norm of social cohesion rather than of social control.

We have similar initial warrant to depict law as involved with problems more of procedure than of substance, again an apparently counterintuitive assertion. The model does not claim that the content of some laws is not concerned to prescribe the *what* of social action. But such substantive content cannot be what sets law apart from the other norms of social regulation. All the norms contain at least some rules of similar substance. It is not always possible, on learning the rule, to know what kind of norm is being presented. Rules against murder can be legal, customary, or religious and perhaps even a matter of etiquette (as Llewellyn and Hoebel recognized) if, for example, a host–guest relationship is in force. In other words, substantive rules demanding refrain from homicides can be equally ideal, typical, minimal, and polite.

For this reason, substantive rules cannot make up the distinctive element of law. Once that expectation has been challenged, we are freed to reconsider the problem de novo. A claim is made here that the special contribution of law to social regulation flows from its procedural rather than its substantive dimension. This assertion is, at least, in line with modern philosophy of law. For example, Shirley Letwin, drawing on the work of Michael Oakeshott, depicts legal rules as "adverbial":

> Instead of commanding the subject to perform anything, a rule designates the manner in which certain activities are to be carried out by those who wish to engage in them or a manner of punishing certain actions that are forbidden. A law against murder does not command anyone to refrain from killing, nor does it prohibit all killing. It stipulates that whoever causes the death of another person in a certain manner under certain conditions will be guilty of the crime of murder. It prohibits causing death 'murderously.'"

With law characterized as a cohesive-procedural, minimal norm of social regulation, the remaining norms of social regulation can be similarly distributed among the graphical quadrants depicted in figure 20.1. Taken as a whole, each of the types has its characteristic solution to the problems to accomplish the following:

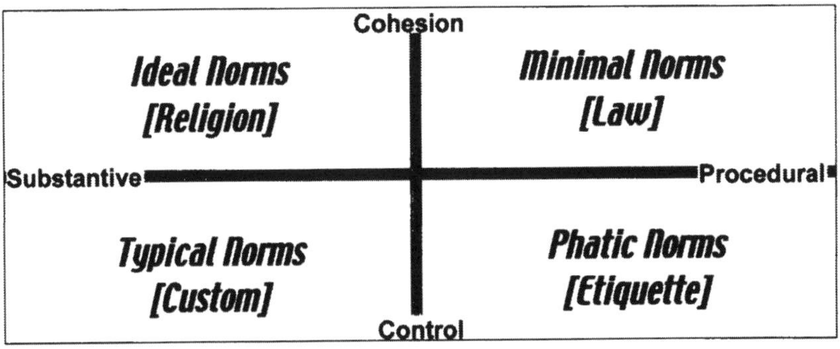
Cohesion
Ideal Norms
[Religion]
Minimal Norms
[Law]
Substantive
Procedural
Typical Norms
[Custom]
Phatic Norms
[Etiquette]
Control

FIGURE 20.1
Coordinated Norms of Social Behaviors

- Inculcate behaviors that foster social bonds (i.e., "good" behavior).
- Demarcate the boundaries of behaviors beyond which one becomes antisocial (i.e., not only fails to foster the good but also actively poisons the existing bonds).
- Sanction those who cross the boundary. Nothing, in other words, should lead the social scientist to an initial expectation that "sanction" is a unique property of law.

Each kind of norm further has its particular arena of social effectiveness and generates its characteristic fruits of social organization. Which predominates in any given situation depends on several factors, including the following:

- The psychology of the actors (what will they respond to?)
- The nature of the disruption (is it due to ignorance, carelessness, or willful transgression?)
- The power of the institutions relative to the needs of the problem (which has the ability to solve the transgression, to impose the required solution, in a timely and effective manner?)
- Whether the goal is to *prevent* or to *heal* a breach

The graphical model eliminates the need to answer these questions in terms of autonomous categories. Rather than an either/or formulation, it intrinsically encourages a both/and response and allows the mapping of individual cases into a defined normative type. Further, it permits any specific social behavior to be diachronically represented as it moves between the different forms of social regulation on the basis of changes in its fundamental elements (thereby incorporating Pospisil's legal dynamics). Because each of the norms preferentially governs a specific slice of social interaction, all are required for adequate functioning. Social centripetality is achieved, says Max Gluckman (1959), albeit using other terminology, by the crosscutting obligations incurred by the coordinated types. Each type of norm generates its own bonds of social relationships, and it is the latticed network of all of them that allows the group to cohere over time. Conflicts arising along one line are contained—or at least temporarily restrained—because of normative ties between the same parties incurred along another. The default expectation then becomes that no viable society exists without the functional equivalents of religion, custom, etiquette, and law. The principled structural relationships described by the model move analysis of these connecting lines and institutional dependencies out of the metaphysical and metaphorical and into real social space.

Fairness as the Unique Task of Law

Granting the characterization of law as a cohesive-procedural minimal norm of social regulation, we are now equipped to isolate the special contribution of law toward creation of a stable social structure. Recall that one goal of social regulation, broadly phrased, is to strike a balance between the individualized goals of each member and the needs of group life. An inescapable tension arises both between the designs of the individual members of the group and between each individual and the corporate entity that is the group. Law addresses this need through procedural rules that generate a socially constructed phenomenological experience of **fairness** of the established social order.

Society imbues the individual with desires for valued attainments, both material and immaterial, but also frustrates many from realizing those ambitions—either at all or as often as he or she would like—by forbidding certain methods to attain them, such as theft and murder, or by assigning those desirables to others. If any group is to endure over time, those privations must be experienced as acceptable (or at least tolerable) to its members. Otherwise, little would prevent the losers in these conflicts from leaving or revolting. Either outcome would be cumulatively devastating to the longevity of the group. This, according to Llewellyn and Hoebel, is the "major difficulty of all law—the problem of really getting a fresh start in relations between litigants after disposition of a trouble-case. This is the problem not only of keeping settled what has been legally settled, but of killing off the grievance tension." Better still if expectations can be shaped ab inicio to minimize later frustrations.

Anthony Kronman says that, for Weber, "at the root . . . of all legitimating explanations is the demand, a demand felt by the fortunate and the unfortunate alike, that there be a *reason* for these inequalities. . . . [It] is not the fact of suffering, by itself, that human beings find intolerable. . . . Rather, it is the threatened meaninglessness of suffering and good fortune alike that is unacceptable." Persons have demonstrated a willingness to accept inequalities and unfavorable outcomes *when they view the process resulting in those ends as having been fair.* The claim made in this section is that it is the distinctive (not sole) function of law, as a norm of social regulation, to foster and inculcate perceptions of fairness, especially as regards the structural inequalities in the social system and the unfavorable outcomes of disputes. Fairness does not guarantee a "win," only that the complaint was, in some way, at some level, heard, considered, and resolved according to known standards—that is, the outcome is "just" as determined by the rules operable within that group. O'Barr and Conley have documented the power of this motivation when observing that formal winners still felt cheated if they have not been allowed an opportunity to adequately voice their felt injuries. It is easier, in other words, to accept losing if one is at least able to play the competitive game against one's adversary for the desired resources, including recognition of personal dignity. Law is that game, and scholars such as H. L. A. Hart identify "the idea of fairness [as] essential to law" (Letwin 2005).

Fairness has been frequently discussed as an important issue in group dynamics. Perhaps the preeminent of these discussions is that by the political philosopher John Rawls. One of Rawls's goals was to describe the conditions under which a society can be stable from one generation to the next. Such a "well-ordered society" is one that is "effectively regulated by some public (political) conception of justice, whatever that conception may be" (Rawls 2001). Basic to this stabilizing conception of justice, Rawls believes, is the idea that the organizing structure of society should be "fair." A fair structure in his model does not guarantee that all persons will be equally situated but only that any inequalities that do exist in the system shall, among other criteria, operate for the benefit of those least advantaged. Rawls's works articulate how such a system could be devised (in an "original position" behind a "veil of ignorance") and what rules of social organization would necessarily follow from that approach.

The present thesis assumes, as does Rawls, that a fundamental problem of social living is ensuring the stability of the group over time and that one key to that longevity lies in perceptions of inequalities as fair by those disadvantaged by the social structure. Social scientists like Rawls are not concerned with fairness in any moral or philosophically absolute sense (if any such could be established) but only with the *perceptions* of fairness held by members of a particular group. The elements of that evaluation in any specific setting are thus an ethnographic problem and not a philosophical puzzle. It does not require that law treat all persons equally but only that the inequalities should not be fundamentally unsupported by the basic propositions held by the group as a whole (and not only by certain classes). Legal anthropologists do *not* ask, Is this system fair? They ask, What are the criteria used by members to determine whether any given outcome is fair by the standards of the group, "whatever that conception may be."

By focusing on fairness, we are able to identify a type of social regulation that is presumptively unique to the legal norm. Other modes of social regulation, while equally effective in contributing to that larger goal, do so through means other than the promotion of perceived fairness. Religion regulates society, in this model, by force of norms emanating from an unimpeachable source: God (or some similar ultimate concept). Having a source superior to the normal human condition explains why religion is able to contain pronouncements about idealized human behavior. The point is that one should merely obey, as did Abraham when ordered to kill his son. The apparent unfairness of a specific dictum or set of circumstances is not regarded as relevant. One negotiates with God at one's peril, even to the extent that demands for coherence or orderliness—or fairness—are unacceptable, as Job learned.

Custom regulates society through norms handed down from a similarly unrebuttable source, namely, the time-immemorial wisdom of the forefathers. It is the presumed history of their actions that generates the concept of the typical behavior. The pressure here is that one should do what has always been done if for no other reason than because it was done that way and the group survived. To be perceived as altering the sequence—however much it actually changes—might raise fears of frustrating that outcome and severing the identity-forming line of ethnic continuity. As with religion, the rightness or fairness of custom is rarely the primary concern. Behavioral compliance is the goal, not psychological acceptance. For that reason, both religion and custom fall on the substantive side of figure 20.1's graphical representation.

Finally, etiquette catalogs how one should behave in public situations, especially when dealing with outsiders (explaining its placement as a procedure-centered norm). While it is possible to set such rules aside among intimates, an outsider expects their observance because the rules provide the most efficient mode of communicating mutual social intelligibility. Like language, it rarely makes sense to ask if a rule of etiquette is good, right, or fair, its social value flowing rather from its being a lingua franca between parties who ordinarily do not directly interact.

All the norms of social regulation have their special provenance, and if, as Rawls and others have strenuously argued, one such need is to generate perceptions of fairness, that task must fall to law. This is not all law does, but it is what is special about law. Perceived fairness, then, is the unique function of the law and as such is suited to serve as the disciplinary focus of legal anthropology: What are the boundaries of circumstances that individuals are willing to accept as fair? How are perceptions of fairness inculcated and fostered? What are appropriate responses to instances of unfairness? What is the relationship between fairness judgments and formal rules? And, most broadly, how do legal institutions evolve to promote perceptions of fairness so that parties in dispute or otherwise disadvantaged will accept the unfavorable outcome?

Summary and Conclusions

The suggestion that the law's special characteristic is fairness follows from the ideas in part III's ethnographic review. Malinowski underscored law's important relationship to support the *"rightful* claims" of persons and to foster the group's social cohesion. Llewellyn and Hoebel concluded that less law is better for a society and that law has definite limits to its effectiveness in fostering social cohesion, findings that raise the question of the other categories of social regulation and their relationship to law, a puzzle of special concern to Pospisil. The insight that law seeks to enforce not a behavioral ideal but instead a social minimum appeared in Gluckman's account of Lozi justice, while Bohannan and Nader reminded us of the central interest in law to find the socially acceptable outcome even more than the empirically correct one. Against such background, a view of law such as that offered in this chapter seems almost inevitable.

A recurring narrative theme of this text has been that the dispute orientation of legal processualism has restricted the anthropological view of law to such an extent that legal anthropology lacks the best tools to address the most pressing of today's issues. The potential for dispute studies to dissolve the discipline has been noted before. Those who believe that an anthropology of law has a unique contribution to offer to the fuller understanding of sociocultural organization are therefore motivated to identify an alternative core concept around which to design research.

Fairness may be just such a productive substitute. Although it could be studied in an ad hoc manner, its proposed role as the central concept for legal anthropology follows from the characterization of law as a cohesive-procedural, minimal norm of social regulation with the special charge to make psychologically and emotionally acceptable structural inequalities.

How does this approach to the cross-cultural phenomenon of "law" resolve the shortcomings associated with the current dispute orientation? There is no longer a translation problem since law reemerges as the object of study rather than a related concept of disputing with an ill-defined relationship to the overarching category. Second, fairness studies facilitate examination of both the positive and the negative functions of law since, as research has shown, it not only addresses the maintenance of social cohesion—the positive function—but also throws light on the negative function through the concept of fair sanctioning. Finally, fairness promises to be a more fruitful perspective from which to analyze today's emerging problems, such as those involving human rights, intellectual property, and terrorism, not least because it can cultivate interdisciplinary relationships with other specialties via identified points of common interest.

Suggestions for Further Reading

The literature on social cohesion is voluminous. Accessible summaries include Michael A. Hogg, *The Social Psychology of Group Cohesiveness: From Attraction to Social Identity* (1992).

Fairness has also generated a significant literature. Norman J. Finkel has written several works from the perspective of the psychology of the individual: *Not Fair! The Typology of Commonsense Unfairness* (2001); *Commonsense Justice: Jurors' Notions of the Law* (1995); Norman J. Finkel and Fathali M. Moghaddam, eds., *The Psychology of Rights and Duties: Empirical Contributions and Normative Commentaries* (2005).

References

John M. Conley and William M. O'Barr, *Rules versus Relationships: The Ethnography of Legal Discourse* (1990), at 127–31; Max Gluckman, *Custom and Conflict in Africa* (1959), at 2, 47–48; Max Gluckman, *The Judicial Process among the Barotse of Northern Rhodesia* (2nd ed., 1967), at 346; E. Adamson Hoebel, *The Law of Primitive Man: A Study in Comparative Legal Dynamics* (1967), at 28; Michael A. Hogg, *The Social Psychology of Group Cohesiveness: From Attraction to Social Identity* (1992), at 1, 21; Anthony T. Kronman, *Max Weber* (1983), at 41–42; Shirley Robin Letwin, *On the History of the Idea of Law* (2005), at 334–35; Karl Llewellyn and E. Adamson Hoebel, *The Cheyenne Way: Conflict and Case Law in Primitive Jurisprudence* (1941), at 45; Bronislaw Malinowski, "The Problem of Meaning in Primitive Languages," *The Meaning of Meaning*, ed. C. K. Ogden and I. A. Richards (1923 [1949]), 296–336, at 315–16; Leopold Pospisil, *Kapauku Papuans and Their Law* (1964); Leopold Pospisil, *Anthropology of Law: A Comparative Theory* (1971), at 87–95; John Rawls, *Justice as Fairness: A Restatement* (2001), at 9; Norbert Rouland, *Legal Anthropology* (1994), at 119; Tom R. Tyler, *Why People Obey the Law* (1990), at 178; Max Weber, *Max Weber on Law in Economy and Society*, ed. Max Rheinstein (1954), at 5.

CHAPTER 21

Overview and Prospects

*It is perfectly proper to regard and study the law simply as a great
anthropological document.*

—*Oliver Wendell Holmes (1921)*

Overview of the Past

Legal anthropology has a long and distinguished history as an intellectual
task. It seeks to analyze the normative order of society, both distinguishing
it from other order principles (such as power) and parsing the whole into
the different types of norms of social regulation. Throughout, the principal
focus of this endeavor is the category of "law" and the holistic picture of
society in which it is found.

Beginning in an environment that denied traditional cultures the honored status of having law, modern legal anthropology built on earlier exercises in philosophy and sociology to definitively rebut that parochialism.
With law no longer the privileged possession of the "civilized" nations, attention moved to more interesting problems: What does the term refer to, and
what sets that category apart from the other norms of social regulation (like
custom, religion, and the rules of etiquette)? How does it make its contribution to the ordering of society in terms both negative (cleaning up "social
messes" by settling disputes) and positive (preventing conflicts by inculcating the minimal rules of acceptable sociability)? Is there a limit to the number of discrete legal systems within a given society?

To address these problems in a systematic manner, legal anthropology
developed its own methodology by combining participant observation with
the case method borrowed from the law school curriculum. Although this
technique yielded a generous supply of data, anthropologists grew dissatis-
fied with the theoretical limitations the case method imposed. Eschewing a
top-down, rule-centered perspective, fieldworkers expanded their view of

law to include a bottom-up, process-oriented unit of analysis. Instead of the moment of the "case," attention now shifted to the longitudinal "dispute" and how individuals negotiate conflicts through the culturally available options for resolution.

An alternative research tradition also emerged, one that emphasized legal pluralism over dispute resolution. The problems studied here were fundamentally rooted in the experience of the colonial empires of the eighteenth century and their wish to pacify local populations with as little effort as possible by attempting to rule by enforcing their own "customary law." Sensitized to situations that included multiple legal systems, anthropologists began to understand that the functional requisites of law were being fulfilled by a wide variety of social contexts, from the family to the neighborhood, labor union, and fraternity house. Law was literally everywhere we cared to look.

The last significant transition within the discipline occurred when—largely under the tutelage of Laura Nader—legal anthropologists turned their eye from the traditional, exotic locales so beloved of anthropology toward the home culture. In this exercise of "studying up," Nader and her students sought to learn how users of the legal system pursued their quests for small justices in consumer complaints, mediation, and other nonlegal means of resolving disputes and offered suggestions to improve the legal systems for the disempowered of society's citizens.

Legal anthropology has indeed come a long way in the short run of its existence. What might the future bring?

Predictions for the Future

Looking ahead, some few predictions seem warranted based on the developments of the past. Beyond doubt, the heyday of the ethnographic studies of tribal legal systems has passed. Local ethnographies today are as likely to look at stylistic rather than substantive differences between communities as they adapt overarching state systems to their local needs.

Much more attention will be given as well to the applied issues of "studying up." For a nation that produces a disproportionate share of the world's lawyers and that dominates the legal culture on a global scale, the U.S. legal system remains remarkably unstudied from an anthropological perspective, although excellent initial efforts have been made on this front. One challenge for legal anthropology will be to identify the embedded parochialisms within a system with a public reputation for its impartial rationality. The hope is that, faced with that contradiction, decision makers will be more sympathetic to the lifeways of other peoples who, unlike the Western powers, lack the might to impose that vision on outsiders.

Participant observation will yield to other research techniques that can shed light on sites of formally inaccessible yet powerful influence in the tradition of Nader's Berkeley consumer project. Methodological eclecticism will become more common and will include a renewed respect for "library research." Modern society generates gargantuan quantities of documents, papers, records, and reports that can serve as data for quality anthropological inquiry.

Despite the decades of astonishingly accomplished work by legal anthropologists, much remains to be explored. Students of the subject will experience no lack of tantalizing new questions to be addressed. A few such suggestions have been incorporated into this text as topics for applied anthropological practice.

Fairness over Sanction

The excitement of the intellectual process lies in formulating and testing new ideas. Chapter 20 offered a different way to conceptualize the field of normative social regulation that both distinguishes the varieties of norms and relates them into a coherent framework. All in all, the model promises to function well as an interpretive map of this sociocultural terrain.

The real test of this and any other hypothesis is in the falsifiable predictions it generates. One such prediction is that reliance on legal institutions will be a function of the rate of social change. Richard Kagan noticed that in European history, reliance on law grew as society experienced greater transformations:

> I am suggesting . . . that the changes set into motion by economic expansion and population growth were the fundamental cause of much of the increase in litigation recorded in Castile's courts. . . . Peasants in England and France experienced similar tensions . . . and in these countries the evidence also suggests that litigation in the sixteenth century was on the rise.

The fairness-centered model helps to explain this observed pattern and predicts that it recurs in similar contexts. Change too rapid to be tracked by any of the other norms of social regulation (custom, religion, and etiquette) results in an increased reliance on legal norms, which have as their virtue a mechanism for reasonably quick reaction to any change in the social milieu. A too-rapidly changing society or one that does not cease such rapid change long enough to allow normative regulation to be assumed by some nonlegal category will find that everything becomes a legal issue to the exhaustion of law. Donald Black has said that "law varies inversely with other social control. . . . The fewer alternatives, the more law. And the more people resort to law, the more they come to rely on it. They develop a condition of legal dependency. In this sense, law is like an addictive drug." And, as discussed earlier, an overreliance on law is a sign of a possibly unbalanced society.

Societies that seek to make morality a subject matter for legal enforcement will thus be predicted to be experiencing a particularly volatile phase of their cultural history.

Whatever the fate of this particular model, legal anthropology has need of more theories that will help make sense of our increasingly complex global society with its novel justifications for war, intervention in the name of human rights, "mind colonialism," and hegemonic property systems. Whether the issue is truly law or merely the way that its language is manipulated for other purposes, deep understanding falls within the expertise of the legal anthropologist.

References

Donald Black, *Sociological Justice* (1989); Oliver Wendell Holmes, *Collected Legal Papers* (1921); Richard Kagan, *Lawsuits and Litigants in Castile, 1500–1700* (1981).

Index

Made in the USA
San Bernardino, CA
25 September 2014